CASH
FROM YOUR
KITCHEN

CASH FROM YOUR KITCHEN

Catherine Harris

HOLT, RINEHART AND WINSTON
New York

Copyright © 1984 by Catherine Harris
All rights reserved, including the right to reproduce
this book or portions thereof in any form.
First published in the United States in 1985 by
Holt, Rinehart and Winston, 383 Madison Avenue,
New York, New York 10017.

Library of Congress Cataloging in Publication Data
Harris, Catherine, 1953–
Cash from your kitchen.
1. Caterers and catering.   2. Self-employed.
3. Cookery. I. Title.
TX911.2.H376 1984   642'.4   84-22594
ISBN 0-03-004432-4

First American Edition

Designer: Nancy Ruth Jackson

Printed in the United States of America
10 9 8 7 6 5 4 3 2 1

ISBN 0-03-004432-4

TO MICHAEL

CONTENTS

INTRODUCTION

Catering is exciting, challenging, and creative. It is also hard work. I've catered hundreds of occasions from large weddings to intimate suppers. These jobs have taught me about people and business, as well as about food and cooking. They've also supported me and contributed to my family for the past seven years.

As much as I've earned from catering, and as much as I have enjoyed it, catering is not my whole life. If you are interested in having it become the totally consuming career it can so easily be, this book will give you the basics for a start. (In Chapter 21 I discuss how to begin expanding the business in ways that will make it the more-than-full-time career it once was for me.) But I've also written this for those who, like me at present, would like to have flexible, satisfying, and lucrative work in order to support other interests or buy more free time.

Many people come to me with questions about how they might start catering. Some are pursuing careers in the arts that are not yet earning them adequate incomes. Others are mothers who want to find some work they can do from the home and so not be locked into a nine-to-five schedule away from their children. Others love cooking more than their present jobs and wonder how they can go into business and do something they really *like* to do. Though each of these groups of people is considering a different degree of commitment to catering, their basic questions are all much the same. It is to answer these questions and describe my own experiences that I've written this book.

Catering from your home, whether you do it a lot or just a little, is very personal work. *You* are essentially the business. The cooking itself and the image you project through contacts with clients, the presentation of the food, and even the service are an expression of who you are.

But, before I begin, let me say something about the current mystique surrounding the chic young caterers that seem to be surfacing everywhere lately. I see articles about them every few weeks and I've often thought I'm glad I'm not starting up now. Not because I think the market is glutted with eager and excellent caterers (in fact, I think the market is just beginning to expand), but because I find all these new caterers so intimidating—at least as they are presented in the articles. One caterer from New York City is quoted as saying, "Cooking is like love; you should enter into it with abandon or not at all." Lines like that seem to have very little to do with actual catering (or cooking, for that matter). Remember, when people sit down to eat something you've prepared, it is not the hype or the boas and black ties of the guests that count, it's the food. If you can cook good food and enjoy doing it, you might very well make a good caterer.

SECTION I

IS CATERING FOR YOU?

CHAPTER 1

AN UNLIKELY BEGINNING

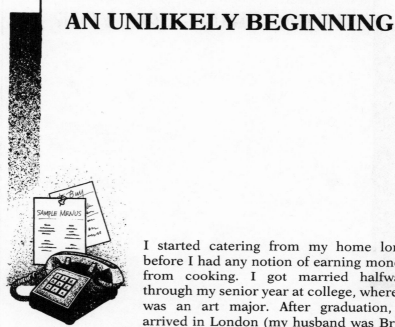

I started catering from my home long before I had any notion of earning money from cooking. I got married halfway through my senior year at college, where I was an art major. After graduation, I arrived in London (my husband was British) with my degree and prizes tucked under my arm and the praise of my teachers still ringing in my ears.

But my confidence was shakier than I'd thought. In terms of the work expected, being a wife was like being an employee with no clear job description. It was more and yet less than any job I'd ever had. More, because no job was ever finished. The work filled twenty-four hours seven days a week; every chore was simply done over and over. It wasn't hard work; it was just never completed. The "job" of wife was also less satisfying because there was no real acknowledgement of the quality of the work by an objective outside world. No grades, no prizes here! And certainly nothing like the salary my husband brought home at the end of every month! I chuckle now when I think of my naïveté then: like many women of my generation I had been trained by my family and my education to expect more from myself and from life. How was I supposed to go about "doing 'wife' well"? First, I would definitely have to learn how to cook.

While I had never had occasion to do much cooking before, I had been fascinated for years with how different types of cuisine were cooked.

During my college years, I worked as a waitress in several good restaurants. I watched the cook and his assistants at work and learned a great deal about how a professional kitchen operates. Of course, the hundreds of hours spent serving meals among experienced waitresses taught me how to serve well.

The next stage of my culinary education came during a year's leave of absence from Yale, which I spent in Italy. At first I lived with an Italian family and would sit out in the kitchen (practising my Italian) and watch the "Mama" of the family prepare the elaborate noon meal that served twelve of us. She loved to talk, especially about food, since she spent so much of her life shopping for, cooking, eating, and cleaning up the meals. Though she taught me many of the basics of Italian cooking, I don't subscribe to all of her culinary rules; they were sometimes somewhere between the religious and the superstitious. She emphatically believed that adding salt and sugar to the same dish was as close to a sin as you could get in the kitchen. The maiden aunt in the family would, from time to time, collapse into long bouts of crying—after which she would drink a tall glass of olive oil. This habit puzzled me so much that one day, when I couldn't contain my curiosity any longer, I asked "Mama", and she explained matter-of-factly that La Zia drank the olive oil after bouts of crying so that she wouldn't rust.

I believe the real Italian cuisine of fine ingredients cooked simply to enhance delicate flavors is one of the finest in the world. As I travelled around Italy, stopping in small towns, I would ask where I might find the best "trattoria". Often I would be shown to a simple doorway with no sign. Inside there would be only a few tables, and no menus. Instead, I would be told what was offered by the *padrone* (usually the husband of the woman out in the kitchen). He would present with a flourish each simple but exquisitely prepared course, one after another. After the meal, I would peek into the kitchen to congratulate the large and sweating woman in front of the stove full of steaming-hot pots. All too often they would press me to try the other courses I hadn't ordered, while describing in detail (which I only partly understood) how each was made. I would leave promising myself not to eat for three days!

Later during my year in Italy, I lived with a widow. It was under her quick eye and sharp tongue that I learned how to shop. Each evening, as we shopped for our supper, she would scold me, or even slap my hand, if I lingered over a pile of peaches she felt were inferior. Often I suspected it was due more to some grudge against the vendor who hulked behind the piles of fruit than to the quality of the fruit itself, but I did learn to pick fruits and vegetables.

Remembering these happy experiences with food, I began, in

London, to learn to cook. I started by reading the cookbooks that had been wedding gifts: *Joy of Cooking* and *The New York Times Cookbook* (still among the staples of my collection). At the beginning, I didn't know what braised, sautéed, or poached even meant, much less how to do them. But I kept reading and I got a sense of things. Sometimes the same dish in different cookbooks varied enormously, so I often combined ideas from several recipes. Now when I go to cook a dish, I read the recipe in several cookbooks and get an idea of how I want it to look and taste. Then I close the books and start cooking. Like anything else, practice doesn't so much "make perfect" as give you the confidence necessary to explore on your own. I've never been much for precision measuring (except for the standard cases where precision is important, such as how much baking powder to put in a cake batter). Most recipes are always a little stingy about the ingredients I especially like. Mushrooms, for example: I don't think I've ever had too many mushrooms served to me as part of a dish at a restaurant. If a recipe calls for one-quarter cup of mushrooms, I add at least twice that.

This experimental attitude, especially combined with my inexperience at the start, did, I admit, get me into trouble occasionally. Once, the delightful woman who had been my husband's nanny (and was an excellent cook herself) came to dinner. As I opened the oven to bring to the table the chicken potpie (I don't need to tell you how long it had taken me to make it), I discovered the only evidence of the crust was the bit stuck around the rim of the deep ceramic dish. The whole top crust had fallen through and was now only a congealed goo, half-drowned in chicken gravy. I sat miserable and red-faced while the others acted as though the crust-rimmed gaping hole were normal.

But I learned by my mistakes (the next time I put in an upside-down glass to support the weight of the large crust). Soon we started to entertain more and more, sometimes having as many as five courses at a dinner for guests who were important business associates of my husband. Spinach soup with fresh dill, crab mousse, blanquette de veau, hot lemon soufflé...

Though I enjoyed cooking, I enjoyed it less if I had to spend the whole day in the kitchen, so I discovered a few basic guidelines that I use in my catering today:

- For every time-consuming, complicated dish you can make, there are three equally delicious, easy, and foolproof ones.
- To double or triple a recipe takes almost no more work than making only enough for the immediate meal. Each time I

make a dish, I make as much as three times the quantity I need and freeze two-thirds of it. For any meal I have to serve I take two of the courses out of the freezer and make just one large batch of the third. You might use this idea for the cooking you do for your family. Or, it might be possible to create your business to include specialty frozen foods.

- Cooking, more than many tasks, expands to fill the time available, yet few dishes improve by being ready early and kept warm, so I learned to cook quickly. In London, I would work in my studio until noon on a day when we were giving a dinner party for forty. At first this was hard, for my worries about preparing the food made it difficult to concentrate, but gradually I became more and more able to shut out all thoughts of the party that evening while I worked on my sculpture. I would say to myself, "At noon I will think about that and there will be plenty of time *then* to do all I need to do." This ability to shut out everything but what I was working on at the moment proved invaluable when I started catering. Life goes on at home whether you have a catering job or not that day. To make and wrap lunches and pack everyone off, you have to be thinking about *them*, not the cooking you aren't doing. First things first; then think about the cooking and only the cooking. Now, after I've done the planning and the ordering of food and rental equipment, I forget about the job until I do the shopping the day before. Worrying was the hardest part about catering at first, but more of that problem later.

I've never had any formal training as a cook. A good cook has good instincts and good sense. I learned to cook well because I love good ingredients, new tastes, and eating delicious food. I learned to cook efficiently because I wanted to do other things with my life than cook. This means if you're going to cook for a big party, a big family, or just the two of you every day, you should make food delicious and beautiful, but never more complicated or exhausting than necessary.

Cooking should be fun. As you will discover from some of my hair-raising stories, it can't always be that way in the catering business. I'm a better cook when I enjoy it, so I take a few days' break when the pleasure has gone out of preparing meals. At home we always manage to eat whether I cook or not. I've never heard of anyone starving because the kitchen had been boycotted for a few days.

But back to my story. After two years, my marriage ended and I left my home in London with its freezer full of countless frozen suppers in carefully marked packages. I arrived in New York City (it seemed like a good place to be as an artist) with few possessions and even less money. I fixed up a studio loft in an old factory building downtown.

The only thing I had in abundance in those days was energy. In my kitchen was an ancient gas stove I was given in exchange for a drawing. My refrigerator proved to be no steal at thirty dollars; its tiny freezer compartment grew ice so fast the plastic freezer door was frozen shut by the end of the first week. By the end of the first month I gave up the notion of a freezer entirely. (The worst part about not having a freezer was that when I wanted ice cream, I was obliged to eat the whole container at one sitting.)

It was in this less than ideal kitchen that I began my catering business. I typed up flyers with suggested menus described in delicious detail and handed them out to anyone I met. I made up a card, calling my new business Creative Catering (not, when I think of it now, a very creative name), and I promptly went out and got a part-time job teaching art, since the doors were not being broken down by eager customers right away.

But one day a friend of a friend called, and I had my first job: a buffet supper for seventy people. I'd never cooked for quite that many before. But there always has to be a first time, so I agreed, sounding on the phone matter-of-fact and very professional, as though I was fitting this into my busy schedule of catering jobs. Only when I'd hung up the phone did I notice that my knees were a bit weak from fright. And excitement!

I chose twelve different exotic dishes, cooked for two days solid (packing my refrigerator to the gills as I went), hardly slept, I was so nervous, and prepared more food than a hundred famished football players could have plowed through. It was a great success. I trudged up the stairs at 3 a.m. the next morning in my stocking feet (because my feet ached too much to wear shoes), and opened my door to find heaps of dirty (borrowed) pans and an all-pervasive smell of shrimp cooked in beer. Little did I think I had embarked on what would be an amazingly successful enterprise.

I charged $300 for that meal, and was embarrassed to ask such an exorbitant price, but the cost of the same meal would be close to $1,200 today. I undercharged for those first jobs, tried to do all the work myself, usually cooked too much food, and had nightmares, the night before, of the guests arriving to find empty serving platters. The list of imagined horrors is too long and too excruciating to tell, but none of them has ever come true. People always ask if there have ever been any complete disasters. I still knock on wood when I say "No", but now, after seven years of doing these catering jobs, I not only don't have nightmares, but realize that while *something* always goes wrong, it can always be remedied and the day can be saved. Seldom if ever has the client even known of the temporary crisis.

I've often thought there must be an easier way to earn a living, and I'm sure there is, but I've found none that offered so much of what I want in a job. The money is undoubtedly the best part about catering. I seldom earn less than $250 per day and sometimes it's over $500 after expenses. While these prices may be high for you at the beginning, I can show you how you can earn this amount much sooner than you think.

At first the income from catering meant that I could afford to pay the rent, to eat out occasionally, to buy new clothes—and even an old Pinto station wagon. Later, when I married again, catering meant a washing machine and a dryer, my studio rent, trips to Mexico and Greece, and eventually the down payment on the commercial building where I have a new studio. I don't need to cater as often as I used to, and I have weeks at a time free to work on my art, be with my husband, and take orders from my two-year-old son.

More than anything, catering has meant a kind of freedom. No one is watching me punch a time clock, and I have the money to buy something or go somewhere whenever I really want to. There is freedom, too, in knowing I can do something well.

CHAPTER 2

COULD *YOU* COOK FOR MONEY?

When people come to ask me about catering, I tell them there are four basic qualities it takes to be able to cater successfully:

1. You should be a good cook.
2. You should be well organized.
3. You should be able to work hard and under pressure.
4. You should have the nerve to do things you've never done before.

Here is what I mean:

1. A good cook should have a sense of the way things ought to taste and look. If you are a slave to recipes and precision measuring, I don't recommend cooking for large numbers of people. It helps to have a flexible, imaginative ability to improve something that's not quite "right" yet. But though a certain amount of intuition is indispensable, none of us knows if our intuitions are reliable at first. Intuitions are developed through experience. (I give you, in Chapter 16, Special Tips, several examples of how the properties of certain ingredients change when they are used in larger quantities. I also deal with how to judge the quantities of food needed to serve large groups.) After you've followed a few of the recipes outlined in Section V, you should have a better sense of the quantities needed for larger numbers of people.

2. Many people think of themselves as totally unorganized. Some women with one or more children, who run a household, and do cleaning, shopping, laundry, and chauffeuring, *still* think of themselves as unorganized!

8

Being organized is something you learn and continually improve. I have gradually learned to get a lot done each day. While the following suggestions for efficient use of time may seem more than you need at present, if you decide to cater, your life will be much busier. You'll have to be more organized about the things you're doing now.

A major key to being organized is to concentrate on one thing at a time. If, while you are packing lunches, you remember the washing, and then actually go off to collect the dirty clothes, but set them down when you notice plants that need watering, you will probably not get any of the three jobs done as quickly or as well as you would have if you had done one thing at a time.

When I seem to have hundreds of things to do—drop off the dry cleaning, pick up a roll of film, buy the baby's vitamins, call Mr. X or Mrs. Y—I sit down, usually the night before, and put everything on a list. On busy weeks I divide the paper into columns, one for each day. Each day has a list under TO DO, TO BUY, TO CALL, and TO WRITE. I put down everything I can think of under each heading. Monday's list is always the longest; by Thursday the days are almost empty. (Some jobs, like letter-writing, have a way of getting postponed from day to day.)

Writing lists serves three purposes: first, there always seem to be fewer things than you thought there were. Second, you can organize each day so that there is not much wasted energy: you make one trip for all your shopping and errands and make all your calls at one sitting. But, third and most important, once each chore is written down on a list, you can stop reminding yourself to do it. Then you can concentrate fully on what you are doing at the moment, and do it better.

Another key to getting things done is to decide what are the most urgent jobs. Work on those first. Do the most important tasks when you are at your best, not tired or distracted. Running a business means that your life will become more organized and compartmentalized. When this happens, it's a good idea to give yourself at least one day a week off. I forget my lists and become a completely inefficient person on Sunday.

3. Catering is hard work and almost all of it is done under pressure. Learning not to panic when something goes wrong, being able calmly to continue when, an hour before you are supposed to serve, you are covered with flour up to your elbows and are still rolling dough, take practice. But eventually you *do* learn. The key to working under pressure is, again, to focus on one thing at a time. Panic is very simply the reaction you experi-

ence when you're worrying about what you still have to do instead of concentrating on what you are actually doing at the moment. Nothing gets done faster or as well when you panic.

Here's where the lists are so important. Cross off what you've done (usually more than you'd realized) and roughly estimate how long it will take to do what remains. If you still think you won't be able to get it all done in time, call a friend to come and help. When you first are getting ready to start catering, it's a good idea to make a list of people and friends you can call on to come and help in an emergency.

Sometimes, even after you've checked your list and decided that everything can be done in time, emotion gets the upper hand and you still feel panicky. When this happens to me I repeat to myself, "Don't worry, everything will get done." For some reason this calms me and the panic fades. After I've resolved that flush of adrenalin, I find I settle down and continue to enjoy the excitement of the challenge.

4. You should have the nerve to do things you have never tried. Often I've been asked to cook a special dish that I've never made before. I always say yes, without letting on that I've never made it, despite the fact that I may be uneasy. Once, I was catering a wedding reception for 120 people and the client asked me to make the wedding cake. (Here in Canada, wedding cakes are dark, rich fruitcakes.) I'd never made a wedding cake, but I had made fruitcakes at Christmas, so I said yes. (Normally I suggest clients have their standard wedding cakes made at a professional bakery, where they make them in bulk and charge much less than I do, but the bride at this wedding couldn't eat nuts and no commercial bakery would make a separate batch without nuts. If the client wants an unusual cake, such as carrot cake, or wants it decorated in an unusual way, you may enjoy the many creative possibilities of doing it yourself. I would tread cautiously in this domain, however, unless you can get some professional advice and have plenty of time to practice.)

For that first wedding cake, I soaked the dried fruit in a combination of brandy and apricot nectar before adding it to the cake batter; cooked, it was delicious. I carefully sawed off the slight mound in the center of each layer so that it was perfectly flat. (At home, after the job, we enjoyed the scraps I'd cut off, crumbled over ice cream with a little apricot liqueur.) I've since learned that when you put the batter into the pan, you leave the center lower and push the batter higher up at the edges; when it's cooked, it's almost perfectly level.

The icing turned out to be more of a problem. Though I'd never had trouble with Royal White Icing before, the weather was *very* humid, and the icing wouldn't harden enough for me to pipe scrolls on it. I phoned the client and suggested the cake be decorated with delicate fresh flowers. She loved the idea, and thus, out of necessity, was born a fresh and attractive idea I've often used since. I now regard the requests for dishes I've never done as a challenge. If you're uneasy, you can always experiment in smaller quantities for your family first.

I sometimes wonder if I will be able to produce, as if by magic, all the food I've promised. Even now, very occasionally, I lose my nerve for a few private moments. I try not to think of chic caterers floating among the guests serving dishes with unpronounceable names. I think, instead, of the usual catered fare: dried-out triangles of white bread held together with bright-orange processed-cheese spread. I remind myself that, at the very least, I can do better than the people responsible for *that*.

CHAPTER 3

PERKS AND PITFALLS

There are obvious positive and negative aspects of catering—such as money and hard work. But some of the less obvious ones are equally interesting to know about.

PERKS

You are your own boss; this means that you have all the responsibility, but also that no one else tells you what, when, or how to do anything. It is scary at first, but exhilarating and enormously satisfying, and, unlike most businesses, catering doesn't need to control all your time and energy. There are busy times when you work very hard, but then there are quiet times during which you are free to do whatever you like. You can decide not to do a job if the other demands in your life are too pressing. Once you are known and in demand, being unavailable doesn't mean you are less sought after—quite the contrary.

When you are not catering, you have virtually no overhead (if you are catering from your home), and launching a catering business requires very low initial expenditures—unlike opening a restaurant. You don't need to mortgage the family home or risk much capital to begin. Expansion and new equipment can be purchased as gradually as the profits allow.

Your family can eat the highest-quality food at wholesale prices. Whenever I do a big job, it makes sense to buy the food wholesale. I order, at the same time, products that are used frequently by the family—anything from ground beef to cans of apple juice. The saving is often as much as thirty percent off what we pay at the local grocer; it's the same or better quality and usually is delivered without charge.

Whenever I do a job, I always make extra and freeze it for future use by family and friends. In our freezer now we have two quiches Lorraine, three spinach pies, one pan of moussaka for ten people and one for five, and two pumpkin pies—all from jobs done in the last month or so. When we have friends over, I pull these out, don't cook much, and enjoy the parties more.

One side effect of catering that has made cooking for the family easier has been the efficient organization of my kitchen. My racks and cupboards are full of good knives and equipment I've purchased for the jobs. There's no doubt that you will become a better (and faster) cook if you do much catering.

There is in addition, of course, a large social side to the business. Catering has enabled me to see inside some pretty fabulous homes. I've met hundreds of people from different backgrounds and professions. It's interesting and fun to see the clothes, jewelry, homes, and furniture of a set of people with whom I generally have no other contact. I enjoy the excitement of parties—and how delightful not to have to make any small talk! At some parties, guests come out to the kitchen and talk with us with greater ease than if we were guests (I guess they don't like small talk either). One is indeed a part of the party, yet an outsider—an interesting position from which to observe.

Finally, there is personal satisfaction. I like to cater partly because I like to feed people. If you've gone to real trouble to prepare a good meal, there are few things more satisfying than having people come back for seconds and thirds. People *notice* the extra care and trouble you take.

PITFALLS

Most of these I've learned how to avoid over the years; perhaps you can avoid them from the start.

Your spouse and family may (or may not!) have been very enthusiastic about your starting a catering business, but I guarantee you they will become hostile to the whole idea if you are not careful. First of all, the house may suffer neglect. Less cleaning and laundry will get done. My recommendation: find a cleaning person. If you're doing much catering, the cost will be relatively small and it will buy you time, energy, and peace of mind. One good job, or a couple of small ones, buys a year's worth of cleaning.

When you're shopping and cooking all day, feeding your family, oddly enough, becomes more difficult. They see and smell all sorts of delicious foods and, understandably, they want some, too. Make extra, or raid the freezer of anything you might have put there against a rainy day. You can even send out for the ubiquitous pizza. But I recommend that you do your best to feed the folks at home. The busier and more preoccupied you become, the more neglected and less loved your family will feel. In the heat of the battle, I used to find myself barking commands like, "Take that !*?! wet raincoat out of my kitchen!" But finally I had to confront the fact that no one really understood the pressure I was under. It's more fruitful to enlist the necessary help than to lose your temper—and valuable time.

One drawback to catering that I didn't expect was how food became less appetizing when cooked in large quantities. I love chicken, but after cooking and deboning eighteen of them, I want to eat just about anything else for supper. Even if you have a knee-buckling weakness for chocolate éclairs, I guarantee you that if you were sat in front of a tray of three hundred, you would feel less like eating even one. This anomaly is very important to remember when serving food. This is why it's more appetizing to serve from dinner-size plates than from huge trays. Another problem is that when you cook all day, the tendency is not to eat real meals. Instead, you nibble, or you may feel light-headed and suddenly remember at 11 p.m. that you haven't eaten since breakfast. I recommend you prepare yourself a little lunch and eat it in any room *but* the kitchen. Same goes for supper. The break will refresh you, too.

My worst experience of becoming disenchanted with a food I was preparing happened during the first two months of my pregnancy. Everyone wanted cold salmon platters that spring, party after party. One morning I felt green even *before* I opened the door to the kitchen, which smelled of all the salmon I'd cooked until late the night before. I had to skin and debone twelve of them before the breakfast I finally never had. I haven't eaten salmon since.

One last pitfall I mention because it took me by surprise at first. It also taught me some unpleasant facts about our social hierarchy. Very often guests don't realize that you have prepared the food that you're serving. This would presumably accord you a little more dignity. Some guests you serve will regard you as anything from a talented cook and business person to the kitchen help. Whenever some red-faced, inebriated man pats my bottom and calls me "honey", I confess my blood boils, but just for a moment...now. I try to ignore it as though it never happened, which is I'm sure what he'd wish for if he too were sober. Unfortunately, many people regard those who serve as faceless "non-people". I don't (and probably couldn't) fight this attitude. Neither do I play the part of the meek and submissive servant. I offer the food more as though I were a surrogate hostess than as though I were just the "hired help". The people who hire me feel comfortable if I'm at ease among them.

Running your own business, you are salesperson, organizer, administrator, cook, server, dishwasher, and bookkeeper. While your family and the client see some of your roles, only you see them all. There are always congratulations from the host and the guests, but when the last pan has been put away, it is always a very personal triumph to have seen the whole job through from start to finish.

SETTING UP FOR BUSINESS

CHAPTER 4

THE BUSINESS OF THE BUSINESS: Legalities, Insurance, and Records

INQUIRIES INTO LEGAL QUESTIONS

There are several preliminaries to attend to before you do your first job.

ZONING: IS IT LEGAL TO CATER FROM YOUR HOME? You will need to find out what the zoning and health regulations are in your area with regard to catering from your kitchen at home. Different areas have different regulations. In some areas it is illegal to sell food that has been cooked at home. While it is common knowledge among caterers that many, especially in urban areas, do cook for others from their homes "somewhat outside the law", you should find out from your local health authority what the zoning laws in your area are. Here is what I discovered during fairly extensive research into the questions of legality in the municipalities near me.

First of all, the codes varied enormously from area to area. In one municipality, it's illegal to prepare food for money in a private home (when I asked about people who have live-in cooks, the official, somewhat embarrassed, said that technically they were illegal). In another municipality, it's legal for a caterer to buy the food and then take it to the place where it will be served to prepare it. When I pressed an official to define this more clearly, he admitted that if I was cooking food in my own home they couldn't prove it wasn't for my own consumption. At which point he winked and I realized that they turned a blind eye to such small-scale operations.

In a third municipality, the official I spoke with said that there was no law against catering from my home if I didn't display a sign to indicate that this was a food business (i.e. a restaurant) and if I didn't disturb my neighbors.

It soon became clear that no single rule applied to all locations. I have clippings from as far away as Houston, Texas, where bake sales are illegal in one county and legal a hundred feet away over the county line in another.

If it is illegal in your area, the law requires that you find an outside kitchen which will be inspected. This doesn't necessarily have to be as expensive as it sounds; there are often little-used kitchens in churches and other public institutions which you may be able to rent at a very reasonable rate. You may decide to begin your business from your own home and then move to an outside kitchen when the demand and the profits allow for it. And, of course, it may *not* be illegal for you to sell food cooked in your home. Some caterers have successfully avoided the problem of unfavorable zoning regulations by preparing at least part of the meal at the location of the job. They describe themselves as "itinerant cooks", a legally acceptable occupation. If you plan to create a bigger business, you will have to be "legal" in order to be able to publicize as you should.

THE PURPOSE OF THE LAW AND INSPECTION If you rent an outside kitchen and get a license, your kitchen will be regularly inspected. This is for the protection of those who will consume what you prepare. This list of health requirements is a useful one, whether you will be inspected or not. First, there are specifications for equipment, washing facilities, garbage disposal, lighting, and ventilation. Then there is useful information about potentially hazardous foods such as dairy, fish, and certain poultry and pork products. For instance, cold food should be kept at 45°F (7°C) or below. Hot foods should be kept at 140°F (60°C) or above. For transport, insulated boxes are essential to maintain food temperatures. Food should be cooled rapidly, either in the fridge or freezer or by placing the pans in ice-cold water.

Refrigerator space is at a premium on big jobs, so it is advisable to buy a second fridge (used ones are available). For a recent big job I rented five of them, which were brought to the house. For very large jobs, I find renting a commercial kitchen is essential.

INSURANCE: NECESSARY PROTECTION Despite the great care you may take to follow all health recommendations, there is always the possibility that someone may get sick from something you've prepared, or that an employee could get hurt, or that you could have a fire in your kitchen. (Home insurance doesn't cover your business.) Discuss this with your insurance agent and get competitive quotes and advice. My agent recommends between three and four million dollars' liability coverage. This is one of the very few overhead costs, but it is a very necessary one.

SETTING UP AND KEEPING RECORDS

Keeping complete records is important for a variety of reasons, and it is not onerous if you keep them up to date job by job. It is a good idea to set up some sort of system right at the beginning.

TAXES You'll be earning money that you will need to declare and pay tax on. This isn't as depressing as it sounds. By declaring an income, you can deduct expenses. Here are just some of the possibilities for deductions, aside from the expenses directly related to each job:

Part of your home (both the kitchen and an office)
Kitchen renovation
Kitchen equipment
Part of the expenses of your car
Recipe trials

And if you are really earning a lot, you may be able to justify much more, including such extravagances as trips to big cities for ingredients and new ideas. Your accountant and local taxman and any government brochures on small businesses can give you guidelines.

But in order to be able to deduct these expenses you have to keep very accurate records to support your claims. This means keeping every grocery receipt from market trips when you shop for catering jobs. I keep a file for each job and simply deposit all receipts in it at the end of the job. Another file is Kitchen Supplies; another, Recipe Trials. I also keep all of the electricity, telephone, and gas bills for the house and deduct part of these.

SAVE TIME WITH RECORDS AS REFERENCE Since each job has its own file, which includes everything from the market list to the after-the-job calculations, if I want to give a price quote on the same dish, or a similar menu, all I need to do is look up the job where it was served and get all the facts. (Of course price changes and inflation have to be considered.) Records of previous parties are useful, not just for prices but also for quantities. I state how much I prepared and how much was left over. There are also notes about idiosyncrasies of different clients. Each job is filed under the client's name (with the date next to it).

I began a Recipes file as I developed my own versions of different recipes; I don't strain my memory as often this way.

CHAPTER 5

POTENTIAL CLIENTS AND YOUR BUSINESS IMAGE

There is potential clientele in all but the most rural areas. How can you tell if there will be enough demand for your services to make it worthwhile to begin? The existence of other caterers locally is one way, but certainly not the only one. Specialty food shops are evidence of substantial interest in, and money available for, good and unusual food. If these shops sell gourmet take-out food, you may have a market for your services right there.

Investigating your area will help you decide what image to adopt—or even what type of business to start. Will you specialize in "haute cuisine", with elegant and expensive meals exquisitely served, or in homey foods emphasizing local specialties, served buffet style. You may decide to offer the more traditional catering services which can include everything from the food preparation to the service, the decorations, and the floral arrangements. A number of caterers provide home delivery or take-out service of food that is bought frozen with careful instructions for cooking. Some deliver take-out food which arrives miraculously hot and ready to eat. You could establish a name for yourself as cook or caterer by providing superior take-out food at local stores. If you choose, this could be the beginning of a more full-service business.

Once you've finished your preliminary investigations, decide what type of business yours will be. Then think up a name. Very often names are plays on well-known expressions. Some caterers begin by doing one specialty item. Jill Roman of Houston, Texas, began cooking cheesecakes from her home. As business expanded with regular orders to many restaurants, she rented a kitchen/shop and is now doing a thriving full-service catering business. The name of her company? "How Sweet It Is". Other clever names include: "By George", "C'est Cheese", "Let Them Eat Cake", and "Just Desserts". The name for your company should be easy to remember, and easy to say. You may want to design a logo which you can use on your card, labels, aprons, and stationery.

Next, sit down and make up a set of sample menus for several different types of occasion: formal sit-down, informal buffet, large and small groups, expensive and less costly. Though I give a whole group of menus in Section IV, Sample Menus, I would suggest your first menus center around those dishes that are already your specialties. Gradually this group will expand. You will probably want to practice on your family any new dishes you've added.

You'll have to estimate rough prices for these. Usually, any potential customer is as interested in prices as he is in the selection of dishes. (I discuss pricing in Chapter 10, Pricing: How to Figure What to Charge.)

FINDING CLIENTS Once you have your basic menus with prices, the next step is, of course, the client. How do you find him, her, or them? Expensive publicity is not advisable at the beginning, if ever. For the sake of your nerves as well as your budget, I suggest starting with your friends and acquaintances. First of all, they probably already know what a good cook you are, and they will be supportive and friendly. But even among your friends, be confident and businesslike. Describe with enthusiasm some of the proposed menus. Get their mouths watering, but make sure they know they will have to pay for such fabulous food. My experience has taught me that, both for my self-esteem and for the value that others place on what I do, it's better to charge a fair price than to work for free or for just the price of the ingredients. You may have to work for a little less at the beginning, but do charge reasonably for your labor. When someone is considering hiring you they are attracted to enthusiasm and confidence, but discouraged by self-effacement and any signs of uncertainty. It makes good business sense to describe how people kept coming back for fourths and fifths of your chocolate mousse, not how you struggled over it or how long it took you to make.

It's not just people you know who are reached when you sell your idea to your friends, it's the people *they* know. Someone in their office is getting married, or a grandmother's friend is having a fiftieth wedding anniversary. In New York City I got all my jobs at first through friends; however, only at the first party did I actually know any of the guests. The jobs themselves are always your best publicity.

If you would like to start into business more quickly, and not wait for the slow, word-of-mouth approach, there are many ways of seeking out the business of strangers. Clients seem to fall into three main categories. First, there are the people who know fine food and can afford to pay for it. They are often professionals or business people who are too busy to cook for themselves. In metropolitan and surburban areas, the place to reach these people would be where they go to buy their food. Gourmet and specialty shops may not object to your leaving your card with some sample menus, especially if you promise a return of free publicity or business for them (if you use some of their products, you can recommend their store to clients, for example). Depending on the type of store, and your relationship with the owner, you might be able to set up a table with free samples of some of your specialty dishes (Saturday morning would be a good time to do this). It certainly couldn't hurt business for the stores, and you would have the added advantage of being able to have your potential clients meet you in person *and* taste your delicious food. Specialty food shops have a very specific clientele, just the group who tend to hire caterers.

Another group to try to reach are those people who are looking for caterers because of some special event that calls for catered food—a wedding, a Bar Mitzvah, a baby shower, a Christmas office party. Go to bridal shops, florists, and bakeries that specialize in wedding cakes, to stores and departments that specialize in party supplies, and to party rental companies, and try to leave cards and even sample menus. Chat with the owners. The store owner's impression of you will be more important than your card. Perhaps there is a local newspaper that would do a feature on what you are doing. You want to get known in your area. Don't be discouraged if all this seems like a lot of work: it is only at the beginning that such aggressive tactics are necessary (though you always need to be on the lookout for any potential way to get publicity). The energy you invest in publicizing your business will correspond to how quickly you want to build a full-time business.

The third main group of clients are the institutions: museums, schools, hospitals, churches, YMCAs, and, of course, businesses. The more of these you can go around to in person, the better. Catering is a business where personal contact is crucial. You may want to phone ahead of time to get an appointment with the person in charge of social functions at which food is served. What you should always stress is the very personal and unusual care taken in preparing what you serve. Describe a selection of foods (and how they will be presented) to demonstrate the beauty and imagination of the different dishes and combinations you can provide. These "personal touches" are the main advantages that catering from the home has over the standard commercial caterers.

The possibilities for finding clients are endless; you could even go to meet established caterers in your area (especially if their approach to food is like yours). If you get along well, they may be able to recommend you for a job that they were unable to do because they were too booked.

In between forays outside to drum up business, there are a few things to be working on at home, to get ready for that first phone call asking you to do a job.

CHAPTER 6

EQUIP YOUR KITCHEN

At first you will probably need very few new pieces of equipment. I've listed below the items I feel are essential or very useful. If you do bigger and bigger jobs, you will probably want to move to the commercial grade of utensils and pans (I discuss commercial appliances later). I have a weakness for beautifully made, heavy-duty kitchenware. Restaurant supply stores are a wicked temptation for me. Their merchandise tends to be more expensive, but it lasts forever and is a joy to use. Make major purchases of more heavy-duty equipment only after the profits and needs are great enough to justify it. I borrowed or bought equipment job by job, as it became necessary.

When I first started catering here in Montréal, my kitchen was not much better equipped than it had been in New York. The fridge was tiny. The problem was always how to keep everything cool so that it stayed fresh. Eventually we went out and got a large second-hand fridge, but at first I would layer vegetables between garbage bags of ice to keep them cool. Once, fourteen ducks arrived thawed when I'd ordered them to be delivered frozen solid. There was no room in the fridge, so I had to cook them ahead of time. It was always a juggling act. Inside the fridge everything was so tightly packed it took five minutes to find a package of cream cheese.

The answer to the problem of cold storage wasn't to have rows of refrigerators but to do the cooking in a shorter period of time. I buy all the ingredients the day before the party, except for fish, bread, and salad greens, which I buy on the same day they will be served. Of course, for big jobs this has meant hiring friends to work with me, but more about that later.

Here is how I would suggest going about choosing what appliances are best for you to buy. If you want to investigate commercial-grade equipment, look up "Kitchen Equipment—Commercial" in the Yellow Pages and inquire about used equipment. Or, go to auctions of restaurants going out of business. For domestic-grade equipment, I would go to the public library and look up what you want in a consumer's guide where most brands are tested and rated. Machines with new features are appearing all the time. Cooking magazines are filled with advertisements about new "wonder" machines. In general, everything gets heavy use and so should be of good quality. Buying the best will save trouble and even money in the long run. In my own kitchen, things like wire whisks, long-handled spoons, and large, deep pots and bowls are commercial grade, while my food processor, electric mixer, and blender are heavy-duty domestic grade. Quite simply, the cost of commercial appliances is very high even if they are not new, and since you often do small jobs for which an eighteen-inch-diameter commercial mixing bowl would be excessive, you would need your small one anyway.

In domestic-grade appliances I look for metal rather than plastic for any part of the casing that is under stress. My son, at six months, sitting in his highchair, managed to pull my electric mixer off the counter by tugging at the cord. The part of the base where the motor is attached broke. The base is lightweight plastic, while the motor is heavy and metal. Granted, having it drop on the floor was an unfair test; still, the general wear and tear of catering will be pretty hard on your machines.

I look for more powerful motors because they can take larger loads of food without straining. These heavy machines remain stationary, whereas lightweight ones shimmy across the counter. I've also always been suspicious of appliances with fifteen speeds when four or five will do.

Take the appliance apart as though to wash it, then reassemble it. Keep an eye out for the parts that will be easily lost, or are difficult to clean. The fewer the parts, the better. You might wash your food processor ten times a day, and you'll feel like cursing any fiddly parts. One possible advantage to buying your appliance in a department store is that you may find a knowledgeable salesperson who can explain the pros and cons of different machines. Once you've selected a machine, you can call around to discount stores for price comparisons.

A last note on appliances such as food processors, blenders, and mixers: listen to the motor when you are using them. If the motor is obviously straining, remove or redistribute some of the mixture you've put in; even the best appliance's motor can burn out if it is overloaded.

STOVE The features and sizes of conventional domestic stoves are adequate for most catering cooking; the most important requirement is a large oven. Two ovens are useful. Be careful before investing in a commercial stove; their size is awkward for most domestic kitchens and they are actually less versatile than domestic ones (and more expensive!).

REFRIGERATOR The bigger the better. While the freezing compartment is not cold enough to freeze quickly and keep foods at peak quality for long periods, I use the slightly warmer refrigerator freezer for bringing frozen desserts to a somewhat softer frozen state. If you have to freeze anything in order to be able to slice it very thinly (smoked salmon, for example), the small refrigerator freezer is a better temperature than the deep-freeze. A second fridge (often used ones can be found cheaply) is extremely useful if you do much catering for large parties or if you do more than one job a week.

DEEP-FREEZE A deep-freeze seems essential to me now, though I have catered without one. Organization, with each item carefully labelled and dated, is very important when using a freezer. The uprights are easier to organize and to find what you need in. The more energy-efficient chest type needs baskets which fit inside: one basket each for breads, meats, poultry, stocks, prepared sauces, sweets, casseroles, etc. Baskets make things easier to find, and keep delicate foods—like pie shells—from breaking.

FOOD PROCESSOR If you've ever worked with one you'll agree it is a miraculous machine for saving time. Six cups of breadcrumbs in less than a minute, two pounds of cheese grated in seconds, thirty-two onions chopped with hardly a tear...However, it takes experience to learn how to use one well. Food-processor cookbooks that include step-by-step pictures of processing different sorts of food are very useful if you are not familiar with processors. Not everything is best cut up or puréed in a processor. Processors tend to remove the air from moist ingredients, such as the yolks of hard-boiled eggs that have already been mixed with mayonnaise, and they can quickly become gooey and unappetizing. Because processing is so fast, you can easily over-process and remove all texture from the food. You should stop often and then "pulse" for only a few seconds at a time in order to get the right consistency. Slicing and chopping in a processor seldom produce as delicate or as uniformly perfect a result as you can achieve by hand. Fresh dill and chives, for example, should be chopped by hand; they are very delicate, and quickly become mush in a processor. Parsley, too, if used for garnish, is best chopped by hand; but if you are going to chop three cups to go in, say, a moussaka, you can chop this in a processor. I have found that short pastry dough can easily become tough in a processor after the water is added; I still prefer to work with the pastry by hand at the water-adding stage. If you are unsure how a mixture will come out in the processor, try a small batch first. Though time is of the essence, quality is even more essential. In buying processors, I look for machines with few parts, for easy cleaning and quick assembly. Large-capacity bowls save time, but the motor needs to be powerful to take the added strain.

ELECTRIC MIXER It should be heavy-duty and stand on a base, though you may want to have a portable one to take with you on jobs. Extra mixing bowls of varying sizes designed for the mixer are useful. I find the food processor has eliminated the need for most of the extra accessories that came with my mixer.

BLENDER It can purée most foods to a much finer texture than a processor; if there is plenty of liquid in the mixture, the blender will actually add air. A pulse setting is essential. I find it is often necessary to stop the motor and push the mixture down.

The list below is meant to help you take an inventory of your own kitchen. Not all the items are essential before you begin; what will be useful will make itself apparent to you as you go along.

APPLIANCES

large refrigerator	electric can-opener
stove	juicer
food processor	meat slicer
electric mixer	fondue pot
deep-freeze	warming tray
blender	electric frying pan

UTENSILS

measuring spoons
several wooden spoons
several large spoons, including slotted spoons and ladles

full range of sizes and shapes of *sharp* knives, some serrated
several sizes of rubber spatulas and scrapers
several metal spatulas, one long
two vegetable peelers
stainless-steel whisk

BOWLS

several for the electric mixer
a good variety and number of large and small bowls—some glass,
    some stainless-steel, some deep

BAKING EQUIPMENT

baking sheets (heavy-duty)
at least two long, deep (minimum 3 in. or 7.5 cm) multi-purpose
    pans
a variety of shapes and sizes of metal and glass pie and cake pans
loaf pans, soufflé dishes, spring-form pans, quiche dishes, muffin
    pans, cooling racks, and a Bundt pan
attractive casserole dishes

PANS FOR THE TOP OF THE STOVE

at least two large frying pans and several small ones (cast-iron are
    especially useful)
a range of sizes of saucepans, some heavy, some enamel
several large, deep pots (remember: glass and enamel pots are
    good to use with acid foods such as spinach, tomatoes, and
    rhubarb and other acid fruits)
double-boiler
steamer
pressure cooker and wok (optional but excellent)

CONTAINERS

Plastic containers from ice cream and cottage cheese usually
    have good, tight-fitting lids and are extremely useful. You can't
    have too many.
Large plastic boxes and long, shallow plastic trays are very useful
    for spreading out and stacking hors d'oeuvres. They can often
    be found very cheaply at fish stores.

OTHER EQUIPMENT

meat thermometer	funnels of several sizes
candy/frying thermometer	mallet for pounding meat
scales	pastry brushes

colanders
sieves of three or four
    sizes
scissors
melon baller
skewers
piping bag with several
    different metal tips
    (plastic-coated canvas bag)
stainless-steel grater
    with four sides
cutting boards
plenty of potholders,
    dishtowels, paper towels
a steel, or other knife sharpener,
    for knives and scissors

cheesecloth
molds (for aspics, ices,
    desserts)
garlic press
roasting pans
salad spinner
a carving fork
string or twine
measuring cups
plastic wrap
aluminum foil (regular
    and extra-wide, heavy-
    duty)
wax paper
corkscrew

SERVING DISHES

casseroles
platters
decorative bowls

salad bowls
serving spoons and forks
baskets

Very simple white or glass serving dishes are extremely useful. Almost anything can be rented, so don't worry if your supply of serving dishes is small. For convenience and cost savings, you will probably want to build up a collection of these dishes slowly. They should be simple enough to show off your food and not clash with the client's own dishes.

Once again, let me say *wait* before buying much. Discover what you consistently need. Browse around in restaurant-supply stores and kitchen departments to become familiar with what is available.

Especially at the beginning, when you find that you need things you don't have, use your local rental company. You can charge the client for rental costs if you let him know beforehand.

CHAPTER 7

ORGANIZE YOUR KITCHEN

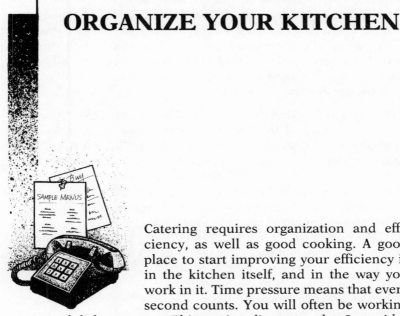

Catering requires organization and efficiency, as well as good cooking. A good place to start improving your efficiency is in the kitchen itself, and in the way you work in it. Time pressure means that every second counts. You will often be working on several dishes at once. This section discusses what I consider are the "musts" for the organization of a good working kitchen. These suggestions are as helpful for your everyday cooking as they are for catering. While you may not want to do all I suggest, at least these ideas may make you more aware of how you can make your kitchen a better place to work in.

Since I began catering, I've been in hundreds of people's kitchens. I never cease to be amazed at how little time and thought has gone into what goes where. The drawer next to the stove holds garbage bags, the potholders are behind cookbooks or tangled up with utensils in a drawer several steps away from the stove. Knives, wooden spoons, matches, string, and stray keys are often tangled together in one drawer.

Granted, those who hire me to cook are usually not dedicated cooks themselves, but *anyone* who ever works in the kitchen will enjoy it more if the space and the equipment are organized for practical use.

The biggest problem for those who do a fair amount of cooking is the overloading of all cupboards and drawers. If a client cooks much herself, when I go to her kitchen and open the cupboard doors looking for the salt, I'm threatened by an imminent avalanche of spices and condiments. They are often so densely packed that to pull one from behind means knocking three others off the shelf. Almost always the spices are above eye level, defeating all but the very determined from searching out the basil or the cumin at the back. When I first put my herbs and spices in alphabetical order on open racks within reach of the stove, I actually began using more of them more often—the dill in the tuna-fish salad, oregano in the cheese omelette . . . The more available the condiments were, the better we ate!

THE STOVE AND THE SINK AREAS The more I cooked, the more I became aware of the wasted motion of opening and closing cupboards and drawers, and the wasted time I spent rummaging in the clutter of utensils. We all know the frustration of not being able to find what we want when a pan of food on the stove needs stirring immediately. The thing is to do something about it.

1. Utensils should hang on a rack convenient to the stove. Potholders should hang near the stove, too.
2. Have knives on a magnetic rack where they are visible and don't bang each other and become dull. You risk being cut by a badly placed knife in a jumble of utensils. The knife rack should be installed near the cutting surfaces.
3. Spices and herbs should be on open racks near the stove, in alphabetical order.
4. Dishtowels and paper towels are usually best by the sink and should also be on racks or in dispensers. Your drawer of spare dishtowels should be close to the sink.

THE POTS AND PANS Obviously not everything can be hanging on the walls. While this is the best arrangement for pots and pans, not many kitchens have sufficient wall area near the stove. In most domestic kitchens, it's awkward to use the ceiling hanging devices. Organize your cupboards by removing all the pots and pans you seldom use. Put these in the less accessible parts of your kitchen, or down in the basement. We all keep pans which we are determined to use some day because they are so pretty or were such a good bargain. Yet we seldom, if ever, do use them. In fact, we use only a small selection of favorites. Keep these next to the stove and, if possible, don't nest them. Stacking one pan in another in a third *looks* neat, but you need two hands (at least!) to extract the one you want, and you may have toppled over another stack to get it. Lids (if you ever do find the one that matches the pan you've selected) can get hidden between pans or come crashing onto the floor. I keep all my pans separate, with the lid set on each. If your cupboards are still much too small to do this, even after you've removed all the pans you seldom use, you can try having a couple of hooks for pans attached to the inside of your cupboard door. Glue a wide strip of felt where the pans touch the door, so that they don't bang loudly each time you open the cupboard.

FOOD PRODUCTS The first step to organizing the food in your cupboards is to sort through those densely packed shelves, one by one. Anything used frequently in cooking should be at the front of the cupboard closest to the stove. For me, that's the oil, salt, pepper, vinegar, Worcestershire sauce, ketchup, cornstarch, beef extract concentrate, bouillon cubes, and HP Sauce. In my kitchen, flour, sugar, and brown sugar stand in large jars on the counter and butter is in a covered dish. These are the *only* things that are on the counter near the stove. In the whole kitchen, only a toaster oven, cutting board, electric kettle, and coffee-maker take up space on the counters. This leaves as large an area as possible clear for working. Many kitchens have decorative objects and rows of seldom-used appliances and canisters out on the counters. If this sounds like a description of your kitchen, I recommend that you carefully consider removing all but the appliances and canisters you use almost daily. Clear space in a kitchen always encourages me to cook.

All kitchens have cupboard space that is inaccessible unless you stand on a stool or crouch on your knees. Keep the orange extract, the colored sparkles for cake decoration, and the other specialty baking ingredients and seldom-used food products in those less accessible spaces, separate from what you use daily. Keep the more frequently used baking ingredients grouped together near where you make up your cakes and breads. Be ruthless about either throwing out—or at least putting completely out of the way—all those products that you haven't used for years or use only once every six months or so. Scraps of cellophane, or leaking plastic bags of rice, noodles, cornmeal, raisins, and popping corn add to the clutter and confusion in cupboards. These foods can all be stored in Mason jars; no labelling is necessary because you can see what you have, and everything is kept neat and fresh. If you need package instructions, cut these out and tape them to the jar. Group ingredients together on the appropriate shelves. In the pasta section, for example, you may have spaghetti, rigatoni, pasta shells, and fettuccini. Or, in the rice section, have the long- and the short-grain, the wild, the brown, and the pudding rice grouped together. Good organization of ingredients will make your cooking more inventive. Reaching for the rice, you may choose a mixture of wild and long-grain, or white and brown, because you can *see* them.

By putting dry ingredients in jars, you can buy them in bulk and store the remainder of the packages in a cool, dry place until the jars need refilling. In the long run this is a money-saver.

LIGHTING The standard design for kitchens has long been to have counters around the walls illuminated by a fluorescent light in the middle of the ceiling. This would be fine if you never had to stand at the counters to work, where your own body keeps the light from falling on the very thing you need to see. For about ten dollars apiece, you can find small fluorescent fixtures that fit up under the cupboards over your counters to light your work areas. Especially important are the cutting surfaces and the sink. Spend some time and a little money to have your kitchen well lit. It will make it an easier place to work for long hours.

GARBAGE You make a lot of it on jobs. Using a large plastic garbage bin with heavy-duty bags seems to be the best system. Pull this from place to place and sweep the waste off from work areas right into it. Restaurants use garbage bins on castors.

ORGANIZING CATERING EQUIPMENT For big jobs, most of my equipment is larger than we ever use at home, so I don't keep these pans and serving things among those for the family. If possible, organize these on closed shelving in any clean and dry space in your home. I always clean every pan and utensil that I will use for a job before starting it.

SETTING UP YOUR OFFICE I strongly advise you to set up a permanent office area with a telephone. (It's actually best outside the kitchen.) Files in a file cabinet and your engagement book on hand will mean you can handle calls for work in a businesslike and effective way.

ON THE DAY OF THE JOB Clear all working surfaces and set up a table in the next room (or use your dining table) to spread out finished dishes that don't need refrigeration. As I work throughout the day and think of items I'll need on the location of the job, I fill cartons set aside for this in the next room.

USING YOUR FREEZER

An important part of a kitchen organized for catering is a deep-freeze – either in the kitchen or right next to it. Though I've catered without a deep-freeze, I don't think I could any more; it has become an essential time- and money-saver, and so I buy meats in wholesale bulk when they are in season and freeze them. When I cook, there are countless times that I will triple a recipe and freeze two-thirds of it to pull out for a catering job or just a dinner party. Our best bakery for cheese straws is a long drive across town, so I always buy a larger quantity than I'll need and freeze the rest. Catering-job leftovers are divided up into family-sized portions and popped into the freezer for days when I don't feel like cooking. I keep stores of ingredients that I use in small quantities, such as caviar, Parmesan cheese, almonds, dates, and coconut, in the freezer. Other ingredients such as butter that I buy in bulk and hate to run out of are kept there too.

It is a good idea to invest in any of a number of good cookbooks for freezers. They explain at length about what foods freeze well, how to freeze them, for how long, and at what stage of the preparation.

Here are some basic guidelines to remember. Freezing will remove the moisture of any part of the food exposed to air. This causes "freezer burn" and general deterioration of the product. Use heavy plastic bags and make sure that sharp bones don't pierce through to break the air seal. I squeeze or suck out all the air from the bags. Plastic containers should be filled almost full, but not to the brim, because food expands when frozen and the lid may be pushed off.

Good organization in your freezer means the difference between efficiency and waste. I can't understand why chest-type freezers aren't sold with organizing baskets. Though, as I have mentioned, you may find baskets that fit your freezer, you may have to get them custom-made. I've found the cost to be well worth it. Look distributors up in the Yellow Pages under "Freezers". If each item is carefully labelled, dated, and put in the right basket, you are saved the unpleasant and impractical job of removing every item to find the one you were sure was there. I keep an inventory of what is in the freezer, crossing off an item when I remove it and adding items when I put them in.

Instead of investing in many aluminum pans, I freeze casseroles, cakes, soufflés, etc., in their pans or dishes. When they are frozen solid, I place the pan in warm water, remove the block of food, and wrap it well in double plastic bags. When I need to use it, I simply unwrap it and place it back in the original pan. Freezer bags can be washed, dried, and reused if still intact.

Remember, things become more brittle when frozen. This includes everything from plastic containers and aluminum foil to pie shells.

Using a freezer well takes practice and a little forethought. Sunday night I may remove two or three meals' worth of frozen food at a time, leaving each in the fridge to thaw slowly for that week's dinners.

CHAPTER 8

ORGANIZE THE WAY YOU WORK

Once the kitchen is well set up for work, you can find ways to work more smoothly on each job you do there, whether it's fixing lunch for your family or a dinner for a hundred.

Become aware of inefficient motions. I like keeping much-used utensils and spices on open racks at hand, because it saves opening and closing drawers and cupboards hundreds of times. But there are countless other wasted motions that can wear you down needlessly.

Sometimes, if I'm working at the cutting board and find myself crossing back and forth to the sink time after time, I try to figure out how I can avoid it. Not only is inefficient motion more time-consuming and tiring, it's monotonous. Even during relatively simple jobs I think my mind wanders just briefly during the walk back and forth to the sink. When I get back to the cutting board, I have to remind myself of what I was doing before I went. These extra motions use up a surprising amount of energy. But improved efficiency is as important for your enjoyment as it is for undisturbed concentration on the task.

A good set-up for working is especially useful for the many repetitive tasks that cooking requires: removing the shells from hard-boiled eggs, for example, or cleaning lettuce leaves, or cutting off the ends of beans. When inefficient motions are multiplied many times over, they become a real cause of slow work. Boredom takes over. Approach each job with fresh concentration and focus on figuring out the most efficient way to set it up. Let's take removing the shells from seven dozen hard-boiled eggs, an

36

apparently simple job. Try studying the motions you make as you peel a couple of eggs for lunch. Watch every step from start to finish. When I have a large number of eggs to shell, here is the set-up I use:

Clear the work area.

Put the pan of cooked eggs at the far left, an empty bowl for the shells at center left, a bowl of water for rinsing the eggs at center right, and a container for the shelled, washed eggs at far right. (Incidentally, one of the best ways to get the shells off hard-boiled eggs is to plunge them into cold water immediately after the eight minutes of boiling; when they are cool enough to handle, tap and roll each along the counter with slight, continuous pressure to break the whole shell.)

When the shelling is complete, clean-up is easy: merely dump the shells in the garbage and rinse out the two bowls and the pan. I use such a simple example because I've seen people that I've hired go back and forth to the sink to rinse each egg as it's peeled—and there are bits of broken shell on the counter and the floor and in the sink.

By concentrating completely on setting up a job at the beginning, you will leave your mind free while you actually do the repetitive task. You can take a mental rest, think of other things. Some of the same rules apply even when the job isn't repetitive. Before you start, clear the area, and collect all the ingredients, measuring cups and spoons, scales, and appliances you will need for the recipe. Every time you have to go looking for an ingredient while you are making up a recipe, you lose track of where you are in the process just for that moment, and you must remind yourself of it when you return.

WASHING UP Washing up the pots, pans, dishes, and utensils as soon as each stage of a job is finished is very important—especially during large jobs when all the basic equipment is used again and again. For big jobs I hire someone to do almost nothing *but* the washing up. This frees me to concentrate on preparing food.

CLEAR OUT THE REFRIGERATOR Before you do your marketing (for your family or for a catering job), clear out the refrigerator of stray leftovers. Consolidate them or put everything into smaller containers. You'll be reminded of food you may have forgotten. For catering jobs, put all the family's food on one shelf. When putting in the food you've just bought, group types of food together—all the dairy products on one shelf, for example. Keep together multiples of any single ingredient—three bunches of watercress, four containers of sour cream. As I have mentioned, on the big day of work for a catering job, have a table clear in the next room so that you can spread out finished dishes and pans of food (that don't need to be refrigerated), to get them out of the working area. Again, if you begin to cater more than one job a week, you will probably want to purchase a second fridge. I got a used one with no freezing compartment.

KNIVES Even good cooks often underestimate the importance of using the right knife for the right job, and of having all knives very sharp. Go to a store or knife department and have the different knives explained and demonstrated. Cooking shows on TV provide excellent instruction in the choice and handling of different knives. Notice how sharp their knives are. Cooks have different preferences as to how to sharpen knives: I use a steel at frequent intervals while I'm cooking; many like stones. If you are just a bit lazy about sharpening them, I recommend doing them the night before and at least once during a "break" on any work day. You'll soon start to notice when a knife loses its edge even slightly. It will quickly become a habit to flick the knife over the steel or stone. A sharp knife saves time and frustration, and makes the food look more attractive. If you're cutting something and it is a struggle, experiment with different types and sizes of knives; try different types of motion.

Just as you can eliminate unnecessary motion around the kitchen simply by becoming aware of what you are doing, so you can think up more efficient ways to cut up various foods.

After peeling carrots, I take four, tap the tops in line with the side of the broad chopping knife, and, in one rocking motion, remove all the tops. I do the same thing with the tails. A similar method works with string beans. I line a dozen or so up quickly so that a single chop takes all the tails off at one end; then I tap the uncut ends of the beans into line and chop all those stems off.

For garlic, take the same broad chopping knife and set the flat side on the cloves; give it a sharp blow with the heel of your hand, remove the dry husks, and repeat the blow to crush the cloves; then a few swift rocking chops will give you several finely chopped garlic cloves. All in a few seconds!

Simple, and perhaps obvious, techniques; but the sort of thing that can save precious time.

GIVING EACH TASK ITS MOMENT OF FULL ATTENTION One of the dilemmas of a housewife's existence is that she spends so much time on small details that don't demand her full attention.

My absent-minded habits and the clutter in my cupboards were stumbling blocks that I wasn't paying attention to because I was so anxious to get to other more important things (for which there was never enough time). Once I started concentrating on the small tasks, in both domestic and professional work, there was more time for the creative work I wanted to do. Perhaps even more importantly, I was getting more satisfaction from the small tasks (most of them anyway), because I'd used some creative thinking to do them.

There still never really seems to be enough time: I try to hurry through wiping up the counters, giving the dog her water, and then putting my son into his snowsuit before we go out. (The dog's patient, but my son complains no matter *how* efficient I am!)

CHAPTER 9

MAKING UP MENUS

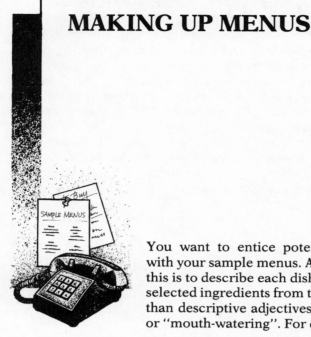

You want to entice potential customers with your sample menus. A good way to do this is to describe each dish in detail, using selected ingredients from the recipe rather than descriptive adjectives such as "tasty" or "mouth-watering". For example:

Drambuie Dream—a lightly frozen custard made with cream, eggs, honey, orange juice, and Drambuie. Garnished with toasted almond slivers.
Parmesan Cream Chicken—boneless chicken pieces with bits of smoked ham in a wine and Parmesan cream sauce.

The name of the dish is usually not enough to describe it, and any name in another language should always be roughly translated.

You may want to design some menus with themes, such as a harvest or a Near Eastern meal. Keep in mind how different dishes go together; if the main course is rich and combines many different flavors, such as a moussaka, you will probably want to keep the accompanying dishes fairly simple. Each meal should be a good balance of tastes, colors, and textures.

Yet, while sample menus entice clients and show them what you can do, I would recommend finding out about an occasion *before* making any firm menu suggestions to the client. There are a great many factors to consider and certain basic information you need to find out on the first phone call. It is really the client's idea of what the party will be like that will determine the menu you select. I discuss this all-important first conversation with a potential client in Chapter 11, The Caterer/Client Relationship.

But, before that first phone call, you need to design several menus for a number of different occasions. You can use these for publicity and for reference if the client asks for suggestions right away. Here is what to consider in making up these menus.

PRICE I suggest that your sample menus include several selections in three price ranges, euphemistically called

Very Reasonable—Not very expensive, for the cost-conscious
Excellent (but not exorbitant)—Medium-priced, for the more adventurous
The Best (sinfully extravagant)—They want to go for the works.

People are impressed by any meal that costs $50 or more per person. Though you may never get to prepare a menu like that, it lends credibility to your image as a caterer for potential clients to see that you *can* make something so elegant and extravagant. It also makes the $20-per-person meal sound very reasonable.

You may want to have your list of main courses divided into these three groups according to price. This enables you to substitute one entrée for another quickly (without having to change the price), if the client just *hates* lamb or fish or cheese.

Less Expensive Ingredients not too expensive. Preparation fairly easy. Quiche, roast ham, chicken curry, spaghetti.

Medium-Priced Expensive ingredients. Easy to prepare. Standing rib roast, baked salmon. OR Inexpensive ingredients and time-consuming to prepare. Moussaka, lasagne, Parmesan Cream Chicken.

Deluxe Expensive ingredients and time-consuming preparation. Homard à l'absinthe (fresh lobster with a Pernod cream sauce). Rolled breast of veal with prosciutto and mozzarella.

Clients seldom realize to what an extent it is the labor that makes the meal costly for the caterer. If a client wants to impress his guests with his extravagance, but does not really want to spend very much, you can offer, at the medium price range, a meal that is easy to prepare and yet includes the impressive and costly ingredients.

A FEW APPARENTLY EXTRAVAGANT SUGGESTIONS Many clients hire a caterer because they want to have a meal presented without having to worry about it; but there are some who would like their guests to be impressed. Nearly everyone wants his guests to feel pampered. Below, I've listed some of the foods that impress; some are expensive and some are only apparently so.

Salmon Though fresh salmon is fairly expensive (except at the height of the season), it is regarded by most people as even more "deluxe" than its price actually justifies.

Smoked Salmon This is always a treat—and *is* expensive—but, because a little goes a long way, it is not as extravagant as most people think. (It can, however, be laborious to prepare.)

Caviar Lumpfish caviar, either red or black, can be served in very small quantities so that it, too, is an apparently extravagant choice that costs little.

Shrimp Expensive, and can be time-consuming to prepare if you buy it fresh—which means that it has to be shelled and deveined as well as cooked. Shrimp has earned its reputation as an extravagant choice with good reason. It is always popular: pounds of shrimp will quicky "evaporate". If you choose a recipe in which tiny frozen shrimp are mixed with cream cheese and stuffed into a pastry puff or put on a slice of cucumber, the ingredients and labor are slightly less costly.

Crab Meat Like shrimp, fresh crab is time-consuming to prepare as well as costly. Canned or frozen crab meat can be mixed with cream cheese and used as stuffing for a wide variety of canapés. This way it is still a treat for the guests, without being too expensive for either the caterer or the client.

Duck Perhaps because ducks are not common supermarket items, or maybe because they are time-consuming to prepare, they are considered an unusual treat, as are Cornish game hens.

Rabbit The possibilities for different sauces and new tastes are almost unlimited. Preparing rabbit well takes a little practice, however.

FOOD FROM OTHER COUNTRIES Greek stuffed vine leaves, baklava, Chinese lichee nuts stuffed with cream cheese and almonds, or Italian antipasto all use ingredients and cooking methods that make them interesting and impressive. If you live in a city where there are stores which cater to particular nationalities such as Italian, Greek, Indian, or Chinese, explore them for unusual ideas and ingredients.

"REAL" FOOD By this I mean whole pieces of meat, fish, or chicken which have no "filler" of pastry, crackers, cheeses, or bread. As hors d'oeuvres at a cocktail party, these are elegant and appear deluxe. They are great for the waistline-watchers, too! At a buffet supper, a table with a large ham roast, smoked turkey, or roast beef set out next to plates of the sliced meats gives the impression of abundance and extravagance.

DIFFERENT-LOOKING PREPARATIONS Anything which is a curiosity or a conversation piece because of its shape, decoration, or taste is striking, and reflects well on the caterer. So does a large selection of different hors d'oeuvres. Dates filled with a mixture of cream cheese and Cointreau and decorated with orange peel are always attention-getters.

Price, variety, imagination, unusual and extravagant choices—these are what to be sure to include in your sample menus. You will also want to include some traditional meals for the more conservative of your potential clients.

Next, I list the considerations which, in addition to those above, will influence your menu choices for specific jobs.

HOW MANY PEOPLE WILL THERE BE? Some dishes are more practical for feeding to large groups than others. Guidelines are suggested before each recipe in the recipe section. As a general rule, the larger the group, the more conservative the choice of main dish should be—if there is only one main dish. Seafood can seldom be the only offering at a large gathering; there always seems to be someone who can't eat fish. Serving two main dishes allows you to present a seafood entrée; this also creates the impression of an unusual and varied meal. Two entrées, however, take longer to prepare, so this meal will also be more expensive.

WHAT IS THE GENERAL AGE GROUP? Tastes and the quantities eaten vary with different age groups. For example, "over-forty" groups tend to eat fewer raw vegetables and don't usually count on a cocktail party to take the place of dinner. They also drink more hard liquor than either wine or beer.

The "under-forty"—and especially "under-thirty"—groups will often end up eating supper at a cocktail party. While the women want lots of raw vegetables and the less-fattening offerings, the young men can be bottomless pits. So, for fairly large cocktail parties, if there will be a number of young men present, have a supply of pâté and cheeses, with bread or other substantial food to fill them up. Even taco chips with dip may keep hunger at bay. You can usually use leftover pâté and cheese at home; most hors d'oeuvres are not good the day after. It's safe to get plenty of extra pâté as insurance against running out of food. Pâté freezes well; cheese doesn't.

At gatherings of older people it's better to serve food that is neither too rich nor too difficult to chew. I find that people over sixty and under twenty-five are less adventurous about unusual foods.

WHAT IS THE OCCASION? Will people be expecting to eat? Will the guests be coming in hungry from a day of swimming or skiing? I recently prepared a dinner for fifteen guests out at the country home of a regular client of mine. It turned out that the guests had been windsurfing, sailing, and swimming all day, and so virtually *attacked* the food, heaping it onto their plates. Every guest came back for thirds of the Boeuf Bourguignon! Fortunately I had taken along the extra I'd made for the family, "just in case". As he looked into the empty pot when I arrived home, my husband didn't share my sense of relief that I had not run out of food. (I had assured him there would be plenty left over as he sampled it before I left.)

People usually expect to eat less at cocktail parties than at birthdays or weddings. At weddings, though there is usually a mix of age groups, people respond to the emotional tension by eating a lot. I've seen wedding guests down handfuls of exquisitely prepared hors d'oeuvres out of sheer nervousness. Explain this to your client; if he doesn't choose to have a meal, suggest either sandwiches in addition to the hors d'oeuvres, or a cheese-and-pâté board. (Always take the latter if the host doesn't want to pay more. Sandwiches are difficult to keep looking fresh and neat, and they are time-consuming to make. Leftover sandwiches are not much good.)

WHAT WILL BE THE TIME OF DAY? Whether the guests are to arrive at 11 a.m. for a brunch or at 11 p.m. for a surprise birthday party will greatly influence your choice of menu. At cocktail parties that start as late as 7 p.m., people tend to be ready for their dinner. Explain this to the client and include some more substantial food to stave off their hunger. (If the client is hoping not to spend too much, suggest that the party start at 5:30 or 6:00 p.m. The guests may not be as hungry.)

Brunches are notorious for lasting all day, with guests arriving at all hours; any hot food will need to be kept warm without deterioration.

THE TIME OF YEAR? It may be December when you make up the menu for a wedding that will take place in July. You will simply have to use your imagination to design a menu that will be right for a hot, sunny day—as you sit looking out the window at the snowdrifts.

I discuss seasonal foods at greater length in Chapter 12, Shopping for Ingredients, but the time of year will also dictate whether people will want to have hot food to warm them up, or light, fresh dishes because it will be too hot to eat much. In warm weather, some foods don't last well if they have to sit out: among these are cucumber, cheeses, melon, gelatin molds, sandwiches, mixtures with mayonnaise, and raw vegetables, though crudités can be kept on a bed of ice.

KEEP SURPRISING THEM You'll want to keep track of what you've served a client before, so that you can be prepared to offer an entirely new menu next time. If you cater much in the same area (and since much of the business comes from guests from one party you've catered wanting you for another, your clientele will often be repeats), you will need to have a large repertoire of selections.

REALISTIC PREPARATION When considering menu choices, be sure that you've not left yourself with too many last-minute preparations. If you have to make a hollandaise sauce, stir-fry vegetables, and make and fill crêpes all at the moment before serving, you might have to sacrifice some of the quality of one dish by keeping it warm while you do the others. In the menus I design, I try to include only one selection that has to be prepared at the last minute.

WILL THE GUESTS BE WATCHING THEIR WEIGHT? Many people prefer food that is neither too rich nor too heavy (who doesn't think of his waistline at least a bit?), so try to include some selections for those who want to eat more lightly. These may be crudités, a salad, plenty of fresh vegetables, or simpler meats and seafoods without rich sauces. If I am approached to cater a ladies' luncheon, I can safely assume they would prefer a selection of light delicacies to meat in gravy. This is becoming more and more true of men's business lunches, too. We are funny creatures about indulging ourselves. During the day (except for a Sunday brunch), people will most often show remarkable self-discipline; on evenings out, however, diets are usually left at home. For evening meals, provide some lighter dishes for the strong-willed, but don't be *too* restrained about desserts and sauces.

(If you are worried that catering may cause your waistline as well as your bank account to grow, I think you'll find just the opposite will be true. Catering is such active physical work, you may actually improve your overall muscle tone and energy level. You will often be too busy even to think about eating yourself! If you're like some women I know who cater, you'll become more discriminating about what you eat. And while I never would suggest that someone begin catering in order to lose weight, a slimmer you may be a fringe benefit.)

WHAT TO AVOID Unless you have a small group that is already sitting waiting for you to produce the food, there are some foods to avoid trying to prepare because they are just too difficult to keep in perfect condition while you wait for the guests to be ready. In general anything which becomes dry, heavy, limp, or gooey at room temperature should be avoided for large groups (when the timing is difficult). Here are some foods best served immediately:

Hot soufflés are very impressive if you can control the timing, as at a small dinner party; they are disasters if they have to sit out in the cold air.

Hollandaise and related sauces are not easy to make in very large batches and do not keep their texture well if they must be kept warm for any length of time.

Raw cucumber should be served within an hour or two of preparation.

Pastry filled with a hot cream sauce mixture becomes soggy if not eaten when it's piping hot.

Anything fried in deep fat is better served immediately.

Prosciutto wrapped around melon quickly becomes soggy.

Pastries, unless just out of the oven, become chewy during humid weather—as do toast rounds.

Sandwiches with damp fillings, such as tomato, tuna fish, or even jelly, quickly become soggy. Crisp fillings for sandwiches such as cucumber or watercress soon become limp. Sandwiches are best made as close as possible to the time they will be served.

Aspic and other gelatin mixtures lose their form and even sometimes melt at room temperature on a hot summer day.

Melted cheese becomes tough if not eaten just out of the oven.

If this seems like a lot to remember every time you make up a menu, don't worry: most of these considerations become automatic. At first you may want to use the following checklist when talking to the client about your menu suggestions.

CHECKLISTS FOR MENU-MAKING

Questions and information you should find out from the client on the first phone call:

1. What is the general price range?
2. How many people will there be?
3. What is the general age group?
4. What is the occasion?
5. What time of day?
6. What time of year?

Questions to consider (in addition to those above) before offering your menu suggestions:

1. Can you describe these dishes in delicious detail?
2. Is there variety of taste, color, texture?
3. Are at least some of the selections a little unusual and apparently extravagant?
4. Is this menu entirely different from any menu you offered the client previously?
5. Can you realistically prepare and serve each of the courses?
6. Have you included some selections for the calorie-conscious?
7. Have you avoided any food which will deteriorate quickly under the conditions of the time and place?
8. Have you carefully calculated the price per person (see Chapter 10, Pricing: How to Figure What to Charge)?

PRICING: How to Figure What to Charge

All the caterers I know agree that deciding on a price for the complex combination of costs, labor, services, and transportation isn't easy. Just as the menu is best designed according to the specific job and client, so the way you calculate the price is often best adjusted for each individual job. At the beginning you will under-price (and occasionally overprice) some jobs. Until you have prepared baby potatoes with sour cream and caviar, canard à l'orange, or cheese straws several times in different quantities, you simply can't know how much work they will be. But you will be surprised how quickly you will learn to estimate jobs without careful figuring. Glancing at a menu now, I can tell you what price I'd charge per head, but I never do it so quickly in front of the client. I always call back later after (apparently) meticulous calculations. At the beginning I did (and you should) calculate very carefully the cost of ingredients, the hours of labor, and other expenses. After a job is finished, compare the estimated expenses and hours spent working against your actual receipts and records. This tells you how much profit you are making per hour, and any adjustments you should make in pricing the next job. It also shows you where you are spending the most and how you can cut costs or time spent in preparation.

BASIC METHOD FOR PRICE CALCULATIONS This calculation is for the cost of the food and its preparation and doesn't include other services that I discuss later. Most caterers I've spoken to multiply the cost of the ingredients by three to get the cost of the meal. (In other words, your labor in preparing the food is twice the cost of the ingredients.) I have modified this rule slightly, because I realized that the cost of the ingredients represented only part of my out-of-pocket expenses on a job. In addition, there is the gasoline I use while shopping, and the electricity I use for the stove, appliances, water heater, lights, and dishwasher. There is also tinfoil, plastic wrap, paper towels, and dishwashing detergent. To cover these costs I add a surcharge of fifteen percent to the cost of the ingredients.* For example: for a luncheon for twelve people, the cost of the ingredients is $69.50; I add fifteen percent of that (i.e. $10.45), to equal approximately $80.00 for the total out-of-pocket expenses. The total price for the meal is three times this and equals $240.00—or $20.00 per person.

COST OF INGREDIENTS Some of the ingredients you use will be part of your staples at home already. Other times you may need to use only a tenth of a bottle of brandy. How do you charge for these? Only if the ingredients you buy are likely never to be used again can you fairly charge a client for the unused portion of the package or bottle. I once did an elaborate Chinese meal for a client and charged her only for the small portions of the saifun noodles, sesame seed oil, dried mushrooms, and rice wine vinegar I used; the unused portions of these ingredients sat for months in the back of my cupboards. Now, if I have to buy something I don't expect to use again soon, I charge the client the full amount and give them the unused portions of the packages.

I often need to use brandy in my recipes and, since it keeps well, it is economical for me to buy the largest-size bottle. If I estimate that the client's meal has used up a quarter of the bottle, I will estimate the client's *cost* as one-third, to compensate me for having bought the whole bottle.

Figuring out the cost of ingredients before a job in order to give a price quote is time-consuming, but it is absolutely necessary until you have become experienced enough to make an accurate estimate. To make the process as efficient as possible, I sit down with the recipes of all the dishes I plan to make. I make two lists: TO BUY and ON HAND. The first serves as my market list. The second is a list of the ingredients I'll use that I have in the house already. An ingredient like butter will usually appear in several of the

---

*Note: This addition of fifteen percent on top of grocery bills for those extra expenses is what I have roughly calculated as a fair and realistic charge; I have not heard that this is common practice. You may want to figure out your own system.

recipes, so I list the quantities, then add them up for a total weight to be bought. After the lists are complete, I mark down an estimated price next to each ingredient and add these up for the approximate cost of ingredients. I always estimate slightly on the high side; this protects me against any underpricing I might have done.

While I am shopping I do rough calculations of what I'm spending on, say, the three packages of walnuts or the four pounds of Cheddar cheese. I then compare this to my estimation, which is written next to the item on the market list. This way I know when I have been radically or even slightly off on a price for any item.

Obviously, catering will help you know what the going prices of most food products are. If you are anything like I was at the beginning, you will need to do a little homework on a number of items. Next time you go shopping, take along a list of basic ingredients and jot down the price per ounce or per hundred grams, and then use this as a reference sheet, updating it from time to time. Needless to say, prices are always changing—and usually going up. For seasonal foods (this includes vegetables, fruits, meats, poultry, and fish) there can often be abrupt changes. Call your market to check on prices if you are uncertain, or if you intend to buy the ingredient in a fairly large quantity. Depending on the size of your freezer and your cupboard space, you may want to stock up when you see specials of a much-used ingredient.

Keep detailed records of what you spend on ingredients. This serves two purposes: first, you will know if you are charging enough to make a reasonable profit after expenses; second, you will have good records for income-tax purposes. Keep all your receipts. I often shop for the family at the same time as I shop for a job, but I keep everything separate and get two receipts. Paying by check is a good way to assure that you have a record of what you've spent, but also keep receipts with a note on the back identifying which jobs they are for.

I sit down the day after a job and add up my receipts, the estimated use of foods on hand, plus additional expenses. I subtract this amount from the total amount I was paid for the job and divide that by the number of hours I spent working (including planning, shopping, and meetings with the client, as well as cooking time).

For example, for our luncheon for twelve:

The price for the meal was	$240
Expenses were	$ 80
Profit was	$160

I then calculate how much I earned per hour. I spent eight hours on the job before arriving at the client's. Therefore I earned $20.00 ($160.00 ÷ 8) per hour. I discuss what the client pays me for the hours spent on location in Chapter 14, Serving. I don't think you should ever earn less than $10.00 per hour; if you find you are earning much less than that, I'd charge more. The responsibility, the long hours, and the pressure you are obliged to work under are reason enough to be well paid. Remember, too, cooking is a skill you've spent years developing. If you find your earnings per hour are too low, you can change the menu, the price, or the way you work, for future jobs.

This method of calculating my profit showed me that I could vastly increase the amount per hour I "paid" myself by hiring one or two other people to help me in the kitchen in the food preparation. I might work six hours less; yet the cost to me of the person helping might (at $5.50 per hour) be only $33.00. That is approximately what I usually pay myself for one hour's work. As I discuss in Chapter 13, hiring people to help in the food preparation is one of the soundest decisions you can make from the standpoints of economy and energy expenditure.

These are the basic guidelines for pricing a menu. Now here are some of the factors that may influence your pricing decision, according to each specific job.

PRICE BIDS If you get a call asking you to suggest a menu and quote a price, you might be wise to assume that this person is shopping around—especially if the call is not from a previous client. You may ask the person who calls if he is getting other quotes, explaining that you may want to give several suggestions at different prices. Bidding for a job sometimes means taking time and trouble to design and price a menu that you will never prepare. If I especially want the new exposure that a particular job might provide, I will do my best to offer an impressive selection at a modest price. Whatever other jobs come from people who found out about my company at the first party will compensate for a low profit margin on that original job. But remember, the lowest price is not the only factor in competitive bidding. Don't be shy about describing the delicious and unusual food you can provide, or how beautifully displayed it will be. Personal service and individual touches are something you can offer that a larger commercial caterer can't match. Make what you offer sound worth paying more for.

WHO IS THE CLIENT? I believe all caterers are influenced to some extent in their menu choices by how well-off (and apparently unconcerned about money) a client is. Unless a client is a regular for whom high quality, not price, is the main concern, be careful not to assume that wealth means extravagance. Often, the wealthiest people are the most careful about prices. (All the caterers I know have astonishing stories of that curious combination of extravagance and stinginess found among some of the wealthiest of their clients.)

Just last week a friend of mine (who is a very fine caterer) told me this story of a very wealthy client for whom she works fairly often: Mrs. Y lives in a vast penthouse apartment in one of Montréal's most exclusive apartment blocks. Her clothes are designer silks and she drips with diamond jewelry. Yet, despite her wealth, she always tries to bargain down the price for meals. She never tips those who serve and never fails to argue over the bills. On this particular evening, while passing through the kitchen, the hostess saw a bottle of Cointreau that my friend was going to use for the dessert. Mrs. Y asked if she could offer some to her guests. When the party was over, the hostess carefully wrote out a check for the cost of the food and the service. Then she asked how much it would be for the Cointreau one of her guests had drunk after dinner. My friend, surprised by the question, said, "Seventy-five cents." At which point, Mrs. Y looked around for her change purse, opened it with her diamond-ringed fingers, and counted out three quarters.

Companies are very likely to be shopping around. Usually the person who calls to get the price quote for an office party or business luncheon has been given the job of finding the best meal at the lowest price (with the emphasis usually on the "lowest price"). It is in this person's best interest, however, that the food be very good. So, it is up to you to convince him that your food and service will offer the best deal.

NUMBER OF PEOPLE The price per person for a meal is always very much dependent on the number of people who will be served. Here is where you have to be flexible in how you calculate price quotes. The cost of the ingredients to feed a hundred people may be ten times what it is to feed ten, but the labor won't be ten times as much. Shopping takes just about the same amount of time, and though frying five cups of onions instead of half a cup takes longer, it doesn't take ten times longer. Washing the pan takes the same length of time for either. This is why the caterers who really make money do a certain proportion of "big jobs" (i.e. jobs for large numbers of people). You can only charge so much per head if there are ten people, but if there are a hundred, the profit per person may be quite low but when multiplied by one hundred represents a significant amount of money. The same meal that I'd charge $20 per head for in a party of ten (i.e. $200), I'd charge $10 per person for in a party of a hundred (i.e. $1,000). Even charging only half the price per person, I make more money per hour of work on the party for a hundred. You will want to explain—either in person or at the bottom of your sheet of sample menus—that the sample prices quoted are based on a party of twenty people, and that the price per person will go up if the group is smaller and will go down if the group is larger.

"WHAT THE MARKET WILL BEAR" In talking to other caterers, I found they almost all admitted to charging as much as they felt they reasonably could for each combination of menu and services they offered. In other words there is a general "market price" for each job (for all but the most exclusive caterers). At the start, use the basic system I have explained to you. This method will ensure you are competitive with other caterers. You may want to do a little research into the competition; undoubtedly you would learn about more than just pricing. If you go slowly and modestly at first, you will very soon learn more about what particular jobs are "worth".

ADDITIONAL COSTS TO THE CLIENT On your sample menus you will probably want to list the cost of the meal as three times the cost of expenses, but unless the client will come to your kitchen to pick up the food, let him know that there will be other charges. You should tell him about these when he indicates an interest in hiring you. If you deliver the food but don't stay to serve it, you should charge a delivery fee; this charge will depend on how far you have to go and how long it will take you. When I am serving a meal, I charge a transportation fee only if the client lives at some distance. You may also provide waitresses or waiters, or arrange for rentals and decoration.

GOLDEN CLIENTS Some clients come back again and again for my services. I never take their business for granted; in fact, I try to outdo the previous job each time. These clients offer some of the most rewarding experiences in catering as they get to know you and you get to know them, their tastes, and their home. For these clients, what you cook is served as much for the satisfaction of having it appreciated by people you like as for the money.

TOO HIGH A PRICE TO PAY One of my clients, a woman with an enormous personal fortune, began to use my services more and more frequently until I was doing several lunches, dinners, and cocktail parties for her every week. No one ever asked what I would charge for the meals and I don't think she ever knew (I sent the bills to an accounting firm). Her secretary would call me at nine o'clock in the morning and ask me to prepare a luncheon for four by noon. By the time the recipes were researched, the market list was made, and the shopping was done, and then the food was prepared, transported, served, and cleaned up, the day was over and I was exhausted. Cooking for her began to take over our lives at home. I used to dread the phone ringing in the morning. Though I began to charge her more and more, until a luncheon for two would cost her $100, I realized that no matter how much profit I was making, it didn't seem worth it. Did I want to be a full-time caterer? What amount of money was worth this loss of choice about what I would do each day? Finally she offered to hire me as her full-time cook. I said no. I've had no regrets. I may be poorer, but my life is my own.

SUMMING UP HOW TO PRICE A JOB
A. Factors to Consider
   1. Are you competing for the job?
   2. How many people will there be?
   3. Who is the client?
B. Calculating the Cost of Food and Preparation
   1. Cost of ingredients.
   2. Cost of other expenses (or add fifteen percent of the cost of ingredients).
   3. Add items 1 and 2 and multiply this total by three to get the price to charge for the meal.
   4. Divide this price by the number of guests to get a price per head.
C. Additional Services to Client, and Their Costs
   Itemize charges for delivery, service, rentals, decoration.
D. Keeping Records and Calculating Your Profit
   1. Compare your estimated costs with your actual receipts and records to discover any miscalculations or poor estimates. Make note of these for the future.
   2. Subtract the expenses from the total price of the job and divide this by the hours you spent working on the job to arrive at how much you earned per hour.
   3. Keep all your receipts and cancelled checks together in a folder for that job.

NOW YOU'RE READY

CHAPTER 11

THE CATERER/CLIENT RELATIONSHIP

For many people, giving a party is an undertaking full of stress and worry. Naturally, as a caterer, you want to eliminate as much as possible any cause for anxiety on the part of the client. The more relaxed, competent, and experienced you appear, the more a nervous host will be reassured.

The relationship you establish with the client is one of the most important aspects of each catering job. It can also be one of the most rewarding.

A PROFESSIONAL IMAGE Be professional in all your contacts and discussions with the client. This means being punctual, dressing attractively, keeping accurate records of all points discussed in conversation, and preparing beforehand a list of what topics should be covered on the phone or during the meeting with the client. Be able to quote prices for various items that may have to be rented. The client will think of you as the expert. (It will help if you think of yourself as one, too.)

BUSINESS ON THE PHONE My first contact with a client is almost always by phone. I try to be cordial, relaxed, and business-like. First, I get the basic facts.

The client's name

Billing name and address

Address of the party

Phone numbers—both home and business (make a note of the best time to call)

The date of the party and today's date
What is the occasion? (e.g. a wedding? a going-away party?)
Number of guests?
What time are the guests expected to arrive?
What is the estimated time the party will end?
What is the general age group?
Will they be all male, all female, or mixed?
What sort of food and service does the client have in mind?
Are there any special ideas or favorite dishes the client would
    like you to do?
Does the client have in mind an approximate price per head he
    would like to spend?

After getting these basic facts, I ask if I can phone back, or, better
still, I arrange to meet the client in person to discuss menu
suggestions. I try to avoid giving menu suggestions off the top of
my head during the first conversation. A well-thought-out menu is
almost always more balanced, varied, and unusual. I don't give
even approximate price quotes until I've had time to calculate
from a firm menu. It is always difficult (and may cause ill feeling)
to have to explain later that an original estimate was too low.

For those times when a client is very eager to hear some menu
ideas during the first phone call, I keep a list of hors d'oeuvres,
soups, main dishes, and desserts on hand for reference.

LISTENING IN BETWEEN THE LINES Getting the facts about an
occasion usually requires tact and a lot of listening in between the
lines. You can hardly say, for example, "How old will the guests
be?" or "How much do you want to spend?"

Usually a description of the occasion will give clues about the
age group. A business luncheon usually consists of men between
thirty and fifty. Wedding receptions and pre-wedding parties are
usually a half-and-half mix of young and old. As I've mentioned, a
windsurfing or skiing holiday supper usually means a young (and
hungry!) group.

Expressions like "nothing too elaborate" (i.e., not too expensive) or "something substantial and unusual" (i.e., cost is no
object this time) tell you both the price and the client's general
image of the occasion. Sometimes a client wants "something
really nice, but not too elaborate"; this means a medium-priced
menu.

MEETING WITH THE CLIENT If the client is willing, it is a good
idea to go to his home to discuss the menu suggestions and other
details. By going to the home (and/or the location where the party

will take place), you offer the personal attention that is one of the hallmarks of a good caterer. It reassures and pampers the client. Discussing the various ideas face to face immediately establishes a better rapport than you can achieve on the phone. Also, on that visit to the location of the party, you can scout out what equipment and space you will have to work with. If I know I'll need an electric mixer or other equipment, for example, I ask or look for them in the kitchen during the visit.

Before going to the meeting with the client, here are some of the topics you may want to be prepared to cover:

- Menu: Have your suggested menu priced per head, with one or two alternatives for each dish.
- How many waiters/waitresses/bartenders will be needed?
- What rental equipment will be needed for the food and bar?
- Discuss the beverages: What will be served and who will buy what? When would the host like each served (e.g., champagne as the guests arrive, red wine only with the meal)?
- What tables will be needed for the food and the bar and where will they be set up?
- How will the guests circulate around the rooms from the bar to the food and seating? Will some furniture need to be removed? Will any tables or chairs need to be rented?
- Would the host like you to move the furniture? Or will it already be done when you arrive on the day of the party? (You will need to arrive earlier if you have to move the furniture.)
- Where will the guests leave their coats? Will it be advisable to rent coatracks?
- What dishes and miscellaneous items will the client provide (e.g., candles, paper napkins, serving dishes, serving utensils, ashtrays, etc.)?
- Advise the client to have as much clear surface area as possible in the kitchen. The refrigerator should be as empty as possible.
- Are flower arrangements wanted? Who will see to them?
- Tell the client what time you will arrive before the party in order to set up.

CONTRACTS When the above questions have been answered and agreed upon, it may be a good idea to write the agreement down in the form of a contract. Most caterers I've spoken with use the formal legal commitment of a contract, especially for larger jobs. It means that the food and services to be provided are clearly stated and both sides are protected against misunderstandings and default. Usually a deposit should accompany the signed document when it is returned to you, and this can cover all or some of the out-of-pocket expenses you will incur before the party. The amount of money you will be spending to buy ingredients may help you decide how much to ask for as a deposit. Whether you want to use a contract at all will be up to your discretion. I find they aren't necessary for small jobs but are helpful for larger ones, especially when the agreement is made several weeks or even months before the event itself. (There is a sample contract at the end of this chapter.)

IF A CONTRACT IS BROKEN It will be up to you to decide what to do if a client cancels and defaults on your signed agreement. I have heard of caterers suing for damages, though I expect these were extreme cases. It will probably depend on the circumstances that have caused the cancellation and on whether you have spent money and time preparing the food. (You may choose to keep the deposit to cover these costs.) From my own experience and from what other caterers have told me, cancellations by clients at the last minute are very rare. For a caterer to cancel is so rare that I've never even heard of it happening; in an emergency friends and/or family could help out. What does happen occasionally is that a client will agree to a menu and price and then call to say she's changed her mind about giving the party at all. When this happens, it is usually before any contract has been signed or any shopping done. When a client does this once, it is forgivable; if she does it twice, it probably means she is wasting your time.

WHEN CORDIAL IS MORE IMPORTANT THAN EFFICIENT You want to be businesslike, organized, and thoroughly professional—without becoming officious. A caterer should try to take the burden of responsibility from the client but not her sense of choice and control. Listen carefully to the client's ideas, respond to them positively, and do your best to incorporate them into your plans. I have sometimes planned an interesting and beautiful meal only to find that the client has already got her heart set on a very conventional one. While I can always make suggestions, it's better not to push my own ideas too strenuously. On the other hand, some of my clients have had excellent ideas that I've incorporated into my repertoire.

Above all else, the client should feel confident and at ease with you. Probably the best way for you to promote those feelings is by being natural, being yourself. In the kitchen, you can be efficient, but in the client's living room, be relaxed and not in too much of a hurry. Often clients will chat about all kinds of things as a way to get to know you and feel more at ease. This can sometimes be a problem. Once a client showed me every plate, serving dish, and silver set in endless cupboards and closets. After nearly an hour, relieved that the tour was finally over, I said, "Those will be fine." At which point, she said, on her way into the next room, "Now, the linens." Though occasionally I've met this kind of lonely and uncertain person, who uses the fact I'm hired to "buy" my company, I've much more often met active and bright people.

FAMILIARITY Friendships will inevitably arise between you and some of your clients, but, with rare exceptions, it's usually a good idea not to become too familiar with clients during jobs. If you've ever had someone work for you, you will understand that the more you know about or become involved with the personal life of that person, the more uncomfortable the work relationship may become. There is a delicate balance between being friendly and maintaining a professional distance.

SAMPLE CONTRACT Below I've listed what you will probably want to include in the contract between you and the client.

Name, address, and phone numbers of the client

Name, address, and phone numbers of the caterer

Date of the agreement

Date of the party
  Hour the party begins
  Hour the caterer arrives to set up

Menu

Number of people

Price per person (to be confirmed)
  This price is based on the number of people stated above and is
  subject to change should that number be altered.

Service
  Number of waiters/waitresses—cost per hour
  Number of bartenders—cost per hour

Rental equipment
  Itemized list—estimated cost

Other equipment
  What will be supplied by the caterer?
  What will be supplied by the client?

Other notes
    The client will clear counters in the kitchen. The refrigerator
    will be cleared as much as possible.

Estimated Total

Deposit

The balance of the bill will be sent after the party and will be
payable on receipt. *Gratuities are not included.*

CHAPTER 12

SHOPPING FOR INGREDIENTS

The meals I serve my clients are expensive and I soon discovered that the more people pay, the more discerning they become. This isn't exactly surprising. When I go out to eat in an expensive restaurant, I'm more critical than I would otherwise be of any shortcuts taken by the kitchen—canned fruit in the fruit salad, frozen vegetables, canned stock in the soup, day-old bread, commercial salad dressing...the list goes on and on. There are hundreds of shortcuts that may tempt you when you cater—especially when you shop for ingredients. Sometimes there are bargains in half-price overripe avocados that you think you can get away with using. Other times laziness holds sway and you can't be bothered to go back to the bakery for the bread just before the party. You are the only watchdog over your standards, so it helps to set up some hard-and-fast rules for yourself. I always take plenty of money with me when I shop, so that I feel free to buy the best and not skimp. Bread, salad greens, and fish I always buy on the day of the party. I don't let myself get away with buying these too early. Perfectionism pays off—literally. The clients and the guests *notice* the difference that the fresh pasta makes, or the superbly ripe strawberries, the fresh dill, or the homemade biscuits. If you have high standards, you can afford to be expensive.

PLANNING THE SHOPPING: How to buy the best for less while saving time and energy.

Sometimes you simply have to pay a high price for top-quality ingredients. But buying the best doesn't necessarily mean you

62

can't sometimes economize; it simply means you don't economize by buying inferior quality. The key to getting the best for less
without wasting energy is to plan where and how you shop.

THE MARKET LIST The first step in figuring out a shopping plan
is to organize the market list of what you need to buy. I divide my
list into the following categories.

Fruits and Vegetables	Bakery
Meat and Poultry	Fish
Dairy	Miscellaneous
Delicatessen	Liquor Store
Nuts and Dried Fruits	

Each heading represents either a different store or a different
section in the supermarket. The "Miscellaneous" heading includes such staples as rice, sugar, flour, and other supermarket
items such as mayonnaise, tinfoil, toothpicks, etc.

COST VERSUS CONVENIENCE When I'm deciding where I'm
going to buy an item, I consider not only the quality and price at
each store, but also how much time, energy, and gasoline it will
take to get there. It's not worth driving across town to save $1.80
on three pounds of tomatoes unless they are also the only *good*
tomatoes you can find. Though I never do large shoppings at the
local high-priced gourmet store, I *do* go there to get some specialty items. To buy these items in the little Chinese shop that sells
them more cheaply would mean battling traffic for half an hour.

It's a good idea to plan your shopping route to make few special
trips for single items. I will, if possible, stock up on items that are
only available at a store across town. For example, I can get long
bamboo skewers only in a small Oriental shop some distance
away. When I do go there, I always get several packages so that I
don't need to repeat this trip every time I need skewers.

Next, I plan a route according to the location of the stores. As
much as possible I go to stores close together, so that I only have
to park the car once. The supermarket is my first stop. There I get
the miscellaneous staples and see if there are any of the other
ingredients that I need at both high quality and low price. Supermarkets sometimes have what are called "loss leaders", fresh
food available to the consumer at below cost (thereby hoping to
attract customers who will do their whole week's shopping in the
store). It's always worth seeing what's on special. I was once
feeding chicken to twenty people and discovered to my pleasure
and surprise on entering the supermarket that fresh chicken was
on special at 79¢ per pound. (Of course, I should have read about

this in the newspaper. You may be better organized than I am about this; I no longer kid myself that "one day" I will keep track of all of the specials offered in order to plan the stocking of my freezer and larder around them. But I know it would be a good idea!)

Here are some other things I consider when planning my shopping. When is the party? As I mentioned before, I do all the shopping the day before and buy the highly perishable items on the day of the party. You may set up a different schedule, doing some work further in advance.

What are the store hours? What days are the stores closed? What times of day are the stores well stocked and not crowded? At my local supermarket this is Tuesday through Friday mid-mornings (some stock isn't yet out on the shelves in the early morning).

I go to a central shopping district with a good supermarket as well as specialty fish, meat, fresh produce, delicatessen, and bakery stores all close together. The farmers' market is ideal during the warm months.

After shopping first at the supermarket, since they usually have the best prices, I go from store to store according to its location and how perishable what I'm buying there is. In the summer I either have perishable foods delivered to my kitchen or place them in an ice-filled cooler in the back of the station wagon as soon as I leave the store. If you live in a warm climate, an air-conditioned car is definitely recommended.

I try to shop when I'm not too tired; there are so many decisions and choices that demand clear thinking. If I'm tired, I tend to succumb to the temptation of buying extra "just in case". Bread, lettuce, and pasta are three items I still always tend to get too much of. If you have calculated amounts carefully while making up the market list, trust the quantities you've written down. Some items like butter are difficult to calculate precisely (how much is needed to butter six loaves of bread?). I almost always get extra butter; it freezes well and will always get used sooner or later.

At the checkout counter I pack my own boxes (boxes are more useful later than bags). By doing this, I am able to protect delicate berries or tomatoes from being crushed. I make sure that multiples of the same item are in the same box, that all frozen items are in one box, and that food that doesn't need to be refrigerated is kept separate from food that does. Food that needs refrigerating stays colder and the unpacking at home is much faster and easier.

SMALL STORES One of the things you pay for when you shop at the more expensive small butcher shops or delicatessens is the personal attention and the knowledge the owner has of what he sells. I've learned from these professionals about different cuts of meat, and how to tell whether various types of cheeses are ripe. As I've gotten to know the store owners (since I cater, they are always glad to see me!), I will sometimes explain how I want to cook a dish and will ask what is the right cut of meat for it. At one specialty delicatessen, I just ask which of his soft ripened cheeses will be perfectly ripe for the next night. Now, whenever I have to serve plates of sliced roast beef or ham, I bring in the cooked roasts and he slices them for me on his heavy-duty slicer as a favor.

Becoming friendly with store owners is fun, but it shouldn't keep you from driving a good bargain if you are buying a fairly large quantity of some expensive item, for example two and a half pounds of prosciutto or three pounds of Parmesan cheese. For the owner of the store to give you a reduced price, he has to feel you are undecided about whether to buy the item at his store or at someone else's. I always check the price of what I'm buying before I buy it. Sometimes a little hesitation will bring down the price. (Remember to do it *before*; it's hard to bargain on the price if he has just sliced the two and a half pounds of prosciutto!) I've found that store owners from Mediterranean cultures are more at ease with such "negotiations", so use your judgement. It may not always be appropriate to bargain, but more often than not it is.

SPECIALTY IMPORTED FOODS There are times when high-quality imported foods add a touch of variety and elegance. Certain biscuits, crackers, and cookies (especially if made crisp in a not-too-hot (250°F/120°C) oven before serving) are excellent. With cheese, English biscuits and some of the Scandinavian wafers are good. For pre-dinner nibbles, Oriental snacks—rice crackers with peanuts, vegetables, and even dried fish and seaweed—are fun and offer new tastes. The German and Swiss after-dinner wafers (often dipped in rich chocolate) can provide an elegant accompaniment to a chocolate, praline, or lemon mousse. These are available in the imported-foods section of some good supermarkets. A larger (and perhaps more authentic) variety of imported foods can be found in shops located in neighborhoods of different ethnic backgrounds, such as Italian, Greek, Portuguese, Chinese, and German.

WHOLESALE DEALERS For large jobs you can economize without sacrificing quality by buying the ingredients in bulk from wholesale dealers. The dealers to use are those who supply the good restaurants. Often I've found that the quality of their merchandise is better than I could find at retail stores. To locate wholesale merchants, look in the Yellow Pages under Meat—Whol., Fruits and Vegetables—Whol., Dairy Products—Whol., and Food Products. When you call, you can describe what you are doing, and if they are not interested in your business because the quantities are too small, they will almost always be able to tell you of another dealer who *will* handle your business. When first calling around, remember to ask for restaurant suppliers, because they have high-quality stock. One of the advantages of wholesale merchants is that they deliver free of charge. You can phone in your order (usually the day before you want it delivered) and then continue working in the kitchen, saving the time you would have spent shopping. A note of caution: ordering by phone only works if you remain vigilant that the highest standards of quality are maintained. It's always a good idea to have the dealer close enough that you can easily go over in person if necessary, so call the nearby ones first.

If you are calling up the wholesale fruit-and-vegetable dealer, here are some things to remember (some of these apply to any wholesale merchant):

- Have ready a complete list of what you want to order.
- Be confident and businesslike, pleasant but firm (not embarrassed or apologetic).
- Before giving any order, get price quotes on more expensive items. When I have a really substantial quantity of one item (for example, three cases of strawberries), I'll get quotes from two or three dealers. While it's good to establish a rapport with a dealer you can trust to give you the highest quality, you don't want him to take your business for granted and become less competitive in his prices.
- Wholesale dealers are usually willing to bargain on both price and quantity. They will sometimes say they don't want to break up a case, but they can often be persuaded to do so if you remain firm that you won't buy a whole case.
- It's a good idea always to deal with the same person. He gets to know what you like and you get to know what he means by "ripe".
- Ask frankly if, for example, the avocados are ready to eat or how big and dense the heads of lettuce are.
- Get him to guarantee delivery by a certain time.
- Ask how much the total order will cost so that you can have enough cash on hand.

Very Important: When the delivery is made, *before* the delivery-man has left, check everything. If something is not ripe enough, send it back. The next time it will be ripe enough or the dealer will tell you when you ask for it that it's not.

MEAT AND POULTRY DEALERS Some meat dealers will let you go into the refrigerated room where they cut up your order. (It's cold, so dress warmly!) I have found this fascinating—and the best way to make sure I get exactly what I want (at least until the dealer knows what I like). It's an education—not just seeing where the various cuts come from on the carcasses, but also watching these professionals deftly cut and slice. What better way to learn how to debone, roll, and tie roasts?

Wholesale butchers are not for the squeamish. There are huge hanging carcasses that look distinctly like half a headless, skinned cow hanging upside down. As beef ages, the outside becomes purple and rotten. This means that the meat is probably tender, despite the extremely unappetizing nature of what they cut off before handing you your piece.

If you are unable to go in person to the meat dealer, ask for one man specifically, who will make sure you get the best-quality meat, cut in such and such a way. I always say I want the roasts wrapped in fat for example, and I also want any bones that have been removed included in the box (from which I can make rich stocks to freeze). If there is one person responsible for your order, when it has arrived you can call up to express your appreciation to him and mention anything that isn't to your liking.

DAIRY For big jobs, it often pays to order milk, cream, butter, eggs, and cream cheese in commercial rather than domestic sizes. For example, you can get three-pound or ten-pound containers of cream cheese, instead of the more expensive eight-ounce (250 g) size that you see at the store. Also, having five half-gallons of milk and ten dozen eggs *delivered* saves the energy of carrying these from the store and unloading them.

HOW MUCH DO YOU NEED TO BUY TO WARRANT A WHOLE-SALE ORDER? When I first called wholesale dealers, I was nervous that my orders would be too small. (At the beginning, I actually ordered more than I needed!) I've since found that they are happy to have my business and will simply tell me if they can't break up a case or give me only half a leg of ham. I have no strict rule for myself about when I use wholesale dealers. It just seems the obvious thing to do if I need six pounds of ground beef or twelve chickens.

Now each time I have a job where I'll use the wholesale butcher, I order plenty of extra for the family and freeze it—and I order the type of meat we often use at home *as well*. When I do smaller jobs, I usually have the meat or poultry I need on hand in the freezer—all bought at wholesale prices.

There are seasons for meats and poultry much as there are for fresh fruits and vegetables. Find out from the butcher good times to stock up on pork, beef, lamb, turkeys, hams, chickens, etc. If you like organ meats such as kidneys, liver, hearts, and giblets, they have a much more interesting selection at the wholesale dealer than the one normally seen at the supermarket or the small butcher.

CAUTION The economies of using wholesale dealers can quickly be wiped out if you get carried away and order too large a quantity of anything that can't be frozen without loss of quality. I'm referring especially to fresh fruits and vegetables and to dairy products such as cheese.

You may wish to order staples such as sugar, flour, and rice in bulk, but I'd be careful not to order any food which deteriorates over time (however slowly). Oil, for example, will eventually go rancid once it is opened. Even white flour is best not kept for too long, and whole-wheat flour should be refrigerated. The catering business is sporadic, and you might buy large stocks of staples and then find them sitting unused for months. The money you spend stocking a larder full of supplies won't be in the bank earning interest.

BAKERIES Unless you are passionately fond of (and good at) quickly making elaborate pastries and breads, I suggest you use professional bakeries for at least some of your baked goods. Sometimes to have three or four types of homemade cookie to go with the fresh fruit salad adds just that special, personal touch that makes the time spent worth while. But the bakery has the equipment and skills, as well as the economy of scale, that are difficult to match for cost and efficiency.

Different bakeries have different specialties, so become acquainted with several in your area. Most will make up special orders if you call two days in advance. (Remember: bakeries are often closed on Mondays.)

Here is what I consider when deciding whether to use a bakery for an order or to do it myself:

- Quality. Whose is better?
- Cost. Whose is cheaper? Don't just consider the cost of the

ingredients, but calculate the time it takes for you to prepare and cook the item (a straightforward loaf of bread is always more economical to buy than it is to make yourself, for example).

- Convenience. Can I take the time to make this myself with everything else I have to do?
- Enjoyment. Would I enjoy making it?

FRESH PRODUCE When shopping, I spend more time choosing fresh produce than I do on all the other ingredients combined. Here are some of the ways I tell if fruits and vegetables are fresh and ripe. A high water content is evidenced by firmness, crispness, or tautness of the skin of a fruit or vegetable. It is one of the few ways of telling how long ago a piece of produce was picked and under what conditions of refrigeration it has been kept. The less water, the less fresh it is.

Color and firmness are the best clues as to ripeness. Yellow is often the color of either underripe or not-very-fresh produce.

Leafy vegetables such as lettuce, watercress, spinach, cabbage, Swiss chard, parsley, and endive should be kept moist (not wet) and cool—not *sealed* in plastic wrap or a plastic bag, which can cause them to rot. They shouldn't, of course, be wilted. A damp paper towel in the bag or container will provide the moisture the refrigeration removes. Leafy vegetables are better stored *before* washing. If you do wash them, be sure to spin the leaves completely dry before storing. Leaves should be left whole, not cut or torn, until just before they are to be eaten or cooked.

Outer lettuce leaves, which may be tougher and slightly bruised, probably won't be perfect enough for salads served to clients and can be either shredded along with carrots and served with dressing to the family or cooked until tender with peas in seasoned chicken stock and then puréed in the blender for a delicious soup which can be eaten hot or cold.

Asparagus should be neither very thin, nor very thick. Greengrocers will sometimes pack bunches with the skinny stalks hidden in the middle. Check this by looking at the bottom of the bunch. Check for rot halfway down the stalk by pulling a center stalk out. Be sure the stalks aren't limp and completely desiccated at the cut end.

String beans, carrots, and celery should snap easily if bent, indicating a high water content. While carrots and celery can be stored successfully for some time in the fridge, string beans get tough quickly.

Fresh peas when raw should taste sweet rather than starchy. The pod should look green and seem tender and crisp enough to eat.

Corn on the cob pull back part of the husk; the paler yellow the corn, the younger it is. The kernels should be close together, without spaces in between, and bursting with moisture.

Onions and garlic should hang so that air can circulate to keep them from rotting. For a different color and a milder taste, try using the purple Spanish onions when using them raw, as in salads.

Mushrooms The common button variety is freshest if dry and white, with the cap closed down to the stem. Dark spots mean moisture has started to rot them, and the taste will be changed. Most mushrooms do need cleaning, and it isn't practical to wipe them clean if you are using any sizeable quantity. To minimize the damage and bruising caused by water on mushrooms, I put a handful at a time in a sieve and shake this rapidly under a stream of cold water until the dirt has been rinsed away. The mushrooms gently wash each other this way. I then dry them on a dish towel. I wash them just before they will be used, whether they are to be cooked or eaten raw. For cooking, try the flat-topped, larger mushrooms which have a stronger flavor. These are more often (in my area at least) available in vegetable stores run by people from the Oriental cultures.

Tomatoes It isn't easy to describe a deliciously ripe tomato in North America, one so seldom sees (or tastes) a vine-ripened one. Growers have been breeding strains of tomatoes to make them more and more indestructible and, as far as I can tell, more and more tasteless. The rock-hard, dry, tasteless, and expensive excuse for a tomato you find all year round in the stores should be boycotted by us all. If we stopped buying them, growers would stop growing them. In Italy, the tomatoes (pomodoro, "apple of gold") are so full of flavor and juice that to eat one with a little salt, pepper, and olive oil is a course in itself. Add to this slices of fresh mozzarella and some fresh chopped basil and the tomato becomes a delicious light meal (especially good when served with crusty bread). As is fairly clear, I love tomatoes and do buy them all year round despite my better judgement. I've probably squeezed many thousands of tomatoes seeking that perfect feel of not-too-hard and not-too-soft. My best advice is to look for a deeper red color and not to buy any that feel hard enough to bounce on the floor. In fact, a really ripe tomato smells something like sun on freshly mown hay.

Berries such as strawberries, blueberries, raspberries, blackberries, and cherries each have their short season in summer. I try to satisfy a year's craving for these in a few short weeks by eating them in as many ways as I can think of: plain, in trifle, with ice cream, in a Bombe Surprise, with shortcake and whipped cream, on my cereal...but two weeks after I think I never want to eat another strawberry again, I pass some baskets of the end-of-season ones and sheepishly put two in my shopping cart. When berries are ripe, but not overripe, the skins are taut, the color is deep, they give slightly under pressure, and they have a ripe smell.

Melons are best and cheapest in early fall, but they can be good at almost any time. The way to tell if they are ripe is by pressing the non-stem end; it should give under pressure. Also, you should be able to hear the seeds rattle when you shake them.

Oranges The heavier and firmer they are, the juicier they will be. Watch out for soft or hard spots. The peak season for all citrus fruits is in the winter, so I use them less in the summer and fall months.

Grapes are best and cheapest in the the summer and fall; they should pull off their stems easily, without being brown where the stem meets the grape. Try one to see if it is sweet.

Apples should be firm; any softness means a drier, pulpier texture. Different types of apple have different seasons, but I use them most often in dishes during the cold weather.

Peaches, apricots, plums, and pears are late-summer fruits. They are ripest when the color is deeper, they give slightly under pressure, and they smell sweet.

Pineapples Try picking up the pineapple by one of its inner leaves; if the leaf pulls out easily, chances are the pineapple is ripe. It shouldn't be rock hard (or too soft) and it should have the light, perfumy smell of ripe pineapple.

Cleaning your produce makes sense because of all the pesticides sprayed on them. I do choose the prewashed potatoes instead of the mud-caked ones if the quality of potato is equivalent. The same goes for lettuce, spinach, mushrooms, etc. Cleaning very dirty produce takes valuable time.

Use what's in season. It's a good way to plan your menus. Though you can buy foods that were once seasonal all year round now, out-of-season produce has taken longer to get to the market, so is less fresh, and often it was picked before it was ripe. Of course, it's also more expensive.

Naturally the following isn't a comprehensive list of seasonal fresh produce. Different foods are available at different times, depending on where you live. My list is just a reminder to think along these seasonal lines when you plan your menus.

In the spring and early summer I look forward to asparagus and strawberries as they become more and more plentiful, cheaper, and of better quality. Watercress, fresh, sweet peas, and snow peas are especially delicate and tender at this time of year. Raspberries, blueberries, and rhubarb have such short seasons that you may want to consider freezing them for sauces and fillings for use later in the year.

During mid and late summer my favorites are vine-ripened tomatoes, peaches, apricots, pears, cherries, watermelon, corn, lima beans, zucchini, and summer squash.

Autumn brings with it many of the foods that are well suited to cooler weather: pumpkins, sweet potatoes, cranberries, and a wide variety of squash such as acorn and butternut. Then there are the melons: canteloupe, honeydew, watermelon, and casaba. All are usually amazingly sweet, juicy, and inexpensive in the fall. Apples, pears, and grapes are other fruits to focus on then.

Winter is the time to use the vegetables that are available all year round (they are easily stored and transported from warmer climates). These include: cabbage, carrots, onions, leeks, mushrooms, avocados, broccoli, cauliflower, brussels sprouts, and spinach.

When you cater, the appearance of what you serve is almost as important as the taste, so choose carefully produce that is as attractive as it is delicious.

CAUTION: FALSE ECONOMIES For the family, I enjoy obtaining bargains on very ripe reduced produce, but for catering jobs I'm careful about buying fruits and vegetables that have been radically reduced for quick sale. If the store wants to sell it today, it's probably because they won't be able to sell it tomorrow! "Quick Sale" usually means "Eat Me Today". If you decide to save four dollars by buying the eight baskets of slightly overripe strawberries that are such a bargain, you may discover that by the following day, when you are ready to serve those strawberries, they are close to mush, and the damage to the looks and taste of your dessert is much more than four dollars' worth.

CANNED AND FROZEN FOODS Even the most humble fresh vegetables can be prepared in interesting ways that make them better than canned or frozen ones.

Canned foods have been (over)cooked and packed in water with added salt and sugar, so they have lost texture, color, taste, and nutrients.

The freezing process breaks down vegetable and fruit fibers, so the texture is never as firm or as crisp as that of fresh produce. Also, before freezing, all vegetables are slightly cooked and salted; this destroys some of their flavor.

There are some canned and frozen products which are acceptable and useful, however:

Tomatoes If a recipe calls for long stewing (e.g. spaghetti sauce), and if ripe cooking (pear) tomatoes are not available, you should use Italian canned pear tomatoes. They are a different, stronger-flavored type of tomato which is better cooked and not normally eaten fresh. They are also already peeled, a laborious job if you're cooking a quantity.

Tomato paste To make this on your own is time-consuming and messy.

Lichee nuts and water chestnuts Oriental districts may have these fresh.

Pitted olives are less damaged and shrivelled and more "polite" to eat (no pit to hide in a cocktail napkin), even if they have a less interesting flavor than the open-barrel deli-store variety.

Pickles Avoid lurid green ones. You may make your own pickles; I find I don't use enough of them to warrant doing so.

Ketchup, mustard, HP Sauce, soya and Worcestershire sauces, dried herbs and spices

Mayonnaise There are times when a homemade mayonnaise is preferable (e.g. a dill mayonnaise sauce for poached salmon), but I use prepared "real" mayonnaise for many dishes and find its texture and flavor very good.

Frozen peas are good, especially if quickly cooked with a leaf of lettuce and a little mint. Fresh peas have a very short season and are too time-consuming to prepare for large groups.

Avoid: Canned soups and cake mixes. The flavor of these is unmistakable for even a moderately discerning palate.

Wines and liquors add delicate flavors and exotic tastes, so I use them liberally. I don't buy the cheapest wine, especially when I need it to flavor a delicate fish or chicken sauce. I find that, understandably enough, the sauce tastes like a cheap wine sauce if I do.

SUMMING UP

ABOUT INGREDIENTS:
Use the best, and whenever possible use fresh ingredients.
Use foods at the height of their season, designing and adjusting menus around what's available.
Use canned, frozen, and prepared foods with discretion and restraint.

ABOUT SHOPPING:
Make a market list organized according to where each ingredient is found in the store or stores.
When larger quantities are needed, order food through wholesale dealers.
Figure out a shopping route that allows you to check what's available at the supermarket first and then go from shop to shop with the fewest possible trips by car.
Stock up, when possible, on items that are only available at some distance.
Buy food that needs refrigeration at the end of your shopping trip and highly perishable foods on the day of the party.
Pack your own boxes at the checkout counter.

CHAPTER 13

HIRING HELP IN THE KITCHEN

It was some time near the end of June, a hot, sunny day. Chickens had been cooking in the oven since 6 a.m. I had just deboned eight of them. It was my third job that week, and I'd started cooking for it the night before—after coming home from another job.

I sat on a stool, elbows on the table, greasy hands dripping over the pile of chicken bones, and looked around the kitchen. A case of strawberries to be hulled sat on the counter and there were potatoes in the sink ready to be scrubbed, peeled, and boiled. Stockpots on the stove were steaming up the room. Miscellaneous utensils, bowls, and cookbooks were propped up and scattered around the counters...and I felt fed up, with cooking, with food, with the whole business.

The phone rang. It was the client whose dinner I was cooking, "just calling to make sure everything was all right." Her nervous voice sounded like a child's whine. As I surveyed the piles of unprepared food, I assured her that everything was almost ready, hung up, and decided I needed to get out. Tossing off my apron, I stepped out into the sun and walked to the large park just a block away. I sat down on a bench and soaked up the rich scent of grass and trees. It was the first place I'd been in days *that didn't smell the least bit like food*. Something felt strange. Then I realized that the last time I'd been in the park there had been snow on the ground. I had missed the spring. I had done so much shopping, cooking, serving, and cleaning up that I felt as though I hadn't *lived* the past few months.

As I walked back to the kitchen, I decided something would have to change.

The change I made then I wish I'd made much earlier. I stopped trying to do all the food preparation myself and began to hire people to cut and chop, to butter bread and wash lettuce, to peel potatoes, to hull strawberries, and...to debone chickens.

It was then I began the arrangement I use now. I shop and do any setting-up work the day before a job and hire enough people to enable me to do all the preparation on the day of the party.

At first I hired my friends, but that wasn't always easy because I'm very exacting and I felt awkward about criticizing and giving them orders. Our relationship had to change. I was "the boss". I remember one time I hired a friend who couldn't talk and work at the same time. Each time he would start to say something he'd stop cutting until he was finished and then look around as if trying to remember what he'd been doing before he started. Oddly his presence slowed everybody down (me included!). Yet I couldn't bring myself to say, "If you can't talk and work at the same time, don't talk!"

You will undoubtedly have the frustrating experience of watching someone you've hired work very slowly. I've sometimes thought I could do twice as much as the people I've hired if only I didn't have to supervise! But, in fact, much of food preparation simply takes a certain number of hours to do, and even reducing a task to the fewest possible motions can only reduce the time it takes by a limited amount.

I've found that the best way to encourage people who work for me to be productive is to

- set up the job they will be doing in their own cleared spot in the kitchen, and put all the ingredients and equipment they will need together so they don't have to wander around looking for the peeler or the sieve.
- have two people work together as a team on the more laborious and unpleasant jobs such as deboning chickens or shelling and deveining shrimp.
- change the type of job often enough so that they don't get bogged down in the boredom of monotonous work. People have different preferences about which job they would like to do, so I usually explain what needs doing and ask which they would prefer.
- have a formal break for lunch where everyone gets out of the kitchen and eats something other than what they are preparing. It refreshes us and is a good time to assess progress and to assign what still needs to be done.
- get them to think about better ways to do something. Those who work for me now often have excellent suggestions and

reactions that help me to evaluate and improve what I'm making. Now, if someone asks how I want something done, I ask what *she* thinks would be a good way.

I've finally learned to be more relaxed myself. I need to remind myself less and less often that everything will get finished. I use up less energy needlessly worrying.

I have an excellent and dependable group of people I call on to help me now. I feel congenial with them, and a very pleasant camaraderie develops as we work together; but, for the most part, they are acquaintances rather than friends.

Here are the guidelines I use when hiring people. They should be hard workers and be able to accept direction and criticism easily without feeling hurt. While obviously it is useful if they have some experience in the kitchen, I find clashes of opinion happen more often with those who are "serious" cooks. I've shown those who work with me now how I like things done, so they work almost completely on their own once I explain what the different tasks are. As in most things, intelligence and attitude are the most important considerations.

Especially if you hire friends or acquaintances, it's a good idea to make clear right from the start the businesslike nature of the job. They aren't just "dropping by to give you a hand". They should arrive at a specific time, for example. Money is always an awkward subject among friends. State clearly what you will pay them (I pay $5.50 per hour).

There are some drawbacks to hiring others to help in the kitchen. Because of the interruptions, it gets harder to concentrate on the cooking you're doing yourself. On large jobs when there are three people working, I feel more like a supervisor than a cook. More than three extra people and things become too hectic, in my kitchen at least. After that, the law of diminishing returns holds true: the more people, the less I get done.

Because I still do all of what I consider are the crucial "taste-making" decisions, I try to do the most important of these early in the morning before the others arrive. Jobs for fewer than twenty-five people I still prefer to do myself.

Certainly an advantage to hiring others to help is that one person can be given the job of clearing and washing whenever and wherever it is necessary—leaving me to concentrate on the cooking (and supervising).

Hiring others also seems to reduce the pressure I feel, probably because everything gets done with plenty of time to spare. So, don't wait, as I did, until you are at the end of your proverbial rope before getting help.

CHAPTER 14

SERVING

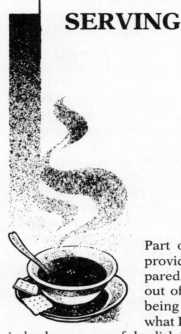

Part of your job as a caterer will be to provide someone to serve what you've prepared. While some caterers don't like to go out of the kitchen to serve, I believe that being on hand to pass around or dish up what I've prepared is the best way for me to judge how successful a dish is. Is the custard too thick on the bite-size pieces of quiche Lorraine, so that people have difficulty picking them up without their breaking? Could the meatballs be a little smaller? The sauce a little thicker? So many of these things are only understood as you watch people eat. This is especially true of hors d'oeuvres. When I'm in the kitchen, the food looks one way. When I step out among the guests, I suddenly see it as though through their eyes, and it appears quite different. How people respond when eating something I've made is the best way to tell if I've got something just right or if it's less successful.

(Another reason for serving what I prepare is that I would have to be working at the location anyway, and if I'm one of the waitresses, I get paid to be there; otherwise the hours spent there would just be part of my job as cook.)

BUFFET MEALS During buffet meals for large groups of people, I make sure I stand behind the table dishing up the food. It's never a good idea to let people help themselves. Too often people (especially the young ones) take more than they can eat. You risk running out of food at the buffet table and seeing large portions scraped into the garbage. One of my first large buffet suppers was for an architects' convention of about a hundred and twenty people. There were three choices of entrée: cold sliced roast beef, Vitello Tonnato, and cold salmon with a fresh dill mayonnaise. I let people help themselves and watched with horror as the first forty people blithely walked by the beef and veal and helped themselves to large chunks of the salmon. (I hadn't even thought to precut the fillets into modest-sized portions.) The hostess herself was the last through the line, and of course by then there was no salmon left. She quickly understood what had happened and, an architect herself, she laughed and said, "I should have told you about letting a pack of architects loose on salmon."

Now, while serving buffet meals, I have a sense of how much food there is and how many people remain to be fed. I can control almost entirely how fast different dishes are finished by the size of the portion I place on each plate. (The big-chain ice-cream parlors and fast-food restaurants understand how one extra tablespoonful doesn't seem like much, but when multiplied by several million may represent tens of thousands of dollars. The same principle holds true when feeding sixty or a hundred people. A dozen portions may be "lost" if the person serving has a heavy hand or even uses too large a serving spoon.)

Without being stingy, it's better to give people somewhat small helpings—especially women, who often are watching their weight. People can always come back for seconds. Yet, when dishing up, I always ask if a helping is large enough or whether the guest would like more. I am delighted if someone wants a big portion, and I let him know that nothing pleases a cook more.

SERVING TIPS As I have said, serving the food myself helps me evaluate what I've prepared and control how fast it goes. Even more importantly, good service can actually make the food taste better. The whole experience of the guests and the host can be made more pleasant by subtle adjustments in how the food is offered and how the waitresses move among the guests.

To enhance the guests' enjoyment of the food, I regard what I serve as a precious delicacy. That may sound farfetched, but imagine a plate of delicately balanced whipped-cream pastries. If you carefully hold it level and move it slowly toward the person to whom you are offering it, it then seems like a treat which draws the attention of the person about to take one and creates a sense of expectation. (It probably even gets the juices flowing, so the food literally melts in their mouths.) The trick is to treat everything you serve with that same sense of its specialness—even a basket of bread. Bring the basket to the level where the guest can look down into it. A common mistake is to offer something to a person who is seated on a low sofa by holding the serving dish so high that the guest must shift his position and stretch to peer over the edge. If, as in this case of the bread, you bend down, holding the basket low in front of the guest, engage his or her attention, and then lift back the linen napkin to reveal the "treasure", the chances are much greater that the guest will be tempted to take a slice.

To engage the attention for a brief instant is another important aspect of serving. My own theory is that we feel positively when we make direct eye-contact with another person. That positive response is transferred to the food. So, if I approach a group of people who are talking and offer a plate of hors d'oeuvres, I don't just shove the plate into the center of the group and expect people to help themselves; I offer it to each person, one at a time. This helps to avoid the awkwardness people feel about who should help himself first. Men don't usually like to help themselves before the women, so I offer it to the nearest woman first, engaging her and each other member of the group by making brief eye-contact while bringing the plate within very comfortable reach. A guest shouldn't have to lean across and risk dropping the appetizer before it reaches her mouth. All of this happens very quickly of course, and the conversation isn't even interrupted. What is left is a sense of... well, graciousness, for lack of a better word.

Often, at crowded parties, there is simply no way to offer food and remove dirty plates without practically climbing through the guests. At such parties, if serving from the left and clearing from the right means stepping or reaching between two people having a conversation, I disregard the rule. When taking away plates that have been finished and then set on the floor or on coffee tables among the guests, I simply try to be as inconspicuous as possible. I won't ask someone to hand me a plate unless I have no other way of getting it.

All motions when serving should be slow, relaxed, and graceful. I may be rushing madly out in the kitchen, but when I enter the serving area I am not in a hurry. Serving hors d'oeuvres at a crowded cocktail party can be like attending a dance where you slip gracefully in and out of the crush. I seldom ask people to move; usually someone blocking my way will sense my presence and automatically move out of the way without being conscious of an interruption.

HIRING OTHERS TO HELP YOU SERVE You will want to arrange for those who will be serving and working with you in the kitchen yourself—and the client will expect you to. It's a help, but not essential, for those you hire to have serving experience. More important is a readiness to do everything from washing the lettuce, to serving, to opening champagne, to cleaning ashtrays, to sweeping the floor. The hours spent on the location of a job are extremely busy, and demanding, and sometimes very long. There is often no time for a break—even to sit down for a moment. (Make sure everyone wears comfortable shoes.) On the job, it is important that those around me can take initiative. They should notice that the bowl of rice out on the buffet table is getting low and prepare a refill dish before I've had time to become aware that the first is almost empty (because I've been at the other side of the table serving the main course).

I don't ever wait until I've scraped the bottom of the bowl before replacing it with a fresh, full serving dish, and of course I never scrape the contents of an almost-empty bowl into the full one in front of the guests (I wait until I'm out in the kitchen to do it).

Those who work with me now *enjoy* being out among the guests. This is essential. I *have* hired people who wanted to hide in the kitchen and had to be told to get out and start serving. I think it's important that those who serve with me are attractive, clean, and neat, with a natural gracefulness and personality enough to project positively. We wear dark skirts (or pants for the men), dark shoes, and white shirts with black-satin string ties. The women's aprons are made of a discreet black-and-white-flowered print material. The men wear straight-front aprons made of a black-and-white pinstripe material. Design or find your own matching aprons. They should have ample pockets. Each bartender, waiter, and waitress wears a small rectangular white pin with our name and logo printed on it in black. We carry business cards in our pockets to hand out if anyone asks for one.

It's a good idea to arrange for the bartenders, waiters, and waitresses as soon as you know you have a job. I explain what time they should arrive at my house in order to leave for the client's, how long I expect the party to last, and what type of gathering I expect it to be. At the location of the party, I explain approximately what will be served when. If you are working with someone for the first time, especially if he or she is inexperienced, you might have a brief training session before the guests arrive (or let them read the first section of this chapter) to make them more conscious of how to serve well. I try to work with the same people as much as possible; that way I know what each does best. And we have a good time in the kitchen gossiping about the guests.

WHAT TO PAY BARTENDERS/WAITERS/WAITRESSES Rates per hour vary from place to place. I'm told that in New York City the rate is sometimes more than $10 per hour. I pay $30 for the first four hours and $6 for each hour after that. I make it clear to the client that gratuities are not included, and if they ask how much to tip, I suggest a tip of anywhere between $10 and $20 per server. This means that if waitresses and waiters work for seven hours, including travel time, it is $30 + (3 hrs. overtime) $18 = $48 + $15 tip = $63, for a wage of approximately $9 per hour. Bartenders, who should have some experience, by the way, earn $40 for the first four hours and $6 for each additional hour after that, plus tip (restaurants will often gladly recommend qualified bartenders).

It is a good idea to have enough cash on hand to be able to pay everyone immediately at the end of the job. Remember to keep careful track of what you've spent in order to charge the client.

Find out the average hourly wages that waitresses and bartenders earn in your area (when calculated with tips and salary combined) and use this as a guideline.

HOW MANY BARTENDERS AND WAITRESSES/WAITERS ARE NEEDED TO SERVE? The rule of thumb is one waiter for every ten guests, but I find that it is better to calculate according to each specific job.

An elegant, full-service, sit-down dinner for twelve people needs two waitresses and one bartender.

For a buffet supper for sixty, I would hire two bartenders and four waitresses.

For a cocktail party of a hundred and fifty people I'd hire four to six bartenders (four if the host wants it self-serve only, or six if he wants two bartenders roving among the guests taking some orders and clearing glasses). I'd probably hire six to eight waitresses/waiters, according to how elaborate the food and how much the host is willing to pay.

In other words, the number of servers needed per guest is lower the larger the group. One reason for this is that it becomes too hectic out in the kitchen with too many. It also becomes more difficult to keep track of who has served what to whom. While more help is not always better, it usually is. I don't recommend trying to economize for the client by hiring fewer servers than I've suggested here. After the food itself, gracious and efficient service is the single most important part of the job. Your reputation is on the line. Understaffing can change the ambiance at a party. Even the best waitress won't be able to hide the fact that she is rushed if people are stopping her to ask for drinks because there is a pile-up at the bar. Ashtrays don't get emptied and dirty glasses don't get cleared. In the past, I have occasionally given in to a client's wish to economize by hiring fewer staff. Now it is a point on which I politely but firmly insist. (After all, I'm going to be one of those who is overworked!) Occasionally, too, people will say that they will look after the bar themselves in order to avoid hiring a bartender. For a party of twelve or so, this may be fine, but for larger groups, I often find that "volunteer" bartenders lose interest, and guests sometimes start asking me for drinks and wandering into the kitchen for ice or more cold wine. These economy-minded clients don't realize how much more there is to a bartender's job than pouring drinks. Dirty glasses have to be cleared—perhaps washed—wine has to be chilled, ice replenished, empty bottles removed. Help-yourself bars quickly become littered with bottle caps, corks, spilled drinks, and dirty glasses. Inevitably the waitresses are burdened with this.

For most dinner jobs the demand for bartenders diminishes at mealtime, once the wine has been served. At that point, one bartender can circulate for the refill requests, while the other can help clear plates or set up the coffee. This is why the staff needs to be flexible in what they are willing to do. By the same token, at a wedding, when all the guests may arrive at virtually the same moment, it is often necessary for the waitresses to help with the drinks. (I've opened hundreds of bottles of champagne. The guests' sense of celebration is so infectious that it can be lots of fun.)

COCKTAIL PARTIES Though I always serve some hors d'oeuvres myself, especially during the peak eating times at a cocktail party, I will usually spend more time in the kitchen than the other waitresses. My job is to cook and keep warm just the right number of appetizers so that a fresh, hot plate is ready just as the empty one comes back.

I also freshen up, fill, and decorate new plates, keeping an eye on the remaining quantities of each different type of hors d'oeuvre and pacing how fast each is used up. Some things go faster than others; smoked salmon and shrimp tend to "evaporate". I save a few plates of these until later in the evening; it gives the impression of more abundant quantities of the most expensive hors d'oeuvres.

I have the light appetizers such as cheese straws or crudités with dip go out first, followed later by the more substantial meatballs or chicken teriyaki—always making sure that different types of hors d'oeuvre are rotated so that someone isn't offered the cucumber with cream cheese and caviar three times in a row.

Cocktail parties have their own natural timing. For the first half-hour to forty-five minutes, while guests arrive and begin their drinks, they don't want to eat much, so only a few plates of appetizers go out at about ten-minute intervals. Then, quite suddenly, about two hours into the party, the alcohol has weakened people's dieting resolve and their dinner-time hunger has caught up with them; they sometimes begin to eat so much they may take two or three hors d'oeuvres from each plate. We go into full swing. All the plates that have been so carefully arranged are taken out in rapid-fire succession. For large groups, different areas are assigned to different waitresses, and they must remember where they ran out of the chicken or the quiche so that they can begin there with the next plate.

Sometimes a group of hungry young men station themselves just outside the kitchen door to pounce on any plate of food that emerges. I enjoy seeing them eat so heartily (even if I'm not sure they always appreciate how beautifully arranged and decorated plates of food are).

I confess that because I want the client to see the plates while they are still attractive, I will usually point the host and hostess out to those who are serving and tell the waitresses to be sure to offer them food when the plates are looking their best. Once twenty or so hands have "worked over" a plate of appetizers, even if a few remain I will bring it back to the kitchen and transfer the remaining ones to a fresh and attractively decorated plate.

After the rush on food, a time comes when people take a break, and it's tempting to think the feeding is over. It usually picks up again later, however, and I bring out any sweet appetizers during this last phase, surprising people with something new and finishing off the "meal" so to speak.

Always carry a small number of cocktail napkins in one pocket (with the business cards). If there are hors d'oeuvres on long bamboo skewers or toothpicks, offer the other pocket to people to drop the used ones in. This saves the guests from awkwardly holding them or setting them down in ashtrays (which looks unattractive). Speaking of ashtrays, one of the jobs of those who serve is to clear regularly all the dirty glasses, to replace full ashtrays with empty, clean ones, and generally to wipe coffee tables and pick up stray napkins and toothpicks. Any accidents, such as a guest dropping a glass, should be quickly and discreetly dealt with. Have the client show you where she keeps brooms and other cleaning materials.

WEDDINGS Weddings are an exception to the rule that people don't eat much during the first hour. People are usually hungry the moment they arrive and tend to eat as much as thirty percent more than I would expect them to at a cocktail party. My theory is that it is due to the heightened emotional tension we all feel vicariously for the bride and groom. When this tension is suddenly relieved (with the sound of popping champagne corks), people seem to feel ravenously hungry.

If at weddings there is to be a series of different activities: the champagne, hors d'oeuvres, dinner, cutting of the cake, toasts and speeches, serving of the cake and coffee, and the couple's farewell, I keep in touch with the hostess and let her know when I think the guests are ready for the next stage. Few hostesses feel confident about this (after all, how many wedding receptions have they given?) and it is reassuring for her to have me circulating constantly among the guests and letting her know that the guests are getting restless for the next phase.

When the bride and groom have made their symbolic cut in the cake, I whisk it away and, as the speeches are being made, cut it up. If the cake is round and tiered, remove the top layer and set this aside for the bride and groom's personal use. Cut an inner circle in the next layer about 2½ in. (6 cm) in from the outer edge. Then cut up the circles into ½ in. (2 cm) slices. The best way to serve the cake seems to be to place each piece on a luncheon napkin or plate and set these on a tray to be passed around.

If dinner has been served and cleared, I've found it's a good idea to keep a plate or two of food aside for ravenous brides, best men, or fathers of the bride who have forgotten to eat.

I've often thought that doing a catering job is like putting on a play. There is the excitement of opening night as the final touches are added to each plate—a sprig of parsley or a twisted slice of lemon. The guests arrive, expectant and glamorous; there is laughter and the clinking of glasses as we go out to begin the performance.

The intensity of the work makes the hours slip by. Several things always seem to need to be done at once. Like actresses coming off stage, the waitresses return to the kitchen and take a quick drink of soda before going back out "on stage" among the guests with a fresh, full plate of hors d'oeuvres.

Yet, while the serving up of the food on location is the most exciting and challenging part of catering, it has its difficult side, too. Being in a situation where I am serving is a test of my own sense of who I am. The purpose of a uniform is to separate you from the guests. Normally, your clothes help to project your personality; a uniform disguises your personality so that you blend with the others who wear the same uniform. The word "uniform" says it all. But, of course, everything that makes me who I am—my personality, intelligence, humor—is still there. Most guests just don't see it. And I must resist the temptation to *make* them see it by intruding who I am into the party. It is not my party; these are not my friends.

Up until I walk out among the guests, it is my "scene"; out in the kitchen, I'm the boss. But, as I serve, I must accept the fact that to most I am faceless—oh, pleasant, and laughing at jokes directed to me...but not really answering them as who I am. I mustn't feel as though I have to prove that "serving hors d'oeuvres isn't all I do".

You may ask, "Why can't I just be myself?" But you do remain yourself. That's very important. I've discovered that you can have a presence and even a sort of dignity that communicates itself without your needing to say anything.

The reason I mustn't talk about myself, or venture my opinions on the subject I hear people discussing, is that for people to include the waitress as one of themselves makes them feel more awkward about being served by her and having her clear away their dirty plates and ashtrays.

I've had a few experiences where I relaxed my reserve and, at the host's request, sat at the end of the evening with the host and the few remaining guests and talked to them about what I do, where I went to college, my work as a sculptor, etc. In each case, and despite the fact that two of them had been regular clients, I was never hired again. I know I did a good job, and that they were very pleased with the food and the service, but I believe they felt awkward about hiring me to cook and serve after they had gotten to know me even a little.

THE CASE OF THE DISAPPEARING GUESTS Occasionally clients will decide that the best way to save money once they've been given a price per person is to reduce the number of guests they say they are expecting. The caterer's only defence against this is to explain clearly (and write in the contract) that the price per person will go up if the number is significantly reduced and will go down if the number of guests is significantly increased (by more than twenty-five people, for example). It's also a good idea to tell the client a specific date after which the number of meals paid for cannot be changed. Hopefully this will prevent what happened to me on the job I describe below. I include it in the chapter on serving because that is the area most affected if more guests show up than were expected.

I was delighted when I got a call from a woman who lives on what is perhaps the most exclusive street in Montreal. (Good exposure, I thought.) All the houses there are enormous, with rolling gardens and spectacular views out over the city. Mrs. Petite's (not her real name) house was no exception, with large rooms, luxuriously furnished. (One thing, however, about those older houses, built during times when servants were plentiful: the kitchens are *small*.)

Mrs. Petite and I had a very pleasant meeting, though she seemed unusually cost-conscious, exchanging cheaper, more ordinary appetizers for any even slightly more interesting ones I'd thought of, and asking for sandwiches rather than any of a variety of cold entrées I suggested, but I didn't sense there would be any problem.

On receiving the contract, however, she began to make a series of economizing changes: for instance, eliminating the dessert and changing the dish rentals to those of the cheapest quality in order to save three cents on each glass and two cents a plate. She also kept reducing the number of guests she was expecting. I guess I hadn't made it clear that the price per person would rise if the number of guests dropped, because Mrs. Petite seemed offended when, after she dropped the number of her guests from one hundred and fifty to one hundred, I told her that the price per person would have to go up somewhat.

In fact, she reduced the number of people expected twice more—the last time on the day before the party, when I'd already bought most of the food. I was beginning to get annoyed, but I was too involved in preparing the food at that point to take much issue over it.

The day of the party was hot. When we all arrived, Mrs. Petite kept coming anxiously into the kitchen to remind me of something or to see how we were doing. To me, in my already tired state, she seemed like one of those nervous little dogs that are constantly yapping and getting under foot, when we had enough problems anyway balancing and stacking up the plates of appetizers in the refrigerator, which she hadn't cleared; we ended up putting coolers with food in a small bedroom off the kitchen. To be fair, my own patience was probably wearing thin because I had done so many jobs in the past few weeks.)

Then the guests began to come...and come. The house and garden filled up, but soon a brief shower sent those who had been outside into the already-overcrowded rooms. The humidity was so high it was like a steam bath in the kitchen, and just plain uncomfortably hot out among the guests, especially for those of us on the move serving and for the bartenders who were mixing a steady stream of drinks. There were jams at the bars, which meant that guests were handing us their glasses and asking for Scotch and sodas as we stood holding plates of food that would be instantly picked clean, often before we had time to get through the crush to the next room.

I had hired staff enough for the eighty-five she had finally said would be there. It turned out when I took a count of the soup bowls that were used that there had been over a hundred and fifty people. I learned later that nearly half of the guests were going to another party and had said they'd have to leave early. Mrs. Petite had simply subtracted these people as though they wouldn't have to be fed—which of course wasn't true; they all ate before leaving.

We waitresses were jostled as we tried to move around, and drunk men would bump up close and crack dirty jokes. As I said, the ambiance of a party can change if there is a feeling of press and rush and if there are too few staff to deal with it. This one had certainly changed for the worse.

Mrs. Petite wanted supper served early (probably because sixty or so of the guests were about to go to the other party). After the supper was eaten, guests began to leave in large numbers while we gathered up soup bowls and glasses from the tables, floors, mantelpiece, stairway, and other less-expected spots around the house (two were in a potted plant).

Afterwards, there was the haggling I expected over the bill. She insisted that there hadn't been eighty-five guests there even when I wondered aloud how, then, one hundred and forty-eight bowls had been used when not everyone had had soup. (Fortunately the rental company had mistakenly delivered the original order for the hundred and fifty people. The order had been changed so often, I'm surprised that the right dishes arrived at all.)

I chalked that evening up to experience. You can do very little to prevent a client from having more guests than she tells you there will be, but it has happened so rarely with me that I don't take any special precautions to avoid it. I guess I consider it one of the hazards of the business.

As the whole staff drove home together that night, punchy and a little hilarious from fatigue, we recounted our misadventures with various inebriated guests. Our laughter washed the evening away.

CHAPTER 15

DECORATION AND PRESENTATION

Your image and reputation as a caterer are based in large part on how your food looks, so it's worth spending time and money on garnishing food and creating displays that have flair and appeal.

The presentation side of catering intimidated me at first. I thought of myself as a cook, not a designer. Now, however, it is a side I especially enjoy. Decorating food and tables is very closely connected to your sense of how what you prepare should taste. (After all, one of the highest compliments you can pay a decorator is, "She has good taste.") If you add just the right crisp green, or tangy lemon yellow, you entice people visually to what you serve through their sense of how the garnishes "taste".

People are impressed by, attracted to, and eat more of, something that has been beautifully or unusually displayed. I was reminded of this once again at a large wedding reception I catered just recently. One of the appetizers was melon balls and pieces of prosciutto on long bamboo skewers stuck into pineapples. I'd set the pineapples on tables, but decided they were too awkward to carry around, so we passed among the guests with the same skewered melon and prosciutto set on plates. An hour or so into the party, the guests had shifted out to the front lawn away from the tent and the tables with the pineapples, so I decided to carry them through to set among the guests. I hadn't gotten more than three or four steps into the area where the guests were when I was virtually surrounded by people oohing and aahing over the beautiful fan of bamboo-speared melon balls. The pineapple was picked almost clean before I reached the table where I had meant to set it down! The same appetizer served from a plate had caused none of the same excitement.

Though I still believe how the food *tastes* is the most important consideration, as I have become confident about that aspect, I've found my attention and imagination drawn to interesting and appetizing forms of presentation. Every time I look through magazines with food advertisements or go out to restaurants, I make mental notes of ideas. Window displays at chic kitchen-supply stores and kitchen departments often show inexpensive accessories and present absolutely free ideas.

However, it's surprisingly easy to forget that the whole point behind decorating food is to make it more appetizing—not just more beautiful. Recently I heard of a catering company which had been so lavish in its decoration that a large hot-house iris had been incorporated into the visual effect of the food on each plate. Though I didn't see this myself, the guest who described it to me thought it was not actually very appetizing. Such decoration is no longer in the service of the food itself.

Not only should decorations be edible, they should actually enhance the flavor of the food as well as contrast with the appearance of what you serve.

One thing I learned during some work as a photographer's food stylist (this meant I cooked and set up the arrangement of food to be photographed for advertisements) is that less is more. Looking at the beautiful photographs in a magazine like *Gourmet*, I've often been struck by how a single sprig of watercress or one curl of candied orange peel on top of a portion of food has infinitely more eye appeal than a random scattering of several leaves and pieces. Restraint can be more effective than lavishness. I find it's often better *not* to try to put every color on every platter. As in many good paintings, if there are many different greens, just a touch or two of red is extremely effective and is all that is needed.

I'm learning all the time myself. Sometimes those who work with me in the kitchen will tease me after I've stood scowling over a serving platter—putting on the olives, then taking them off, moving the green pepper circles, then removing them and putting the olives back on . . .

GARNISHES AND DECORATION I enjoy garnishing and decorating so much now that I leave myself little else to do at the client's before most parties. When I look at an undecorated plate of food, it cries out for a color or a texture or a shape. The formlessness of cold sliced roast beef is complemented by the crisp, green, regular shape of green pepper rings. The "muddy" colors of some of the most delicious sauces can be made to look more appetizing by adding the contrast of fresh green herbs or sieved egg yolks next to chopped egg whites.

For appetizers, the garnish often adds a crucial element of taste. The sprig of dill on the cream cheese or the caviar on cucumber, the grated orange peel on the dates with Cointreau and cream cheese, the rolled anchovy, or the toasted almond may add just the flavor or texture that's needed.

Here are some suggestions for garnishing and decorating:

APPETIZERS OR HORS D'OEUVRES
   crumbled fried bacon
   parsley—flowerets or chopped
   black or green stuffed olives—sliced or chopped
   sprigs of dill
   lemon or orange rind—finely grated or candied
   gherkins or pickles—chopped or sliced
   carrots—curled or shredded
   radish roses
   red and black caviar
   pimento—slivered or chopped
   crushed ice (Though not exactly a food, it can make food seem
      more appetizing.)

SOUPS
   croutons
   sour cream
   whipped cream (salted)
   watercress leaves
   popcorn
   chopped parsley or chives
   chopped tomato or cucumber
   bacon bits
   miniature pastry puffs

ENTRÉES
Any of the above, plus
   toasted, seasoned breadcrumbs
   mushrooms—slivered and sautéed, or mushroom caps oiled
      and rolled in chopped parsley
   green or red pepper rings
   sieved egg yolk, chopped egg white
   lettuce, cabbage, watercress, or endive leaves

baby potatoes—oiled, tiny carrots, cherry tomatoes, asparagus, glazed onions

lemon—wedges, slices, or curls (slit the peel of a lemon slice in one place and twist)

gelatin coating or chopped aspic

plumped dried fruit (cooked in fruit juice and wine)

apricot halves filled with red jam

DESSERTS

sliced kiwi fruit

fresh raspberries, cherry halves, blueberries, or strawberries

peach slivers

mint

glazes (made of cornstarch, fruit juice, sugar, and water)

chocolate curls or chips

orange or lemon slices (or candied peel)

powdered sugar sprinkled onto lace paper doilies (to make a stencilled pattern)

toasted, grated coconut

nuts—toasted, grated, sliced, or sugar-coated (pralines)

chopped fruit—crystallized, dried, or brandy-soaked

whipped cream or icing that is piped in ribbons or flowerets

dribbled chocolate or caramel sauce

TABLE DECORATIONS When you meet with the client, it's a good idea to discuss her plans, if any, for decorating the table. Very often a hostess will take care of the flower arrangements, tablecloth, and napkins herself. If she'd rather you take care of them, get an idea of what type of arrangement she likes. Unless you are well versed in flower-arranging, I recommend you use a professional florist. (Either have the client billed directly, and you add a small fee for your trouble, or, if the florist prefers, you pay her and pass on the bill to the client.)

Flowers are by no means the only, or always the best, table decoration. It's fun to think of a theme around which the menu and the table accessories are chosen.

For a spring luncheon, yellows and pale greens could be the predominant colors. Try putting out bunches of daffodils and baskets lined with green and yellow napkins and filled with eggs or bread. There's also a Pasta Primavera (cold fettuccini and pieces of spring vegetables tossed in a vinaigrette) that looks beautiful in a glass bowl.

A harvest meal might have baskets overflowing with beautiful fresh vegetables. Squashes are attractive, and when the insides are scooped out, they make decorative and unusual serving dishes.

For Christmas I've made centerpieces with popcorn, tangerines, and small red bows scattered among evergreen branches.

As with garnishing, restraint is a good idea. Simple, attractive arrangements complement and highlight rather than compete with or overwhelm the food. I like to feel that the bowls and plates of *food* are the centers of attraction.

I once catered a wedding supper for a young couple during the week before Christmas, and since they wanted to spend as little money as possible, they said they would do the decorations themselves. Well, the bride was, I think, busier than she'd expected to be, so when I arrived with all the food, the apartment was completely bare of any decoration except for a few ornaments on a very lonely-looking little tree in one corner of the living room. The wedding party was rushing around getting ready to leave, and too busy to do much more than say hello, so I occupied myself with the food until finally they went dashing out the door. The large dining-room table would be the focal point of the evening, I was sure, and it presented an expanse of bare white tablecloth. The few plates of hors d'oeuvres I would set out at first would look lost, so I began to rummage through cupboards and closets to look for something to decorate it with. Finally I came up with a pile of candles and some large brandy-snifter-type glasses. I snipped evergreen pieces from the back of the tree and set these in the snifters with the candles. When the lights were dimmed and the candles lit and set around the apartment, it was magically beautiful.

Around Christmastime (which is the busiest season for me) I carry, in the cold back of the car, evergreens and rolls of red crepe paper—just in case. You can get evergreen cuttings wherever they sell Christmas trees.

SERVING DISHES Choosing the right dish to go with the right food can make it decidedly more (or less) appealing. Certain hearty country or peasant foods such as winter stew, chili, baked beans, minestrone, or onion soup are better suited to earthenware or terra cotta dishes.

Bread looks better in baskets. Maybe because the baskets "breathe".

Meat or fish in white or light-colored sauces looks better in dark-colored serving dishes or in silver, whereas a Boeuf Bourguignon looks better in white. Pasta is better in a dark dish. In other words, I find contrast is usually effective.

Any mixture of food which has colored bits tossed through it looks better served from a glass bowl. This includes such dishes as salads, Pasta Primavera, and sherry trifle. I also like serving mousses from crystal or glass.

Cheeses are more attractive (and practical) served on wood. (Once a Camembert turned an unappetizing blue while sitting on a silver tray.) I like to put fruit and other garnishes with cheeses for color.

I seldom use very large (commercial-size) bowls or serving platters. It always seems as though large quantities of food seen all together are less appetizing. The trick is to have several smaller platters and replace each one quickly as it becomes empty. When serving large numbers of people, I have two kitchen helpers refilling and decorating plates. A "runner" between the kitchen and the buffet tables carries out the empty plates and returns with the full, and tells those in the kitchen what is getting low. I keep two dishes of each offering on the table at any one time when serving a large group. This way, there is always a full dish ready immediately.

When I first meet the client at home to discuss arrangements, I usually ask her to show me where she keeps her serving dishes and if she minds if I choose those I think will be attractive. This way I know if there won't be enough and what I will have to rent.

A FEW FINAL WORDS ABOUT DECORATING Don't worry. If the most garnishing or decorating you've ever done is sprinkling on some chopped parsley, you'll find you pick up new ideas very quickly. (Food advertisements are great places for new ideas.) When I make up the market list, I picture each finished dish, imagine the ideal decoration, and mark down what garnishes I will use. On the day of the party I leave myself plenty of time to experiment with what looks right.

CHAPTER 16

SPECIAL TIPS ON JUDGING AND COOKING QUANTITIES

HOW MUCH DO PEOPLE EAT? When people come to me for advice about catering, their biggest worry always seems to be "How do you know how much to prepare?" It would be nice if there were some absolutely accurate formula we could neatly apply to each job. Unfortunately, there isn't—though there are some guidelines. It's much easier to be sure you will have enough than it is to be sure you won't have far too much. Yet leftovers mean less profit, so you want to try to come out with just about the right amount of food.

It seems as though, at dinners, the more people there are, the less per person people eat. I have several ideas why this is true. First, at big parties there have almost always been appetizers and drinks beforehand. People come up to the buffet table with their appetites dulled, and so ask for small portions (probably also thinking of their waistlines). Only the really big eaters bother to get up from where they are sitting to go back to the buffet table for seconds. Also, most people eat more slowly at social occasions than at home and have time to notice that they are full.

Remember, however, more food is eaten if there are quite a few young men in the group, or if the meal is after some sporting activity, or if the food is left on the table for guests to help themselves over a longer period of time.

Obviously, the more appetizers offered, the less dinner people are likely to eat. Older people eat less than young, and women less than men.

95

Here are the generally accepted rules of thumb (plus some of the guidelines I find work) in figuring how much food to prepare per person.

HOW MUCH MEAT PER PERSON? The general rule is half a pound (225-250 g). For a small dinner party with a boneless rib roast, half a pound is certainly what I'd figure. But, if the meat is in a stew or a sauce, half a pound is usually too much. For a small dinner party of under fifteen people, I'd probably still estimate half a pound (225-250 g) of veal for the Blanquette de Veau (veal stew), because I like to have some extra to freeze. Yet, if I were to serve the same Blanquette to seventy-five people, we'd be eating veal stew at home for a month if I used half a pound per person. Though a quarter of a pound (115-125 g) per person is what I actually expect people will eat, I'll usually calculate a third of a pound (150-175 g) per person, or twenty-five pounds (11 kilos) for seventy-five people. If the people are older (over forty-five), I'd only order twenty pounds (9 kilos).

But, remember, that's for meat with no waste. If you're using meat with bone, ask the butcher to estimate for you what the weight would be without the bone. Less meat is consumed if it is in a sauce or if it is very thinly sliced. Stuffings and gravies mean people eat less meat, too.

POULTRY The rule of a certain number of people per pound (or kilo) doesn't strictly apply to chickens or ducks because there is so much "waste" (i.e., bones and skin). If a chicken or a duck is cut up into small pieces and cooked in a sauce, I estimate between five and seven people per fowl depending on its size (3 to 4 lb., or 1½ to 2 kilos). In the Parmesan Cream Chicken, it's more like seven to nine people per chicken, because ham is added as well as the sauce.

FISH Fish is an unpredictable item to serve. Sometimes a salmon fillet or a fish salad goes very slowly as one of several selections and sometimes it is the most popular item. This seems to depend on the type of group. (I've found salmon to be the most popular fish.) Because of the large amount of waste when you buy a whole fish, I calculate a half-pound (225-250 g) per person for small groups. For larger groups, where it is one of several selections, approximately a third of a pound (150-175 g) is enough.

SAUCES When doubling recipes with sauces, make only one and a half times the quantity of sauce. If multiplying the recipe by four, I'd do two or two and a half times the quantity of sauce. I talk about specific ingredients later in this chapter.

RICE, POTATOES, AND PASTA I never cease to be surprised at how little of these are eaten at parties. At a recent wedding reception where I was serving a Rice and Vegetable Salad to a hundred and fifty people, I estimated ten people per cup of uncooked rice and there was still plenty left over. (At home I estimate five people per cup.)

For the average party, I'd calculate seven to eight people per cup of rice, half a potato per person, and a very small handful of pasta or one "nest" per person. This will be more than enough.

VEGETABLES AND SALAD Figure on slightly less than half a cup (about 125 ml) of cooked vegetables for small dinner parties, but about a quarter of a cup (60 ml) at larger gatherings is plenty. Asparagus is popular; four stalks multiplied by the number of guests is a good guideline.

For salad, a small handful per person is enough. Older people eat even less of this.

BREAD A hot, herbed, sliced Italian loaf will usually feed fourteen to sixteen people—more at a big party. I always cut each slice in half; it's easier to manage, and the bread is eaten less quickly.

DESSERTS Sweets at big dinner parties usually come at the end of a long evening of drinking and eating; people seem to prefer small portions. Recipes that are supposed to feed six to eight people will usually feed eight to ten. Usually, people eat about a third of a cup (85 ml). Most of the desserts in the Recipe section are designed for these slightly smaller "party portions".

CONTROLLING HOW FAST FOOD GOES As I mentioned in the chapter on serving, if you do the dishing up of the food, you can control to a large extent how much people eat. I always brief anyone who helps me serve to go easy on the size of the portions and to be sure to ask each guest how much he would like. This way I've found there is much less food left on plates to be thrown out. When setting up the buffet, if I put the bread, rice, or vegetables before the main course, people eat less of the meat. I don't mean to sound stingy—I *want* people to eat and enjoy what I make—but I've just found that people's eyes are often bigger than their stomachs.

WHAT IF THERE ARE SEVERAL CHOICES OF ENTRÉE? This is always a problem, and again there is no strict rule. I've found people eat slightly more total weight of entrée when there are several choices. They like to have some of each, yet some choices are always more popular than others. When serving a cold buffet with entrées of roast beef, salmon, and Vitello Tonnato (veal in a tuna sauce), I calculate the total weight of entrée to be eaten will be approximately a half-pound (225-250 g) per person, or fifty pounds (23 kilos) for a hundred people. I expect there to be more roast beef eaten than salmon and more salmon than veal.

If you see you've miscalculated, as I did at the architects' buffet mentioned earlier, and may run low on salmon but have more than enough beef, you can set the beef plate first and give larger portions of it. Next comes the veal; give a good portion of it, too. This will make a small portion of salmon look less meager. (Anyone who especially likes the fish will tell you, and you can give him a bigger helping.) There are lots of possibilities for juggling portion sizes around so that you won't run out.

Undoubtedly at first, as you look at the food in the store or your kitchen, you will be tempted, as I was, to feel panicky that the roasts or noodles or vegetables in front of you couldn't possibly feed a hundred people. You may even succumb (as I did) to the temptation of buying extra. But, as I have mentioned, if you figured the weights carefully, trust those numbers. If I get extra, I get what freezes well and can be used by the family later.

WHAT HAPPENS TO THE LEFTOVERS? If the client has said there will be fifty people, and fifty people show up to eat the food, whatever leftovers remain are mine. If only forty-five people come, the host still pays for fifty people (because that is how much I was contracted to prepare), but I leave approximately five portions for the host to eat if he likes. It's a good idea to explain your policy about leftovers at the time the contract is signed.

LEARN FROM MISCALCULATIONS If you arrive home with a huge pot of fettuccini, or six loaves of bread, or a large garbage bag of lettuce, you have obviously overcalculated on those items. Take an inventory of leftovers and make a note of how much was eaten to use as a guideline for the next job.

NOBODY'S PERFECT I will still occasionally come back from a job with piles of one course left over. There is no way to predict how a certain group will go for certain types of food. Most things can be frozen. Leftover Italian bread with herb butter is excellent when spread out on a cookie sheet and browned under the broiler. Fettuccini can be frozen and used in casseroles or tossed in butter and cheese. Salad and hors d'oeuvres don't last well. I've had to accept the fact that a certain amount of waste is inevitable.

TIPS FOR ADJUSTING RECIPES
WHEN COOKING FOR LARGER NUMBERS OF PEOPLE

Here, too, there are no hard-and-fast rules, so follow your intuition. Any good cook has instincts about what quantity is right; trust these. I use cookbooks for ideas and as guidelines, of course, but in cooking larger quantities of food I find the food turns out better if I'm not automatically measuring cup after cup of ingredient. I add a seasoning and then taste the mixture and try to figure out if it needs more of that or something not even in the recipe. At first it's better to err on the side of blandness, adding a little at a time. Spicing up a dish is easier than undoing the work of a heavy hand with the chili powder.

Ingredients vary. This isn't a problem if you are making only six portions. When you're making a hundred and fifty portions, differences in the size of the eggs or in the sourness of the fruit can change the quantities needed in ways that no recipe can predict.

Below I've listed some key ingredients whose properties change noticeably when multiplied.

SALT:

- Never multiply the quantity of this automatically by the number of times you multiply the recipe.
- Don't add salt until the last moment the recipe allows, after as many other ingredients as possible have been added. Some ingredients such as cheese, anchovies, and tuna make additional salt unnecessary.
- Taste what you are making (even such things as raw batter) as you add salt a little at a time; some foods taste salty more quickly than others.
- A little salt added to a food that is cooking will have a more noticeable effect than salt added just before serving or eating. During cooking, it has had time to dissolve and penetrate the food.

SUGAR:

- The quantity of sugar also shouldn't be multiplied automatically; a little goes a long way, and too much sugar can hide delicate flavors. Though these are questions of personal preference, in a recipe that is doubled I will use one and a half times the amount of sugar; in a recipe multiplied by ten, I'll use three or four times the amount of sugar.
- Sugar can be used in unexpected places to remove the harsh

acidity from tomatoes or vinegar or lemon. When I have put
in lemon to give zest to a bland sauce, I may use a dash of
sugar to cut any acid taste.

LEMON JUICE:

- Lemon juice, either fresh or the bottled concentrate, is an
  extremely useful addition to many dishes, especially sauces. It
  heightens flavors and cuts bland or too-sweet tastes. I use it
  especially in sauces made with flour or cornstarch. Small
  amounts can be used with milk sauces with no danger of curdling.

EGGS:

- Egg whites beat better—
  at room temperature
  in small batches of three or four at a time
  if you make sure there is no grease on the bowl or the rubber
      spatula
- Thickening—
  Eggs are less satisfactory than flour or cornstarch for thickening large batches of milk for custards or sauces. The trapped
  heat causes curdling more easily than in small batches. For
  larger quantities of custard, for example, small amounts of
  cornstarch may be used in addition to the eggs without loss of
  the delicate texture.
- Hard-boiling—
  Avoid overcooking (evidenced by a gray-green coating on the
  yolk). Cook for seven or eight minutes (depending on the size
  of the eggs) from the time when the water has come to a rapid
  boil. Immediately empty boiling water and run a constant
  stream of cold water on the eggs until they are cool enough to
  hold in your hand. Roll each along the counter, breaking the
  shell, which then easily peels off.

  Placing raw eggs in the cold water when the pan is set on the
  fire seems to prevent the shells from cracking. If this doesn't
  work, try putting salt or vinegar in the water or piercing a tiny
  hole in the shell.

  Slightly undercooked eggs taste and look better than slightly
  overcooked ones.

CREAM:

- To whip:
  For feeding small numbers of people, I always whip the cream
    by hand with a wire whisk. I chill the bowl in the freezer
    beforehand.
  If using a machine—
  Chill the bowl and beaters and have the cream *cold*.
  Whip in small batches.
  Use a slower speed than most electric-mixer manufacturers
    recommend.
  Never leave the cream while it is whipping.
  Stop the machine frequently to test for soft peaks.
- When adding cream to a hot dish, don't let the sauce boil or
    the cream will curdle. Add it at the last minute.

FLOUR:

- "All-purpose" flour is too often treated with too little care.
  Here are some of its properties, ways in which it is mistreated,
  and a quick, lump-proof béchamel (or white) sauce that can
  be made by the cup or by the gallon.
- Flour used in baking and for pastry:
  It is better to make cakes in small batches than to multiply
  recipes several times. A common error made in handling
  flour, especially if using larger quantities, is to over-beat it
  after it has been mixed with liquid. Air pockets in cakes get
  smaller and smaller and the cake gets tougher and denser the
  more you beat—once the batter is fairly well mixed. I always
  stir in flour by hand rather than use the electric mixer. For
  pastry, I will use the processor to cut the fat into the flour, but
  I knead the flour by hand when I have added the water.
- Béchamel Sauce: Cookbooks contain laboriously long and
  cumbersome descriptions of how to make this sauce in which
  you use scrupulous measures and double-boilers, remove it
  frequently from the heat, heat liquids separately, etc. You
  won't have time to be cleaning pans and using extra burners,
  so here is my method. It can be used for any quantity. The pro-
  portions are approximately one part butter to one part flour to
  eight parts milk.

  Melt butter in a heavy pan over medium-high heat, breaking
    up unmelted pieces and stirring.
  When butter is hot but not brown, put in enough flour for the

bottom of the pan to look dull rather than shiny. (The quantities of butter and flour are approximately the same.)

Continue to stir rapidly. At first the butter-flour mixture adheres to the spoon a bit, but gradually it begins to cover the bottom of the pan.

When the mixture starts to bubble, turn down the fire to medium-low, stirring to keep it from browning.

When the flour has an almost granular texture and is not at all gooey, it's cooked. Cooking the flour well is the single best way to avoid lumps. Be careful to have the milk ready, for the mixture browns very easily at this stage. (A browned butter-flour mixture isn't inedible; it merely has a different flavor. I actually like it for a sauce with toasted almonds and plenty of wine on chicken.)

Add a couple of cups (approximately 500 ml) of cold milk (if you've had at least a quarter of a cup (62 ml) each of butter and flour). Turn the heat to medium-high and stir constantly with a whisk.

When the sauce has thickened, add more milk if necessary to get a good thickness. Let the sauce bubble on a medium-low heat for a few moments, stirring constantly. Remove from heat and cover.

I've avoided exact quantities of the ingredients because there are times when you want a thicker sauce and times when it should be thinner. A thicker béchamel has less milk; a rich béchamel uses half cream, half milk. Any sauce you mix with meats and/or vegetables should be thicker because juices from the meat and vegetables tend to thin it. Any sauce that might cool slightly when served (in filled pastry shells, for example) should be thinner (i.e., have more milk), because cooling always thickens a sauce and can make an already thick sauce gooey or heavy.

- Flour versus cornstarch:
  Flour makes a creamier thickness. Use in gravies and in béchamel and cream sauces.
  Cornstarch makes a more gelatinous thickness (it makes a clearer glaze). Better with desserts because of its lighter taste. Use in milk custards, fruit sauces, Chinese food.
  Both should be very well cooked, so leave each to bubble rapidly for several minutes.

RICE:

- Normally to cook a cup (250 ml) of rice I boil between 2¼ (560 ml) and 2½ (625 ml) cups of water. If I cook more cups of rice at one time, however, less water is needed. I assume this is because the surface area for evaporation is greater in relation to the total depth of water if there is only a small quantity. Six cups (1½ liters) of rice would need only about 10½ cups (2.625 liters) of water—i.e., 1¾ cups (435 ml) of water for each cup (250 ml) of rice.
- Sticky or gummy rice is the result when the rice absorbs too much water, so check the firmness of the rice frequently and simply drain off any excess water and leave the pan uncovered. The wettest rice is on the bottom of the pan, so I often turn the rice out into a bowl and place it in an oven on the warm setting.
- I have a low opinion of converted rice, and most supermarket white rice has little flavor compared with the rice available at East Indian stores.
- Cook brown or wild rice separately from white because the cooking time is longer.
- I've found that a bouillon cube and some powdered herbs or spices, such as thyme or paprika, added with butter to the boiling water make ordinary white rice delicious. The bouillon cube usually makes additional salt unnecessary.

DON'T LOSE TOUCH Many characteristics of basic ingredients don't change when used in large quantities. But, when you first start cooking in larger quantities it is easy to "lose your touch" with the qualities of the ingredients. How often do you work with twelve cups of flour or forty-eight eggs, after all? One of the tendencies is to use machines. These speed up the work, but they are sometimes unsuited for the job.

Try to work on the crucial aspects of recipes when the kitchen is quiet and empty. My instincts are less reliable after about 10 p.m., so I don't try to do much actual decision-making then. Concentration and attention allow you to heed your good instincts.

CHAPTER 17

RENTAL EQUIPMENT

For many of the occasions you cater, you will need to arrange for dish and equipment rentals. Most towns and urban centers have several party-rental companies listed in the Yellow Pages. Call around and then visit those you feel are best equipped and pleasant.

CHOOSING A RENTAL COMPANY It's a good idea to establish a business connection with one or possibly two companies. Here are some points to consider in choosing which company to use.

- It should have a large stock, a wide range of prices, and tasteful styles of dishes, glasses, cutlery, and accessories. The stock should be in good condition.
- A reliable and prompt delivery-and-pick-up service with seven-day-a-week availability is essential. Many parties are on Saturday or Sunday and I've occasionally arrived at the client's house to find that champagne glasses or coffee cups have not been delivered. You need to be able to call and have these sent immediately by taxi.
- Look at other equipment such as tables, tablecloths, chairs, large coffee-makers, and portable ovens. At least one rental company with whom you deal should be able to supply more major equipment such as tents and dance floors.
- Will they offer a discount on all jobs billed to your company?
- Are they pleasant and not too pushy? Rental companies will often have numerous direct contacts with your client. It is important that they reflect your image as a caterer.

ADVANTAGES TO RENTING For the caterer and the client, renting is easier. Convey some of these advantages to the client.

- By renting, you know exactly how many dishes and glasses there are; there's no need to rummage through drawers for three more forks.
- Hours of dishwashing time are saved because all dishes and glasses are packed dirty (to be cleaned by the rental company). There's also less chance of running out of glasses; no one has to take time to wash them while people wait for their drinks.
- There's no fear of loss or breakage of family heirlooms.
- Place settings match.

WAYS FOR THE CLIENT TO ECONOMIZE Renting does cost more, so, if the client balks at the expense, here are some ways to reduce the number of pieces needed and the overall rental costs.

- Serve "fork" food; no knives and spoons will be needed.
- Don't have coffee; the small demitasse spoon and the cup and saucer *each* cost just about as much as the dinner plate. If you do have coffee, order fewer cups, saucers, and spoons than there will be guests. About twenty percent of guests refuse coffee.
- Use good-quality paper napkins instead of linen.
- Use the standard grade of glass and dish rather than crystal and Royal Doulton.
- Have the client supply the single items needed, such as serving bowls, platters, and utensils.
- Remind the client that a staff of three people is costing about twenty dollars for each hour they spend washing dishes. Some of the money the client would save by not renting would go to pay for the staff's time spent cleaning up.

BECOME FAMILIAR WITH THE SELECTION OF STOCK AT THE RENTAL COMPANY Get an itemized price list and any brochures that show the different patterns of dishes or styles of glasses. The price list also acts as a good checklist to help you avoid overlooking any small items.

The client often will depend on your taste and judgement in choosing the rental items. The simple dishes and accessories are a wise choice, especially in the cheaper grade. For elegant dinners, I usually recommend the best china and crystal—but still in simple patterns. White porcelain with a gold trim doesn't compete with the food for attention and won't clash with any of the dishes the client provides.

BILLING FOR RENTAL EQUIPMENT There are two possibilities when billing for rental equipment. You can have the client billed directly, or, if the rental company offers a discount on all jobs billed to you, you can charge the client what he would have paid the rental company anyway, and you can earn the ten or fifteen percent for your time spent organizing what needed to be rented. (During your inquiries into different rental companies, you could suggest that a discount might persuade you to choose them as your supplier.)

Finally, make sure the client has a written list and estimate of what he is renting.

GETTING THE BEST FROM THE RENTAL COMPANY It doesn't hurt for the rental companies you use to think of you as a perfectionist who won't accept last-minute substitutions. If they know you will refuse to pay for large coffee cups if they send them instead of the demitasses you ordered, next time the company runs short of demitasse cups your order will be filled first while someone else will get the big cups. The dishes your food is served on enhance the impression you and your food make, so it's in your interest to be particular. Simply calling up to complain about the holes in the linen tablecloth doesn't work as well as refusing to pay for the shoddy quality.

It is important to get a copy of the final order sheet. This helps you double-check that nothing has been omitted and it also is proof if there is any argument about what was actually ordered.

As in all your business dealings, if you always deal with the same person, you can be sure that messages about an order change or other instructions will be received.

Being a good business person doesn't mean that you can't be pleasant and appreciative. The firmest complaints can be made in such a way that the person you are speaking with doesn't feel he personally is being attacked. It is helpful to have your contact in the rental company on your side; there are times when the rules about delivery charges need to be bent or you may need them to supply you with a last-minute order. They like to know that a job well done is appreciated. Don't we all?

CHAPTER 18

BEVERAGES

HARD LIQUOR AND WINE To buy liquor for resale isn't legal without a liquor license, so it's best to discuss what the client needs and have him buy all the alcoholic drinks. I've found most clients are happy to do this because they can control what they get and what they spend this way.

Many liquor stores and beer distributors deliver, and some will refund for any bottles not opened. The client may ask your advice about quantities and choice of both liquor and wine. For wine, part of your pre-job homework might be to go to the liquor commission or the state store and get prices and advice about reasonably priced, good wine that goes with your menu. Every month, it seems, some new wine comes onto the market in the bargain price range. You can experiment with some of them yourself if you enjoy wine.

How much people drink of different types of liquor varies enormously. The hosts know best what type of drinking crowd their friends are. Older groups drink more hard liquor at a cocktail party than do younger groups, who seem to prefer wine. During hot weather people drink more tall drinks, like rum-and-Cokes or gin-and-tonics. For wine at dinner, the rule of thumb is half a bottle per person, but some groups drink much more.

SOFT DRINKS Some rental companies will deliver soft drinks and mixes with the rental order. They will also only charge for what is used, and they know how much to send so that you won't run out. But their prices aren't discount ones, so the client may prefer to order his own. This is the soft-drink and mix selection I usually suggest for cocktail parties:

Coke (and Diet Coke)	mineral water(opt.)
ginger ale	tomato juice
7-Up (and Diet 7-Up)	Clamato juice
tonic water	orange juice
soda water	

I also bring the following bar supplies:

lemons	salt and pepper
limes	shot glass
Worcestershire sauce	bottle openers
Tabasco	corkscrews

In addition, the client provides, or I rent,

dishtowels	ice buckets
tablecloths	glass pitchers for
large plastic tubs	water and juice
for chilling wine	

You should have crushed ice for cooling wine and beer and ice cubes for drinks. The party rental company can deliver these and advise about quantities. Make sure the client has enough freezer space to store the ice, or have the ice delivered only a few hours before the party. I like to rent large, sturdy plastic tubs for cooling the wine and beer. Make sure the client has enough ice buckets (one per bartender), or you can rent them.

One sub-zero night last winter, we arrived to set up the job and asked where the ice was. "Oh, we put it outside," they said. In the extreme cold, the crushed ice was a solid bag-shaped block. We had to hack it apart. Another time, we arrived to find the ice sitting in the front hallway. When we lifted the bag, it broke, and the water and ice landed in a pile on the cream-colored wall-to-wall carpeting. Now I find out *exactly* where the ice will be stored until we get there.

CHAPTER 19

A SAMPLE JOB

Here's one of my jobs from beginning to end.

MR. JOLI'S COCKTAIL PARTY FOR SIXTY PEOPLE ON JULY 8

JUNE 15 Mr. Joli phones. During our conversation I find out that he wants to have a party for his wife's birthday on July 8. He's inviting seventy of their friends (in their mid-forties, I guess by his voice), and expects about sixty to come. He wants it to be a cocktail party starting at about 7 p.m. with "really nice" hors d'oeuvres. I suggest there be a few substantial appetizers, since people will be ready for their dinners by then. He agrees, but says he doesn't want a birthday cake. If the weather is good, he hopes to have guests out on the back lawn as well as in the house.

He gives me his business address and company name for the billing, so I expect he's charging it off as a business expense and therefore won't be quite as worried about the cost.

We make a date to meet at his home on June 18 to discuss the menu and other details.

While the conversation and his general sense of what he wants the party to be like is still fresh in my mind, I sit down and make up a suggested menu, a list of the rental equipment I'd recommend, and the number of waitresses and bartenders needed.

JUNE 18 At his home, we decide on the tentative menu:
Crudités with Guacamole
Shrimp with Cocktail Sauce and Brandied Mayonnaise
Snow Peas filled with Cream Cheese and Caviar

Stuffed Eggs—curried, dill, and devilled
Vol-au-Vents with Creamed Ham
Mushrooms stuffed with Pâté
Chicken Teriyaki with Sauce
Dates stuffed with Cream Cheese and Cointreau

I explain that I will let him know the next day what the price per person for this menu will be and he can make any changes then, based on this price.

I explain my policy about leftovers and that the price per person is based on the number sixty, with the price per head going up if the number of guests is reduced by more than ten people.

We discuss staff. He will need three waitresses and two bartenders (one will circulate taking orders and clearing glasses).

We go into the kitchen; I look at ovens, pans, utensils, and serving platters and ask him to have the counters and the refrigerator as clear as possible. Back out in the living and dining rooms, I suggest where the bar and the food table should be and what furniture should be moved to open up the living room for "traffic flow". If it rains, we decide where to set up the second bar inside. I see he'll need more ashtrays. Since there will be mostly hard liquor, the glass rental order is principally highball, with some old-fashioned and a few wine glasses. (I suggest he get one or two bottles of white wine. Spritzers—half white wine and half soda—are popular on hot evenings.) He has ice buckets and an ice chest to keep the bags of ice in under the table.

Here's my rental list:
108 highball glasses
24 old-fashioned glasses
12 all-purpose 8-oz. wine glasses
5 cut-glass ashtrays
1 6-foot table (the client is providing a table and cloth for the second bar)
2 ten-foot white linen tablecloths (one hangs down to the floor to hide the ice tubs under the table)
1 bag crushed ice for cooling wine, beer, and soda
4 bags ice cubes (rental companies can advise you on quantities)

The rental order is to be delivered the morning of the party. Mr. Joli's deep-freeze has room for the ice.

I'm to buy paper cocktail napkins and arrange for one bouquet of flowers for the table. I make note of the colors in the room.

JUNE 19 I calculate the cost of the food and labor—approximately $600, or $10 per person. The rental costs will be approximately

$50 and the staff cost approximately $220. The approximate total is $870.

I phone up Mr. Joli with the price estimate, and when he agrees, I write up the contract, asking for a $300 deposit.

I arrange for the flowers at the florist and the rentals from the rental company and call around to get firm commitments from one kitchen helper to help me at home, three waitresses, and two bartenders.

Then I forget about the job until...

JULY 6 I call Mr. Joli to confirm sixty as the number of expected guests.

I order vol-au-vents.

I call the staff to remind them and confirm the time we are to meet.

JULY 7 I do food shopping in the morning.

In the afternoon I cut up the chicken and marinate it. I prepare snow peas and set them in water to open and put the dates in the freezer (freezing makes them easier to handle).

JULY 8, 8:30 a.m. to 3:30 p.m. My kitchen helper arrives at 9:00 a.m. and does the following:

- hard-boils eggs, shells them, and cuts the whites into quarters
- slits open dates and puts them back in freezer
- cleans mushrooms, removes stems, fills them with pâté, and sets them on cookie trays lined with foil
- cuts up crudités
- finely grates peel from two oranges
- cleans parsley and chops some for stuffed-mushrooms garnish (All the above are covered and chilled.)

Meanwhile, I

- chop ham, and make cream sauce. These are combined and left in the pan to take to the client's.
- make sauce dip for chicken, put it in labelled container, and chill
- mix the fillings for the eggs, put them in labelled containers, and chill
- make caviar-and-cream-cheese mixture, put it in labelled container, and chill
- make cocktail sauce and brandied mayonnaise, put them in labelled containers, and chill
- mix cream cheese and Cointreau, put mixture in labelled container, and chill until two hours before it will be piped

By 3:30 these jobs are finished and the kitchen is clean. I bathe and dress, and then, with no one else in the kitchen, I go down the list of appetizers one at a time. For each one, I visualize what ingredients, utensils, garnishes, and serving dishes are needed, and I carefully pack each of these.

Besides the food itself, I take for this job:

2 cookie sheets	paprika
a cast-iron frying pan	chives
long bamboo skewers	parsley
cooking oil	lemons
2 attractive bowls	watercress
for sauces	

I always take with me to the client's:

2 potholders	3 sharp knives, large and small
a roll of paper towels	piping bag with tips (check
several dishcloths	to make sure you have
3 large garbage bags	the right ones)
plastic wrap	paper doilies
aluminum foil	rubber spatula

And for the bar:

shot glass	can opener
lemons and limes	Worcestershire sauce
corkscrews	Tabasco

I make sure everything is carefully packed and covered for travelling. I once had to stop suddenly on the freeway and a third of an enormous bowl of trifle sloshed into the cardboard box in which it sat. With most menu items, I try to have all the parts ready but not yet assembled. This isn't always possible, so I drive with the stately, slow demeanor of a hearse.

The staff meets at 4 p.m. at my home and by 4:30 we are at the client's, unloading. I show the staff the layout of the house and kitchen and tell the bartenders where they can find the ice, glasses, and liquor to set up the bar.

In the client's kitchen, before the guests arrive, the other waitresses and I

- put vol-au-vents on the cookie sheets for later warming
- leave frozen, cooked shrimps out to thaw
- arrange egg whites on beds of lettuce and pipe in the different yolk mixtures. Chives go on the curried eggs, extra sprigs of dill on the dill eggs, and paprika on the devilled eggs. Chill, covered.

- set the creamed ham mixture on warm setting on stove
- pipe cream-cheese-and-Cointreau mixture into dates, place them on doilies, and sprinkle with grated orange peel. Chill.

In the half-hour before the guests arrive, we

- put shrimp on crushed ice with wedges of lemon and some parsley and set the two sauce dishes in the ice
- arrange the crudités and dip on large plates
- pipe caviar mixture into pea pods and set these on a bed of crushed ice, decorating the plate with parsley
- warm vol-au-vents

While serving appetizers,

- in small batches we fill vol-au-vents; the pastry gets soggy if filled too long before it's eaten
- after cooking a dozen pieces of chicken in oil, we spear them on bamboo skewers and set these on a bed of watercress with a small bowl of sauce at the side
- in batches of twenty, we broil the mushrooms stuffed with pâté for two or three minutes until the pâté just begins to sizzle. Serve these from warmed silver trays with chopped parsley sprinkled over them.

CLEAN-UP Cleaning up after ourselves is an on-going process all evening. I ask whoever is at the sink to leave everything that has been cleaned on the counter for me to sort through. This way, my knives and spatulas are less likely to be left in the client's kitchen drawers.

The waitresses constantly clear away dirty glasses and ashtrays. As the party winds down, with the few remaining guests settling in for what looks like a long evening, we clean up completely. We'll leave what appetizers remain set on a table among the guests and the bar open for those who still want to drink to help themselves.

As I say good-bye, Mr. Joli asks what tip I would suggest and I say between $10 and $20 per staff member. He hands the tips out and we pile into the car and go. It's 11 p.m. By midnight the car is unloaded and the food put away. I fall asleep as I hit the pillow.

The next day I make notes on the job. How much did I spend on ingredients? How much was left over? How much did the staff cost? What ran out too quickly? Are there any changes I'd make in the recipes or the cooking? I prepare the bill, except for the rental charges. As soon as I receive this bill from the rental company, I send off Mr. Joli's bill.

CHAPTER 20

SOME NEAR-DISASTERS AND "SAVE THE MEAL" TRICKS

On just about every job, something doesn't go as I've planned. Mistakes are how I learned—and in the first years as a caterer I made plenty of them. Here are some of my moments of panic and last-minute solutions.

One of the more hair-raising experiences I've had was at a very elegant dinner party for twelve. I liked the guests and knew they appreciated good cooking. They had just finished their cold spinach soup with fresh dill and I was about to serve the salmon with hollandaise sauce. I had wanted the sauce to be a highlight of the meal, so I'd brought it to a light perfection at home, then carefully set it in its double-boiler on the warm setting of a front element of the stove. The salmon was ready on its decorated platter and I lifted the lid of the hollandaise to find it curdled and rapidly boiling! I broke out into a cold sweat. I could hear the quiet conversation of the guests as they waited for their next course. There was no time to make another sauce; I felt frozen with panic. It sounds silly now to say that a curdled sauce upset me so much, but on a job like that, my whole self feels at stake when I carry food I've prepared out to the guests. The hostess came out for something and could see the distress on my face as I explained what had happened. "Oh dear," she said, "I meant to tell you that burner is faulty; even on low you get the same HIGH heat. Don't worry." With that she went back out to her guests. I beat in an extra yolk, and the sauce, though not perfect, was a fairly good texture. The salmon, which I'd had to keep warm, was no longer as perfect either, but I had no choice; I went through the doors to the guests apparently confident, gracious, and smiling.

There are three lessons I learned from that job. Make sure there are no problems with the stove; make the hollandaise sauce at the last minute; and slightly undercook the salmon before deboning it so that, as it is kept warm, it finishes cooking rather than becoming overcooked. Maybe there was even a fourth lesson: to accept that not everything will be perfect.

Once when twenty-four ducks were delivered thawed instead of frozen solid as I'd been told they would be, I was obliged to cook them earlier than I'd planned. The Canard à l'Orange was to consist of boneless pieces of duck in the orange sauce (this way it could be eaten with a fork). After cooking and deboning the ducks, I cut the meat up into bite-size pieces and then refrigerated it. Then I made an exquisite and elaborate sauce using expensive liquors and the duck bones for stock. On the morning of the party, both the sauce and the meat were cold, and I added the duck pieces to the sauce before heating it all up. This turned out to be a mistake. I had to stir the "stew" mixture frequently; this broke down the already small pieces of duck so that, though it was delicious, the texture was more like duck hash. I still get a cold shiver down my spine when I think of dishing up that duck "hash". There were rave comments about it from the guests, but I try to forget that job.

Here's what I learned, though. Like the salmon, poultry is best if slightly undercooked before deboning if it will be heated with a sauce before serving. I cut the poultry up into larger pieces than I eventually want the guests to be served. This way, after the inevitable breaking up of some of the chunks, the pieces end up about the right size. Also, to minimize the breaking up of stew meats and poultry, I place the cooked boneless pieces in a deep baking pan and pour the sauce over them before warming gently in the oven. No stirring is necessary.

Finally, I now always make sure I know how something is going to arrive, frozen or thawed. Spring meats such as veal and lamb are often frozen when you buy them in the summer or fall.

Once I had agreed to do two jobs on the same day, arranging for the main course of each to be moussaka. I was rushed, so I asked the baby-sitter (who wasn't busy because my son was sleeping) to come and stir the huge pot of béchamel sauce until it thickened. There were probably three gallons (12 liters) of cold milk in a large commercial pot, so it was going to take a while to come to a boil. Busy at other jobs, I would occasionally ask Susan how it was going, to which she answered, "Fine." Finally she said, "It's thick," so I asked her to pour the sauce into a large stainless bowl and add the cartons of ricotta and the several dozen eggs I'd set out. After all the cheese and the eggs were added, I came over and immediately smelled a strong scorched smell. The entire bottom of the pot had burnt. I realized she'd been stirring only the top of the sauce, not reaching the spoon down to the bottom of the pot. (With large quantities this can easily happen.) There wasn't the time—nor did I want to spend the money—to make the sauce over again. How was I to eliminate the scorched taste? First, I added lemon juice, then a touch of sugar, then plenty of salt. I was thankful I'd added no salt yet to the rest of the moussaka, so it was not too salty as a whole. I sprinkled in plenty of nutmeg and pepper and then, after it was all in the pan, covered the top of this custard mixture with grated Parmesan cheese. When people told me it was the best moussaka they'd ever eaten, I just smiled a little sheepishly to myself, but I haven't asked the baby-sitter to help with the cooking again. Also, I make sure the larger the pot of sauce, the lower the heat setting on the stove I use.

Once I salted the rice water twice by accident. At least I guess that's what I did, because I tasted the rice and it was much too salty. To remove the saltiness, I soaked the rice in boiling water, drained it, then soaked and drained it again. I tossed in a dash of lemon juice and some unsalted butter and it was delicious.

Too much salt in stews can be greatly helped by putting in slices of raw potato. (Remove these when the stew is ready to be served.) Add some lemon juice (or vinegar) and a dash of sugar. The anchovies and tuna in the Vitello Tonnato sauce tend to make it very salty. I add sour cream mixed with homemade, unsalted mayonnaise to make the sauce "cooler" and lighter-tasting. Sour cream and yogurt are useful additions to any dish that is too sweet, too salty, or too spicy. (Of course they aren't always appropriate!)

The old cliché "necessity is the mother of invention" is often true enough in catering. I heard of one caterer whose aspic mold didn't set, so she poured it into crystal goblets and served it as a cold soup. Once, when I turned out my apple-and-date upside-down cake, some of the fruit remained in the pan and had to be put back in place, leaving the top looking less attractive than I wanted it to be. So, just before serving the warmed cake, I heated some butter and brown sugar to make a brown-sugar glaze and poured it over the top, dribbling it down the sides. The cake both tasted and looked better than my original recipe.

When, as I mentioned, some of the sherry trifle sloshed over the edge of the bowl en route to a party, I discarded the box with the spilled trifle, cleaned the outside and the inside edge of the bowl, then whipped up attractive swirls of whipped cream to pile on top and sprinkled this with toasted almonds and bits of candied fruit. (We served slightly smaller helpings and even had a little left over!) It is experiences like that which have taught me to leave the decorating of dishes to the last minute.

But sometimes no amount of planning will be enough. The following story is one of my favorites, and demonstrates very well how being a caterer requires calm and ingenuity in the face of some unexpected problems.

THE LOBSTER TALE

December 14, 1982. At 7 a.m., as I was packing the lunches, I warmed the milk for what would later be part of the frozen custard dessert for the party I was catering that evening. My husband, Michael, and I discussed the pros and cons of a vacation in the South, while our son, Nicholas, sensing our distraction, decided to pour his orange juice on the dog.

By 9 a.m., after talking on the phone to our travel agent, and twice to Florida (while I stirred the cooling custard to let out the steam so it wouldn't curdle), we decided a vacation was too expensive. Michael left for work. Nicholas sat shredding the pile of Christmas wrapping paper he'd pulled down from the dining-room table.

At 10 a.m., ready to go at last, Nicholas waddled out to the car looking like a pink penguin in his snowsuit. I swept the snow off the windshield and buckled Nicholas into his seat, and we drove off to his play group. As soon as he was among his friends, I was back in the car and on my way to the fish market.

It was one of those slushy winter days when the car in front of you sends up a steady spray of dirty water to coat your windshield. As I drove along, collecting my thoughts, the windshield wipers suddenly just stopped—diagonally across my line of vision. The visibility was so bad I had to leap out of the car each time I came to a stoplight and scrape clear a patch of windshield.

Finally I arrived at the fish market; it is enormous and always crowded. There are thirty-foot-long lobster tanks three tiers high. The man who came up to help me spoke a completely incomprehensible mixture of French and Portuguese. With verbal communication at a minimum, we carried lobsters of various sizes to and from the scales until I approved of the selection.

After a quick stop at the bakery to buy fresh onion, poppy-seed, and pumpernickel bread rolls, I drove home, still jumping out to clean my windshield whenever I managed to arrive at a light that was red. I could hear the occasional rustle of the lobsters in their plastic bags in the back.

At home, leaving the lobsters out in the cold station-wagon, I prepared the hors d'oeuvres: chicken teriyaki, shrimp-stuffed éclairs, cheese straws, and mushrooms stuffed with pâté. I wanted to leave the cooking of the lobsters (which would be served in a Pernod and cream sauce) until the very end. I confess I didn't relish facing those twelve lobsters, still (at last check) trying in slow motion to climb out of the plastic bags.

About two o'clock the lights, the refrigerator, and the stove went dead. Thinking the situation was temporary, I continued to work, not very alarmed. Then I got a call from Michael across town. They were evacuating the college where he teaches; all of Montréal was without electricity. Later, listening to my battery-operated radio, I learned that up north a transformer had blown and all of Québec was without electricity. While others were caught in elevators, or stranded on the thirty-second floor, and while cars tangled at intersections without traffic lights, I was thinking about the ninety-eight dollars' worth of lobster out in the back of my car and the thirteen guests who would be expecting their supper that night. A waiting game began. While I finished up all the details I could, I listened anxiously to the radio. At first they said power would return by three o'clock, and then, later, three-thirty "at the earliest". I began to call around to anyone I could think of who had a gas stove.

There was something surreal about those two hours of waiting for the electricity to come back on. The house got colder and darker. I felt like laughing; it was one of those "this isn't really happening to me" feelings. I couldn't reach the client, as her switchboard wasn't operating. Meanwhile, I called my friend Graham for moral support. An excellent cook herself, she had always said she wanted to see what one of these jobs was like, so, game for anything, she showed up fifteen minutes later.

At three-thirty, Michael called from the home of Ray, a colleague who'd offered to let us use his gas stove; then, he picked Nicholas up and came home. After loading up pots, frying pans, utensils, seasonings, lemons, bottles of wine, Pernod, and cooking oil, Graham and I arrived at Ray's home—just as it became almost completely dark.

Having thought only about the power for the cooking, I had forgotten about the power for light to cook *by*. Ray found and lit three or four small candles while I filled the lobster pots with water and Graham brought in the last bag of lobsters from the car.

As it turned out, not only was Ray a dedicated cook with a fully equipped kitchen, but he was also from Nova Scotia, and nothing short of an expert at shelling lobster.

Graham was in charge of boiling the lobsters, which she did one at a time in each pot. Ray and I stood with our shirt-sleeves rolled up, elbow to elbow at the sink, cracking open the shells, extracting the meat, and occasionaly squirting each other with juice from the lobsters.

The dim flickering of the candles created a macabre atmosphere as we cracked open the shells and dug out the delicate meat. Behind us, on the floor, other lobsters stirred.

By five-thirty, the cooking and shelling was finished, and bright-red shells filled the sinks. We opened the bottle of Pernod to toast our success. Meanwhile, I melted butter to finish cooking the lobster pieces and ignited the warmed Pernod that had been poured into the pans. That blue flame rising from the pans was magic in the dark kitchen.

The spell broke when the lights came on about six-fifteen. In the dazzling light, we looked at each other and began to laugh. In the dark we hadn't noticed that both of us were covered with various smears of lobster liver; bits of red shell clung to our clothes. We looked like soldiers after a battle with lobsters— which wasn't far from the truth.

Then, looking at the carnage and chaos of the kitchen, I realized that the guests were due to arrive in just forty-five minutes. Leaving Ray and his wife with a dish of lobster in the sauce of cream, egg yolks, wine, and Pernod, Graham and I loaded up the car and drove to my house to pick up the rest of the meal.

After a quick shower, I put on my freshly pressed blouse, skirt, and apron, loaded up the car, and said good-bye to Graham. I drove off to pick up Patricia, who would help me serve. Downtown was eerie, with some blocks still totally blacked out. I was narrowly missed by a car which came barrelling through an intersection where there is usually a traffic light.

I was beginning to feel shell-shocked (an unintentional pun!), but the nightmare was not over yet. I had visited the apartment where the party was to take place, and had asked the client about the service entrance and the elevator from the garage. She explained where they were and said they were very easy to find, so I hadn't bothered to go down in the service elevator to the garage as I usually do. Never again will I make that mistake! The apartment complex was vast, covering two full blocks. The garage door opened automatically, so we entered and were soon lost in a maze of underground levels filled with empty parked cars—*no* people and *no* signs anywhere. Finally, near an exit door, we found some elevators, parked the car, and unloaded the four boxes and the heavy pot of lobster (whose ingredients alone I'd calculated to have cost over $120). The elevator kept trying to close, with great jerks, on the box we'd left there to keep it open while we loaded the other boxes, and in the next half-hour we were to load and unload the elevator another half-dozen times. We rode up to the tenth floor, only to find that all the room numbers were too high. After loading up again and riding back down to the main lobby, we discovered we had entered the wrong wing! The correct wing was what seemed like half a mile down long corridors through countless fire doors, all of which we had to open while carrying the heavy boxes. Finally, after having made two trips down this long corridor, we reloaded the elevator and rode again to the tenth floor. Standing in front of apartment 1017, I thought to myself as I rang the bell (and could hear the faint sound of laughter from guests who'd already arrived and begun to enjoy the party), "The last thing they will want to hear about is what a day I've had," so I just smiled, said hello, and promised to bring out the first hors d'oeuvres in ten minutes.

The hors d'oeuvres, the lobster served with Viennese spinach and a mixture of white and wild rice, the hot breads, and then the Drambuie Dream frozen custard (served before the chocolate truffles and the Irish coffee), were a great hit. I don't think the guests even remembered there had been a five-hour blackout that afternoon.

It was nearly 1 a.m. when I went down to get the car. As I was looking for the right door to reach the garage, a doorman asked what I wanted. "I'm going to get my car," I explained.

"Is that the red Volvo station wagon?"

"Yes," I said, cringing.

"We nearly towed it away; you're not supposed to park in that space. You're a very lucky woman."

I opened my mouth to say..., but instead just smiled. "Yes," I agreed. "Good night."

From this account, you can see how catering will sometimes demand more pressure, ingenuity, and hard work than the client or anyone else will ever know. At the same time, perhaps some of the greatest satisfaction comes from dealing successfully with these challenges.

HOW MUCH SHOULD THE CLIENT KNOW OF NEAR-DISASTERS? Usually problems can be put right before the client even knows of their existence. When something isn't as perfect as I'd like, I don't rush to the client and point it out. I've always felt apologies and excuses are worse than the original trouble. Whenever one aspect of the job isn't as good as I would like, I try twice as hard to make the rest of the meal and service as good as it can be. Clients have always been both reasonable and appreciative.

CHAPTER 21

EXPANDING THE BUSINESS

After having worked on a small scale, perhaps from your home, you may find that you want to move into a commercial kitchen with a retail business. The seasonal nature of the catering business with its literal times of "feast" or "famine" is why some successful caterers I know decided that a retail store with gourmet take-out service and gourmet frozen dinners would carry them through the quieter times (since the market for such food is more regular, not being based on people's desire to give parties, but rather on their desire to eat well).

Before you venture out into large capital investing I would recommend doing some homework. First, look at your own finances. Has the catering business so far been, or shown the potential to be, lucrative enough to support the overhead that a commercial kitchen and a store would demand? Could you afford to run in the red for the first year? Is there a market and a potential for such a store at the location you've chosen? Investigate other caterers in other cities who have done what you are considering doing. Evaluate the reasons for their success. You might wish to write or phone one of them (preferably in another city; don't expect a potential competitor to give you advice). Offer to pay a substantial consulting fee and make up a list of detailed questions. I've often enough been happy to do this kind of consulting work. There is great camaraderie among people who love to cook.

Finally, I would suggest that you evaluate the personal costs of being tied into a pressured, full-time catering business. From my experience, the risks in being totally involved in a business are often more profound than just monetary pressures. If the stress of an at-home business has been great, the stress of meeting large monthly bills will be even greater on you and your family.

CHAPTER 22

CONCLUSION

NOT THE LAST WORD In writing a "how to" book, I wanted to communicate my experiences with authority, without sounding as though I were just this side of a superhuman, ultimate organizing whiz.

While I know what *should* be done on each aspect of a job, I seldom manage to do everything "by the book" myself. (Fortunately, however, good habits become more and more automatic. This should be at least some consolation if you are feeling that there are too many details to remember.) In writing this, I was surprised at how complicated it all began to sound. But, like most jobs, if you take one step at a time, it's quite manageable. A manual on how to care for and raise children would surely make even the most confident of prospective mothers faint-hearted. Compared to the thousands of things you have to know and do to raise a child, catering is a snap.

I've been able to point out bad habits to avoid because I have so many of them myself. I tend to crack the shells off hard-boiled eggs in the sink, though I don't have a garbage disposal unit and know it isn't very efficient to have to scoop out the wet bits of shell.

Several of my pans have loose or broken handles, but I can't bring myself to throw them out (though I curse them daily). I sometimes start a recipe only to discover halfway through that I'm out of a crucial ingredient. This is one of the reasons I know it's a good idea to collect the ingredients *before* you start.

Often enough I put an unlabelled container in the freezer—sure that I'll remember what it is. Occasionally, I have to thaw a "mystery" package.

In other words, I've described what the "ideal caterer" should do, but I'm not always so perfect myself. I didn't want to make this book intimidating because I don't think it is all that difficult for a good cook to cater well. So if you're feeling intimidated, just start one step at a time. You'll find you won't look back.

SAMPLE MENUS

SAMPLE MENUS

These sample menus are designed to take into account such considerations as the season, the number of people, and the type of occasion, also such things as the balance of taste, texture, and richness. Recipes follow for all the dishes mentioned below.

SPRING

PRE-WEDDING BUFFET DINNER FOR 50

Cucumbers stuffed with Crab Meat

Blanquette de Veau

Rice

Brandied Mushrooms

Mixed Green Salad with Mustard Vinaigrette

Buttermilk Rolls

Frozen Drambuie Dream

BUSINESS LUNCHEON FOR 8
Spinach Soufflé
Herbed Lamb Chops
Grilled Tomatoes
Pasta Primavera
Crusty French Bread
Cream Berry Crunch

BUFFET DINNER FOR 100
Antipasto Misto
Parmesan Cream Chicken
Tagliatelli Verdi
Hot, Herbed Italian Bread
Mixed Green Salad
Citron Fromage
Assorted Wafers

SPANISH OUTDOOR SUPPER FOR 45
Gazpacho
Paella
Green Salad
Hot Breads
Strawberries and Kirsch with Wedges of
    Pound Cake

TRADITIONAL SUNDAY DINNER FOR 12
Seafood Bisque
Leg of Lamb with Mint Sauce
Petits Pois à la Française
Carrots Vichy
Baked Stuffed Potatoes
Sherry Trifle

SUPPER BUFFET FOR 60
Asparagus with Hot Herbed Mayonnaise
Swedish Meatballs
Fettuccini
Watercress and Endive Salad
Hot, Herbed Italian Bread
Upside-down Apple-and-Date Cake

SUMMER

PATIO SUPPER FOR 20
Crudités and Taco Chips with Guacamole
Shish Kebabs
Rice Pilaf
Green Salad
Bombe Surprise

COCKTAIL PARTY FOR 60
Shrimp with Cocktail Sauce and Brandied
    Mayonnaise
Snow Peas with Caviar and Cream Cheese
Crudités with Curry Dip
Stuffed Eggs—Curried, Dill, and Devilled
Vol-au-Vents with Creamed Smoked Ham
Grilled, Pâté-stuffed Mushrooms
Chicken Teriyaki with Sauce
Dates Stuffed with Cream Cheese and Cointreau

LADIES' LUNCHEON FOR 10
Green Summer Soup
Shrimp and Rice Salad with Pineapple
Watercress and Endive Salad with Lemon or
    Mustard Vinaigrette
Profiteroles

WEDDING RECEPTION BUFFET DINNER FOR 100
Prosciutto and Melon Balls on Skewers in
    Pineapple
Cheese Straws
Cold Salmon with a Fresh Dill Mayonnaise
Cold Roast Beef with a Horseradish and Sour
    Cream Sauce
Vitello Tonnato
Rice and Vegetable Salad
Tomatoes and Cucumber with Fresh Mint
Hot, Herbed Italian Bread
Wedding Fruit Cake
Lemon Mousse

COLD BUFFET SUPPER FOR 60
Salmon Mousse with Cucumber Sauce
Curried Chicken Salad
Sliced Roast Beef
German Potato Salad
Crunchy Vegetable Aspic
Marinated Green Beans with Cumin and Shallots
Assorted Breads
Honeydew Melon with Strawberries
Rich Chocolate Brownies

AFTERNOON WEDDING RECEPTION FOR 70
Sandwiches—Cucumber and Watercress
                Shrimp Spread
                Chicken Salad with Walnuts
                Curried Egg Salad
                Roast Beef
                Cream Cheese with Currant Jelly

Crudités with Guacamole
Fresh Fruit on Skewers with Kirsch and Sour
    Cream Sauce
Wedding Cake

FALL

HARVEST SUPPER FOR 20

Artichokes with Lemon Butter or Hot Herbed
  Mayonnaise
Canard à l'Orange
Herbed White and Wild Rice
Zucchini with Dill
Pumpkin Soufflé Pie

COCKTAIL PARTY FOR 40

Baby Potatoes with Caviar and Sour Cream
Cucumbers Stuffed with Crab Meat and Water-
  cress
Smoked Salmon
Quiche Lorraine
Spicy Meatballs with Sweet and Sour Sauce
Chicken Teriyaki
Stuffed, Grilled Mushrooms
Fresh Fruit on Skewers with Kirsch and Sour
  Cream Sauce

AFTER-GAME SUPPER FOR 10

Minestrone
Cheese Soufflé
Herbed Biscuits
Apple Crunch with Brandied Whipped Cream

BUFFET BRUNCH FOR 20

Fresh-Squeezed Orange Juice (or Buck's
  Fizz—Orange Juice with Champagne)
Sweet Corn Muffins
Ham and Leek Rolls in Wine Sauce
Spinach, Mushroom, and Bacon Salad
Fresh Fruit Salad
Crêpes with Maple Syrup and Whipped Cream

DINNER FOR 20
Onion Soup
Pork Rolls with Apple and Prune Stuffing
Scalloped Potatoes
Glazed Brussels Sprouts with Caraway
Chocolate Silk Pie

BUSINESS LUNCHEON FOR 8
Oriental Rice Crackers and Nuts (available at
    Oriental stores)
Sweet and Sour Pork Chops
Rice
Mandarin Orange and Avocado Salad
Zabaglione over Sliced Fresh Peaches

WINTER

FORMAL DINNER FOR 12
Shrimp with Garlic and Herbs
Boeuf Bourguignon
Rice
Petits Pois à la Française
Orange Slices with Cointreau and Candied
    Orange Peel
Rich Chocolate Chip Cookies

CHURCH LUNCHEON FOR 30
Crudités with Avocado Dip
Lasagne
Green Salad with Oregano
Hot, Herbed Italian Bread
Lemon Mousse

ITALIAN SUPPER FOR 8
Tagliatelli with Pesto
Osso Buco
Peas
Italian Bread
Zabaglione

GREEK SUPPER FOR 50
Stuffed Vine Leaves (from Greek delicatessen)
Moussaka
Garlic and Herb Bread
Greek Salad
Apricot Cream

INFORMAL COUNTRY SUPPER FOR 12
Winter Stew
Parsnip Purée
Crusty French Bread
Apple Crunch with Brandied Whipped Cream

BEFORE- (OR AFTER-) THEATER PARTY FOR 25
Watercress Soup
Rolled Flounder with Crab-Meat Stuffing in
    Wine Sauce
Herbed Biscuits
Pineapple Rum Sorbet

RECIPES

INTRODUCTION

The following recipes I've found to be very popular and practical for serving on my catering jobs. Since most cookbooks have recipes designed to feed six or eight people, I've focused this caterer's cookbook on recipes adapted for larger numbers of guests. I have also included suggested modifications should you need to multiply these quantities still further. There are few of the esoteric or exotic meals which I enjoy making for friends; I've found these are usually too expensive, too time-consuming, and less universally acceptable for the diversified groups you encounter in catering (besides, clients seldom choose to serve them).

Recipes are in both U.S. and metric measures. If you begin by following the metric quantities, don't switch to U.S. halfway through, *as they are not exact equivalents*. I have adjusted quantities of certain ingredients if I thought it was necessary.

Whenever pepper appears in a recipe, it means *freshly ground* pepper. All oven temperatures are for a preheated oven.

136

APPETIZERS (HORS D'OEUVRES)

Most caterers I know agree that appetizers are the most often asked for and the most time-consuming to prepare. (Which is probably why we get hired!) There is no hard-and-fast rule for estimating how many "bites" of each appetizer each guest will eat. Naturally, if there are eight different selections, fewer of each will be needed. Also, if there will be a meal to follow the appetizers, fewer will be needed than if it is a cocktail party. For appetizers before a dinner, I usually estimate eight to twelve bites per person depending on the age group (older groups eat fewer). For cocktail parties, I would estimate closer to sixteen or eighteen bites per person (i.e., if there are six different hors d'oeuvres, I'll make enough for each guest to have three of each). For very popular appetizers, such as smoked salmon, I would estimate four (plus) per person. The more variety, the more people will eat.

In the recipes below I've stated either how many people each will feed (assuming three bites per person) or how many bites it will make. I expect these recipes to be one of four or five other hors d'oeuvres served at the same time.

COLD APPETIZERS

CUCUMBER STUFFED WITH CRAB MEAT
AND WATERCRESS MAKES APPROX. 60 BITES

Especially cool and fresh-tasting

> 6 medium-sized, firm cucumbers
> 8 oz. (250 g) cream cheese
> 14 oz. (400 g) snow crab, either canned or fro-
> zen, *well drained*
> 1 bunch watercress, cleaned, with stems
> removed
> Dash of cayenne
> Salt, pepper, and lemon juice to taste

- Peel cucumbers (or score with a tool that removes the dark-green peel in strips; the tool looks like this

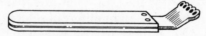

- Slit open the cucumbers lengthwise, cut them in half, and hollow them out by removing the seeds.
- Layer the inside cavity with the watercress leaves.
- Mix the crab meat, salt, pepper, cayenne, and cream cheese, either by hand or by pulsing for three or four seconds in the food processor. (There should still be chunks of crab.)
- Add lemon juice to taste, adjust seasoning, and pulse again.
- Refrigerate all ingredients.
- Stuff crab meat into the cavity of the cucumber and, just before serving, slice the stuffed cucumber into ⅜-in. (1 cm) slices and spoon any extra crab mixture on top of each slice.

> To Serve: The strips removed when peeling or scoring the cucumber are very attractive and they can be used as a dark-green bed on which you set the cucumber slices.
>
> *Notes:* Squeeze out the crab meat until it is completely dry before mixing it with the cream cheese; otherwise the mixture will be soggy.

Keep all ingredients and the final stuffed slices in the refrigerator at all times.

Though the crab-meat mixture may be prepared the day before the party, the cucumber shouldn't be prepared more than a few hours before it will be served.

MELON BALLS AND PROSCIUTTO

MAKES APPROX. 60 BITES

The orange and green colors of the melons skewered with the prosciutto into the pineapple make an attractive (and edible) centerpiece at a buffet.

1 ripe cantaloupe
1 ripe honeydew melon
1 pineapple with attractive green leaves (it
     need not be ripe)
6 oz. (200 g) thinly sliced prosciutto (raw
     smoked ham)
1 package long bamboo skewers (these may be
     washed and reused)

- Slice open the melons and remove seeds.
- With a melon baller, make melon balls (scoop out the scraps and reserve for your own use).
- Cut up the prosciutto slices into 1¼ in.-by-2 in. (3 cm-by-5 cm) pieces.
- Put melon ball 2 in. (5 cm) up on the skewer and fold prosciutto in half and put on skewer (make sure it doesn't touch the melon ball).
- Refrigerate the melon and prosciutto on the skewers.
- Just before serving, stick the skewers into the pineapple, alternating the cantaloupe and the honeydew.

To Serve: The pineapple with the fan of sticks looks attractive set on a bed of crushed ice on a silver tray or bowl.

Notes: Prosciutto (which literally means "before cooked" in Italian) is a delicacy from Italy and Spain. As with smoked salmon, a little goes a long way. The paper-thin slices

draped over ripe wedges of melon make a
delightful first course if served immediately.

Because the prosciutto has been partly
dried, it will quickly absorb the moisture from
the melon if it remains in contact for any
period of time.

The melon should be balled the day of the
party and kept refrigerated at all times until
ready to be served.

After the party, I purée the pineapple (if it is
a ripe one) and make a rum and pineapple sorbet. (See Desserts)

BABY POTATOES WITH CAVIAR AND SOUR CREAM MAKES APPROX. 60 BITES

Jill Roman of Houston's "How Sweet It Is" gave me this idea.

60 tiny new potatoes 1¼ in. (3 cm) in diame-
    ter (out of season, 5 cans of new potatoes)
8 oz. (250 ml) sour cream
6 oz. (200 g) black caviar
Oil
Lettuce, watercress, and parsley for garnish

- Scrub (do not peel) the new potatoes and cook in boiling
water (canned potatoes are already peeled and cooked).
- Slice off enough of the bottom of each potato so that it sits on
a plate without rolling. Scoop out a small indentation in the
top of each potato.
- Roll the potatoes in oil so that the skins remain moist and
shiny.
- Refrigerate.

To Serve: Just before the guests arrive, place
the washed leaves of lettuce on plates and set
potatoes on them. Spoon on a daub of sour
cream, then small quantities of caviar.

You may wish to put parsley sprigs or
watercress on the plate to add a dark green to
the pale green of the lettuce.

Notes: There is a variety of types of black fish roe (lumpfish) available at fish and specialty stores that taste fine and are much less expensive than the authentic Russian caviar.

Save the sliced-off bits of potato for a potato salad.

CRUDITÉS WITH GUACAMOLE OR CURRY DIP SERVES 30

1 lb. (500 g) carrots. Peel and cut to finger-length, delicate sticks.

1 celery heart. Prepare as for carrots.

3/4 lb. (350 g) mushrooms. Clean just before serving, leave on the stems, and cut large mushrooms into halves or quarters.

1/2 lb. (250 g) snow peas. Break off tails and pull down to remove string along straight side.

1 cucumber (the long, thin type with small seeds). Prepare as for carrots.

1 small head of broccoli. Remove stems and cut up into small flowerets.

1 small head of cauliflower. Prepare as for broccoli.

1/2 lb. (250 g) fresh string beans. Remove tails and steam briefly, refresh under cold water, and refrigerate.

2 pint-size baskets cherry tomatoes. Clean and remove stems.

1 red pepper. Cut into thin strips.

1/2 lb. (250 g) fresh asparagus spears (if in season). Use just the tips and steam briefly.

1 small package radishes. Make radish roses.

To Serve: On hot summer days (when crudités are especially popular) sprinkle crushed ice over the raw vegetables to keep them crisp.

I scatter radish roses among the other vegetables for decoration.

Notes: Radish roses can be made in a variety of ways; experiment. Cut a small amount off the top and slice each side part way down, then rotate radish and slice again across the corners before leaving it in water so that it opens. Slice enough off the bottom so it doesn't roll.

All vegetables (except the mushrooms and the cucumber) may be washed and prepared the day before they will be served. They should be refreshed under cold water before they are put on the plate.

GUACAMOLE (AVOCADO DIP) MAKES APPROX. 1¼ CUP (310 ml). SERVES 30

2 large avocados (ripe), or 3 medium. Discard
    pits and skins.
2 Tbs. (30 ml) minced onion
2 pressed cloves of garlic or 1 tsp. (5 ml) garlic
    powder
1 tsp. (5 ml) chili powder
Dash of Tabasco
3 Tbs. (45 ml) mayonnaise
Salt, pepper, and lemon juice to taste

• Mince the onion in the food processor, add the rest of ingredients, and adjust seasonings to taste.

CURRY DIP MAKES 1¼ CUPS (310 ml)

¾ cup (200 ml) mayonnaise
¼ cup (65 ml) sour cream
2 tsp. (10 ml) curry powder
1 tsp. (5 ml) ground cumin
1 Tbs. (15 ml) dark honey
1 Tbs. (15 ml) Worcestershire sauce
Salt, pepper, and lemon juice to taste

• Mix all ingredients together.

To Serve: Be imaginative in your choice of dish for the dip. Depending on the party's tone, you can use anything from sliced-open raw squash bowls to crystal stemware.

Notes: Remember, as you taste the dip, that since it will be used to add flavor to the bland raw vegetables, it needs to be stronger-flavored and usually more salty than it would be if eaten "straight". Of course, if it will be eaten with taco or potato chips, which are already salty, the dip can be less so.

Halve the above quantities of dip if you are going to offer both the guacamole and the curry dip to 30 people. 1¼ cups (310 ml) is plenty for 30 guests, assuming it isn't the only appetizer.

For large groups of young people, buy some bags of taco chips to go with the guacamole. They are popular, add instant variety, and mean you won't run out of crudités.

STUFFED EGGS

These are traditional, but always popular, and there is an almost infinite variety possible. Some of my favorite combinations include: dill, curried, devilled, and salmon (see recipes below), but try mixing the yolk with fresh chives, basil or tarragon, pâté, sardines, red caviar, or grated cheese.

Calculate about ¾ of an egg per person if there will be four other types of appetizer.

There are many theories about the best way to hard-boil eggs. Here is what I recommend:

- Place eggs in cold water to cover—never more than 2 dozen eggs in the pan at one time (they cook unevenly if there are more).
- Bring to rapid boil, reduce heat slightly, and boil for 8 minutes.
- Drain boiling water and run cold water over the eggs continuously for 15 minutes if you are not going to shell them immediately (this prevents them from continuing to cook and turning gray). They are best shelled and opened as soon as they are cool enough to handle.

- Slice eggs lengthwise in quarters. Remove yolks and place them in the dry bowl of a food processor. Process briefly and divide unseasoned yolk mixture among separate bowls to await seasoning. (Adding mayonnaise to the yolks before processing makes the mixture dense and pasty because it removes the air.) For salmon eggs, process salmon scraps until they become a smooth paste and then stir this paste into the yolk-and-mayonnaise mixture.

STUFFED EGGS WITH DILL MAKES 48 QUARTERS

1 doz. large eggs
½ cup (125 ml) mayonnaise
4 Tbs. (60 ml) finely chopped fresh dill, or 2
    Tbs. (30 ml) dried dill
Lemon juice, salt, and pepper to taste

CURRIED EGGS

1 doz. large eggs
½ cup (125 ml) mayonnaise
3 Tbs. (45 ml) sour cream
2 tsp. (10 ml) curry powder
1 tsp. (5 ml) cumin
Dash of Worcestershire sauce
Dash of Tabasco
Salt, pepper, and lemon juice to taste
3 Tbs. (45 ml) finely chopped gherkins
    (optional)

DEVILLED EGGS

1 doz. large eggs
½ cup (125 ml) mayonnaise
2 Tbs. (30 ml) butter
1½ Tbs. (20 ml) prepared Dijon mustard
Dash of cayenne
Salt, pepper, and lemon juice to taste
Paprika garnish

SALMON-STUFFED EGGS

1 doz. large eggs
½ cup (125 ml) mayonnaise
2 Tbs. (30 ml) soft butter
¼ lb. (125 g) smoked-salmon scraps
Lemon juice, salt, and pepper to taste
Garnish of fresh dill or chopped chives

To Serve: I like eggs served from a bed of
greens (it doesn't always need to be lettuce—
chicory, spinach, mature endive, or watercress are just some of the other possibilities).
At the location of the party, just before guests
arrive, arrange the egg quarters on the bed of
greens and pipe in flowerets, alternating different flavors and colors. I toss on a few black
olives for color. Depending on the flavor of the
filling, try using some of the following for garnish: sliced stuffed olives, capers, anchovies,
chopped pickle, pimento, or crisp bacon bits.

ÉCLAIRS STUFFED WITH SHRIMP, CRAB, OR LOBSTER SERVES 25-30

Seafood mixture: Combine the following
    ingredients and refrigerate.
½-¾ lb. (250-375 g) shrimp, or crab, or lob-
    ster—cooked, chilled, and coarsely chopped
8 oz. (250 g) softened cream cheese
3 Tbs. (45 ml) chopped fresh chives
1 Tbs. (15 ml) chopped fresh dill
2 hard-boiled eggs sieved or pulsed in the
    processor
Dash of cayenne
Dash of Tabasco
Lemon juice, salt, and pepper to taste

ÉCLAIRS

¾ cup or 12 Tbs. (190 ml) butter
1 cup (250 ml) milk
1 cup (250 ml) water
1½ tsp. (7 ml) salt
2 cups (500 ml) flour
8 eggs
Egg wash—1 yolk beaten with 1 Tbs. (15 ml)
    water

- Preheat oven to 375°F (190°C).
- Put butter, milk, water, and salt into saucepan; bring to boil.
- Remove from heat and stir in flour.
- Return to heat, stirring until dough forms a ball.
- Beat in one egg at a time, making sure each is thoroughly incorporated before adding the next. (This may be done in the processor; leave the machine running as you add each egg.)
- Put dough in pastry bag equipped with plain ½-in. (1.75 cm) tip.
- Lightly grease baking sheets and pipe the dough onto them in strips 2 in. (5 cm) long and ¾ in. (2 cm) wide.
- Brush with egg wash.
- Bake until puffed and golden, about 15 or 20 minutes.
- Slit open the top of each éclair and fill it full enough that you can see the seafood mixture. You may want to reserve the whole pieces of claw and some whole shrimp to garnish the top of each éclair. (If you've made batches of different types of seafood, this also identifies what seafood was used in each.)

> To Serve: Arrange a pattern of éclairs on paper lace doilies. Add sprigs of parsley or watercress and lemon wedges or curls.

> *Note:* The seafood mixture and the éclairs may be made the day before they will be served, but the éclairs shouldn't be filled until just before serving.

SNOW PEAS WITH CREAM CHEESE AND CAVIAR SERVES 20

$^{1}/_{2}$-$^{3}/_{4}$ lb. (250-375 g) snow peas
2 oz. (60 g) red caviar
8 oz. (250 g) cream cheese
Fresh dill for garnish

- Mix the caviar and the softened cream cheese.
- Cut along the straight edge of the snow peas to open pods.
- Refrigerate ingredients (but remove cream-cheese mixture two hours before it will be served so that it is sufficiently soft to be piped).
- Just before serving, on location of the party, pipe caviar mixture into each pod and arrange the pods upright in a bed of crushed ice. Garnish with dill. Set lemon wedges and watercress among the pods for decoration.

> *Notes:* Sliced cucumber may be substituted for snow peas; simply pipe a floweret of caviar mixture onto each slice. A little black caviar sprinkled on top of the pink floweret is stunning.
>
> Red caviar (lumpfish) is available at any fish or specialty store. Look for whole red eggs instead of paste.
>
> If the opened pods are kept in cold water, they open slightly, and this facilitates the piping of the mixture.

CHEESE STRAWS MAKES 4 DOZ.

$^{1}/_{2}$ lb. (250 g) sharp Cheddar cheese, grated
3 Tbs. (45 ml) soft butter
$^{3}/_{4}$ cup (190 ml) all-purpose flour
1 tsp. (5 ml) Worcestershire sauce
$^{1}/_{2}$ tsp. (2 ml) salt
Dash of cayenne
$^{1}/_{4}$ lb. (125 g) Parmesan cheese, grated
2 Tbs. (30 ml) caraway seeds (optional)

- Combine ingredients and roll into a ball. Refrigerate.
- Preheat oven to 475°F (240°C).
- When cheese mixture chilled, roll out as thin as possible and cut into strips 2 in. (5 cm) long and ½ in. (1.5 cm) wide.
- Sprinkle with Parmesan cheese (and caraway seeds).
- Bake for about 10 minutes or until just browning.

To Serve: Line small, handled baskets with colorful napkins and stack cheese straws in a jumble. If the baskets are so large that the cheese straws look lost, put a false bottom underneath the napkin.

Notes: It is better to make these in small batches than to multiply the recipe several-fold.

Find a bakery to make cheese straws for you if you are pressed for time.

SHRIMP WITH COCKTAIL SAUCE AND BRANDIED MAYONNAISE SERVES 20

1½ lb. (750 g) frozen, shelled, deveined, and cooked shrimp

- Leave frozen until one hour before guests arrive.

To Serve: When thawed, place shrimp on a bed of crushed ice dotted with parsley and lemon wedges. Silver platters and crystal bowls are especially attractive.

Set the small bowls or stemmed wine glasses, full of the sauces, into the ice.

Note: For very special small groups, you may want to buy the (expensive) large, raw, fresh shrimp (see in seafood section for cooking). The cooking, shelling, and deveining is time-consuming, so the price should be high.

COCKTAIL SAUCE

¾ cup (200 ml) ketchup
¼ cup (60 ml) horseradish sauce
2 Tbs. (30 ml) lemon juice
Dash of Tabasco

BRANDIED MAYONNAISE

1/4 cup (60 ml) brandy
3/4 cup (200 ml) mayonnaise
2 Tbs. (30 ml) prepared chili sauce

Note: If both sauces will be served, prepare
only half the quantities suggested.

"ANTIPASTO MISTO" (MIXED SAVORIES)

Cubes of different cheeses
Pickles, fruit, and olives
Chunks of smoked sausage
Rolled salami
Pickled herring
Sardines
Raw, marinated, or pickled vegetables

- Cut the above ingredients into bite-sized chunks and put them
  on toothpicks or bamboo skewers.
- Refrigerate until ready to serve.

To Serve: Stick skewered savories into a large,
round, domed loaf of bread. Arrange greens
under the loaf on a large, wooden board or
platter.

Notes: This becomes a conversation piece and
a way for guests to try new taste combinations.
Make sure all items are well drained before
spearing them into the bread.
Leave a small dish for discarded toothpicks.

HOT APPETIZERS

CHICKEN TERIYAKI WITH BRANDIED MAYONNAISE SERVES 30

1 3-4 lb. (1.5-2 kg) roasting chicken
1 package Kikkoman instant teriyaki sauce
    mix for chicken (or see marinade recipe
    below)
1/2 bottle white wine
1 cup (250 ml) water
1 cup (250 ml) vegetable oil for cooking
1 package bamboo skewers

- Skin, debone, and cut up raw chicken into 1-in. (2.5 cm) cubes and soak these in a marinade made of mix, wine, and water (or marinade below) for several hours or overnight.
- Heat the oil over medium heat; add a dozen or so pieces of chicken at one time and cook for a few minutes.
- Put each piece of chicken on a bamboo skewer and place these on a bed of lettuce.
- Serve with a bowl of sauce sitting on the plate, too.

> *Note:* This chicken melts in your mouth when eaten immediately after cooking, so prepare in small batches.

CHICKEN TERIYAKI MARINADE

4 Tbs. (60 ml) soy sauce
1 Tbs. (15 ml) molasses
1 1/2 cups (375 ml) dry white wine
1 cup (250 ml) water
1 tsp. (5 ml) M.S.G. (monosodium glutamate)
2 tsp. (10 ml) pepper
1 Tbs. (15 ml) garlic powder
1 medium onion, minced
2 tsp. (10 ml) salt

SAUCE

³/₄ cup (200 ml) mayonnaise
1 Tbs. (15 ml) brandy
3 Tbs. (45 ml) ketchup
1 Tbs. (15 ml) Worcestershire sauce
1 Tbs. (15 ml) honey
1 Tbs. (15 ml) lemon juice
Salt and pepper

- Mix together.

CHICKEN LIVERS WITH WATER CHESTNUTS WRAPPED IN BACON
SERVES 30

1 to 1¹/₂ lb. (500-750 g) raw chicken livers
1 lb. (500 g) smoked bacon
1 large can water chestnuts
Toothpicks

- Cut the raw chicken livers into 1-in. (2.5 cm) pieces.
- Slice the water chestnuts.
- Place one slice on each piece of chicken liver.
- Slice strips of bacon into three.
- Wrap each piece of liver and chestnut in bacon and secure with toothpick.
- Set these in batches of 20 on cookie sheets lined with foil.

  To Serve: Just before the guests arrive,
  preheat oven to 300°F (150°C). As guests
  arrive, bake one tray of livers until the bacon
  is crisp, 20-30 minutes. Put the next tray in as
  you remove the first. Batches come out hot
  and fresh at 20-minute intervals this way.

SPINACH PIE SERVES 25-30

PASTRY

6 oz. (200 g) fat—half lard or shortening, half
   butter
12 oz. (400 g) all-purpose flour
1 tsp. (5 ml) salt

- Preheat oven to 400°F (200°C).
- Mix flour and salt.
- Cut fat into mixture with a knife and then rub in with finger-tips (or cut fat into chunks and place in food processor and process) until dough has consistency of bread crumbs.
- Remove from processor, add 3 or 4 Tbs. (45-60 ml) cold water, and knead until dough forms a ball. Chill.
- Roll pastry to ⅛ in. (.25 cm) thickness and line the bottom of a long, rectangular baking pan, approximately 10 in. by 15 in. by 3 in. (25 cm by 37.5 cm by 7.5 cm). Let stand for 30 minutes to avoid excessive shrinking.
- Bake until pastry has set but not browned.
- Remove from oven and lower temperature to 350°F (180°C).

SPINACH MIXTURE

2 lb. (500 g) fresh spinach
2 onions
2 Tbs. (30 ml) butter
8 eggs
3 cups (750 ml) sour cream
1 tsp. (5 ml) salt
1 tsp. (5 ml) pepper
1½ cups (375 ml) soft bread crumbs
5 Tbs. (75 ml) melted butter
½ cup (125 ml) grated Gruyère cheese

- Cook and chop spinach, drain *well.*
- Mince onions and cook in butter until golden.
- Mix onions with spinach and layer over pastry.
- Put eggs and sour cream, salt and pepper in food processor. Pulse until mixed.
- Pour egg mixture over spinach.
- Toss bread crumbs in melted butter and stir in cheese.
- Sprinkle this over egg mixture and bake for 15 minutes at 350°F (180°C), or until eggs are just set.

- Cut into ³/₄ in.-by-1¹/₂ in. (2 cm-by-4 cm) rectangles.

    Note: While serving, keep pan warm in 200°F
    (100°C) oven.

STUFFED MUSHROOMS MAKES 60 BITES

STUFFED WITH PÂTÉ

60 medium mushrooms (approximately 1 lb.
    or 500 g)
1 small bunch parsley
¹/₄ lb. (125 g) pâté de campagne or pâté de foie
    or half of each

- Wash and remove mushroom stems (save for soups).
- Fill each cap with a mound of pâté.
- Broil in preheated broiler 2 or 3 minutes.
- Garnish with chopped parsley just before serving.

STUFFED WITH ONIONS AND BREADCRUMBS

60 medium mushrooms
¹/₄ cup (60 ml) butter
1 large onion
¹/₂ cup (125 ml) fresh breadcrumbs
8 sprigs of parsley
Dash of Worcestershire sauce
Dash of garlic powder
Salt and pepper to taste

- Wash mushrooms and remove stems.
- Chop stems.
- Chop onion and sauté in butter until golden.
- Add chopped stems and remaining ingredients and stir until
  well mixed. Remove from heat.
- Pile the stuffing high in each mushroom cap and broil in
  preheated broiler for 2 or 3 minutes. Serve immediately on a
  bed of watercress.

    Note: Place mushrooms in small batches of 20
    or so under broiler at any one time. Mush-
    rooms become quickly soggy if left to keep
    warm in oven.

MINIATURE VOL AU VENTS WITH FILLINGS MAKES 60

Fillings:
Creamed ham
Chicken and mushrooms
Shrimp in a cheese sauce

Vol au vents, also known as bouchées (meaning mouthful), are pastry shells. Order from the bakery 60 miniature vol au vents. They should be no more than 1¼ in. (3 cm) in diameter. Often, if they are too high, I break them in half horizontally and get, in effect, two bouchées for the price of one. (The holes in prepared bouchées go only a third of the way down. If you cut low enough and poke a hole in the top of the bottom half, you will get two.)

- Just before serving, warm bouchées in a low oven, 250°F (120°C).
- Fill with hot fillings and serve immediately. Pastry shells become quickly soggy if allowed to stand once filled.
- The quantities of each of the fillings below are enough for 60 miniature pastry shells.

CREAMED SMOKED HAM

1½ Tbs. (20 ml) butter
1½ Tbs. (20 ml) flour
¾ cup (190 ml) milk (approximately)
½ lb. (250 g) smoked ham coarsely chopped
2 Tbs. (30 ml) white wine
4 Tbs. (60 ml) chopped chives
White pepper

- Melt butter; add flour and stir until flour becomes thoroughly cooked and has a granular texture. Add enough milk for the sauce to have a consistency that is smooth and not too thick.
- Add wine, chives, and chopped ham and remove from heat.
- Reheat ham mixture briefly just before filling pastry shells.

CHICKEN AND MUSHROOMS

White sauce as for ham
Add to sauce:
1½ cups (375 ml) cooked, coarsely chopped
    chicken
½ lb. (250 g) coarsely chopped mushrooms,
    cooked quickly in butter
2 Tbs. (30 ml) butter
1 Tbs. (15 ml) sherry
Lemon juice, salt, and pepper to taste

- Reheat just before filling bouchées.

SHRIMP IN CHEESE SAUCE

White sauce as for ham and chicken
1½ cups (375 ml) cooked, frozen shrimp
    (thawed and squeezed dry), coarsely
    chopped
½ cup (125 ml) medium Cheddar cheese,
    grated
Dash of lemon juice
Pepper and salt and dash of cayenne

- Add cheese and seasoning to cooked white sauce.
- When cheese has melted, fold in shrimp and remove from heat.
- Reheat just before filling pastry shells.

To Serve: Vol au Vents are attractive served
from paper lace doilies on warmed plates.
Decorate with one or two sprigs of parsley.

Note: For each time you double the quantities
of ham or chicken or shrimp, you will only
need to make 1½ times the cream sauce.

QUICHE LORRAINE MAKES APPETIZERS FOR 30

While I love a quiche with a thick, light custard, the first time I tried to serve it as an appetizer to guests, they were unable to pick up the wobbly squares of custard without them breaking. That experience forced me to put less custard on the crust when I prepare quiche for hors d'oeuvres.

When you want to serve the quiche for a brunch, picnic, or supper where the guests will eat it with forks, double the quantities of custard filling to crust.

- Make and cook pastry as for spinach pie (p. 152). Make sure the pastry comes up the side of the long, rectangular pan 1¼ in. (3.5 cm). This way the custard won't overflow and seep under the crust, causing it to stick. Remember, the custard rises about 30 percent while cooking, before falling again when it cools.

CUSTARD FILLING

12 strips of bacon
2 medium onions, finely chopped
½ cup (125 ml) grated Parmesan cheese
12 oz. (400 g) Gruyère cheese, grated
1 cup (250 ml) milk
6 eggs
1 cup (250 ml) cream
1 Tbs. (15 ml) chives, freshly chopped
¾ tsp. (3 ml) salt
½ tsp. (2 ml) pepper
½ tsp. (2 ml) nutmeg

- Preheat oven to 450°F (230°C).
- Fry the bacon until crisp, and then break it up into small pieces.
- Pour off most of fat and fry onion until transparent in remaining fat.
- Sprinkle bacon, onion, and cheeses over partly cooked pastry shell.
- Mix the remaining ingredients and pour carefully over cheese and bacon and put in oven.
- Reduce oven to 350°F (180°C) after 15 minutes and cook until a knife inserted near edge comes out clean—about 10 min. more. I can tell that a quiche is cooked if, as I pull the pan, only the center has a slight wobble.
- Cut into small squares to serve.

SPICY MEATBALLS WITH SWEET-AND-SOUR SAUCE SERVES 20-25

1 lb. (500 g) ground chuck
¹/₂ cup (125 ml) fresh breadcrumbs
2 eggs
1 large finely chopped onion
2 Tbs. (30 ml) Worcestershire sauce
3 Tbs. (45 ml) chili sauce
1 tsp. (5 ml) chili powder
1 tsp. (5 ml) garlic powder or a minced garlic
   clove
10 sprigs of chopped parsley
2 Tbs. (30 ml) lemon juice
Salt and pepper to taste

- Mix ingredients well and roll into 1-in. (2.5 cm) balls and set on foil-lined cookie sheets.
- Just before they are served, cook for 15 minutes in a 350°F (180°C) oven until just firm.
- Serve with the following sauce and toothpicks on the side.

SWEET-AND-SOUR SAUCE

¹/₂ cup (125 ml) ketchup
¹/₄ cup (60 ml) drained, crushed pineapple
   (optional)
1¹/₂ Tbs. (20 ml) vinegar
1 Tbs. (15 ml) brown sugar
Dash of Tabasco

To Serve: If meatballs and sauce will be left on a table, set them on a hotplate covered with a straw mat or a colorful cloth. If you must carry them around to serve the guests, have one plate with meatballs on it very hot from the oven set on a second plate with a large paper napkin in between to keep the heat from reaching your hand. I use a tiny bright-yellow enamel saucepan with a wooden handle to hold the sauce. I reheat this each time I return to the kitchen for a refill.

Note: For each time you double the above recipe, prepare only 1¹/₂ times the sauce.

CURRIED MEATBALLS WITH CHUTNEY SAUCE
SERVES 20-25

Follow recipe for Spicy Meatballs, but substitute ground lamb for the ground beef, and
substitute 2 tsp. (10 ml) curry powder and
1 tsp. (5 ml) ground cumin for the chili
powder and the chili sauce.
Chutney Sauce: Chop finely ½ cup (125 ml)
mango chutney and dilute it with 1½ Tbs.
(20 ml) pineapple or other fruit juice.

SWEET APPETIZERS

Actually the notion of "sweet" appetizers is a contradiction in terms, because appetizers are literally meant to stimulate your appetite, and a sweet ideally indicates the close of a meal. However, I have found sweet appetizers are very popular at cocktail parties where there have been many substantial hors d'oeuvres served over several hours. People feel as though they've had a meal and literally crave dessert.

By far the most popular sweet appetizer is the dates stuffed with cream cheese and Cointreau. Guests are always skeptical at first and then, once they've tasted them, I've seen women who all evening have carefully resisted one hors d'oeuvre after another take half a dozen of these sweet treats (which must be as high in calories as they are good).

DATES STUFFED WITH CREAM CHEESE AND COINTREAU
SERVES 30

2 boxes (approx. 90) whole pitted dates (they should not be pressed or damaged). Put in freezer.
¾ lb. (350 g) cream cheese
½ cup (125 ml) Cointreau
Finely grated rind of two oranges for garnish

- Put cream cheese and Cointreau in bowl of food processor.
- Blend until Cointreau has been incorporated. Leave this mixture out of refrigerator to soften for 2 hours before it will be piped.
- Make a slit lengthwise in dates and put them back in freezer (freezing makes them easier to handle).
- At location of party, put the dates out on paper lace doilies on plates.
- Pipe the cream-cheese mixture into frozen dates just before the guests arrive (the dates defrost quickly).
- Sprinkle on the grated orange rind.
- Cover with plastic wrap.
- Keep refrigerated until served.

JILL ROMAN'S BAGUETTES WITH CREAM CHEESE, PINEAPPLE, WALNUTS, AND RAISINS SERVES 30

3 long, thin loaves of French bread (baguettes)
    1³/₄ in. (4.5 cm) in diameter
2 lb. (approx. 1 kg) cream cheese
1 fresh pineapple or 2 19 fl. oz. (540 ml) cans
    of pineapple chunks (coarsely chop the
    fruit)
1 lb. (500 g) walnut pieces
1¹/₂ cups (375 ml) yellow raisins
1¹/₂ cups (375 ml) mango chutney

- Soften cream cheese and mix all ingredients well (except the bread).
- Make a slit in the bottom of the loaves and pull out the soft bread inside (this can be used for bread stuffings).
- Fill with cheese mixture and wrap in aluminum foil and chill for 8 hours.
- Slice just before serving.

FRESH FRUIT ON SKEWERS WITH KIRSCH AND SOUR CREAM SAUCE
SERVES 30-35

1 pineapple
1 basket strawberries (probably a pint)
1 cantaloupe
1 honeydew melon
3 apples
3 bananas
3 oranges
4 peaches
¹/₂ watermelon, sliced lengthwise
1 package bamboo skewers

MARINADE
Juice of 4 lemons
½ cup (125 ml) sugar
3 Tbs. (45 ml) kirsch

SOUR CREAM SAUCE
1 cup (250 ml) sour cream
1 Tbs. (15 ml) sugar
3 Tbs. (45 ml) kirsch

On day of party:
- Cut up fruit into bite-sized chunks.
- Keeping each fruit in a separate bowl, sprinkle some of the marinade over them.
- Make kirsch and sour cream sauce.
- Hollow out watermelon, balling the fruit.
- Serrate the edge of watermelon shell.
- Arrange the fruit to line the bottom of shell in color patterns.
- Pour extra marinade over.
- Put kirsch and sour cream sauce into a stemmed goblet and set this in center of fruit.
- Decorate with mint leaves and lemon twists.
- Place watermelon shell on a bed of ice as the centerpiece of a large table. Put skewers in containers beside watermelon shell. The guests skewer pieces of fruit and dip them in the sauce.

SOME FINAL WORDS AND
LIGHTER MOMENTS ABOUT APPETIZERS

There's no question about it: appetizers and sandwiches are very time-consuming and fiddly to prepare. They don't keep in perfect condition for long, and leftovers are pretty un-appetizing. Nevertheless, fully half of what most caterers do consists of these "finger foods", so here are a few guidelines to remember.

- For appetizers, prepare each part of the recipe before going to the location of the party, but don't try to put them together into their final form until you can do it on the plates from which they will be served. (Need I describe in detail the trays

of egg quarters that left my kitchen each filled with perfect
flowerets and arrived at the client's looking like egg salad?)

- For appetizers especially, it's important to hire enough
kitchen help that you can prepare almost everything the day
of the party.
- For appetizers, it's easy to lose track of what a "bite size" bit
actually looks like. "Bites" have a way of getting larger the
more of them you make. I once went to a party (which happily
I didn't cater) where the pieces of raw vegetable in the crudités were so large that only the most uninhibited dared to
open their mouths wide enough to bite them. The smaller the
bites, the longer the food lasts. It's hard for a bite to be too
small.
- Summertime heat is the enemy of all cold hors d'oeuvres. I've
stood in a densely packed crowd of decidedly warm guests
and watched mixtures of cream cheese and caviar literally
melt before my eyes. Before I could retreat to the kitchen, one
unlucky gentleman picked up a snow-pea pod, only to find
he'd left the filling on the plate. My suggestion of serving these
from platters of crushed ice is essential on hot days.
- But crushed ice has its weakness too. It melts. One silver tray
a host had offered for the shrimp and crushed ice had tiny
pierced holes around its rim as part of its decoration—a fact I
failed to notice. I came out from the kitchen to see a steady
circle of drips dropping from the beautiful centerpiece of
shrimp onto the linen tablecloth. Bowls are best for holding
crushed ice. Any serving tray with ice needs to be drained and
replenished *frequently*.

SANDWICHES

I make sandwiches for my husband, my son, and myself every weekday morning. Sometimes I think I've made so many sandwiches that I could make them in my sleep. Occasionally I literally do. But the following recipes and hints for sandwiches are for the dainty, party variety and are quite different from the "7 a.m. specials" I pack for lunches.

Sandwiches served at wedding receptions and parties shouldn't fall apart when picked up (this means no thick wedges of lettuce). The chunks or slices of filling should neither drop down someone's silk dress, nor pull out to hang like a limp tongue from the guest's mouth.

At the same time, there should be plenty of filling, so that the sandwich is both moist and flavorful, not just a mouthful of bread (don't be stingy with the butter).

Speaking of bread, use a wide variety of good bakery bread—fresh the day the sandwiches will be eaten if possible. The best filling can't disguise tasteless, supermarket sandwich bread. A variety of colors of white, whole-wheat, oatmeal, and egg bread, and pumpernickel, and light and dark rye are pleasing to the palate as well as to the eye. (Try white and whole-wheat pita bread, too. These are handy and attractive envelopes of bread.)

For decorative looks, try cutting the bread into different shapes. There are the standard triangles, squares, and finger shapes; then, for sandwiches with cheese or puréed fillings (which can be more precisely cut) you can use cookie cutters for leaf-shaped or round sandwiches or for such seasonal shapes as hearts or stars. And, of course, there are rolled and open-face sandwiches.

Making sandwiches is time-consuming, and if there are many to be made, all before a 3 o'clock reception, extra pairs of hands are essential as well as more fun.

Set up an assembly-line production. (Have plenty of *soft* butter.) Lay out all the bread for a single type of filling. Completely cover both halves with butter; this seals the bread and usually prevents the filling from soaking it. Spread the filling evenly; close and stack four sandwiches before slicing off the crusts (make sure your knife is *very* sharp).

Sandwiches are best placed in sealed plastic boxes and refrigerated as soon as they are made.

Estimate twelve whole sandwiches per standard loaf of bread. Estimating the number of sandwiches each guest will eat depends on the usual list of variables: What other food is being served? What is the age group? The occasion? The time of day? As a general rule, if sandwiches are the main item on a menu for an afternoon reception, you can calculate two (i.e. eight quarters) per person. At wedding receptions (which tend to have plenty of young men), I've learned to expect the "bottomless pits", as we jokingly refer to them out in the kitchen, to take a stack of sandwiches for each hand. As insurance against running out, I'll put a cheese-and-pâté board with crusty bread out for these fellows.

I don't actually encourage clients to have a menu of sandwiches. Few people realize how expensive (in terms of labor) making sandwiches is. Sandwiches served at a reception give the impression of a not very lavish affair. So, understandably, hosts expect a not very lavish price.

Still, it's true: sandwiches are popular—especially the traditional favorites. I've described below my own version of these with a few new twists.

(These first two appeal to older ladies especially.)

CUCUMBER AND WATERCRESS
MAKES 36 WHOLE SANDWICHES

3 loaves of bread (white or whole-wheat may
   be used)
2 bunches watercress, stems removed
4 cucumbers (the long, thin, "English" variety
   with small seeds)
3/4 lb. (350 g) soft butter (unsalted)
Salt and pepper

Notes: Peel and slice the cucumbers into
paper-thin slices.
   Use plenty of butter
   Best made close to time they will be served.

TOMATO WITH FRESH DILL
MAKES 36 WHOLE SANDWICHES

3 loaves of bread (white, whole-wheat, or
   other whole-grain bread may be used)
6 large tomatoes
1 bunch fresh dill, stems removed, coarsely
   chopped
3/4 lb. (350 g) butter
Salt and pepper

Notes: Drop tomatoes briefly in boiling water
and then plunge into ice water; peel off skin.
Cut off top and squeeze to remove seeds. Slice
tomatoes very thinly. Tomato sandwiches are
also best made close to the time they will be
eaten so the bread doesn't become soggy.

SHRIMP SANDWICHES
MAKES 36 WHOLE SANDWICHES

3 loaves of bread (white and/or whole-wheat)
1½ lb. (750 g) shrimp (frozen, cooked)
    chopped coarsely
1 lb. (500 g) softened cream cheese
Dash of cayenne
Dash of Tabasco
Watercress (or alfalfa sprouts in a whole-
    wheat pita bread)
1 bunch scallions or 1 bunch fresh chives
Dash of lemon juice
Salt and pepper
¾ lb. (350 g) soft butter

- Cut cream cheese into large chunks and put in processor with cayenne, Tabasco, lemon juice, salt and pepper.
- Pulse till mixed.
- Add shrimp and pulse briefly.
- Stir in fresh chives and scallions after mixture has been removed from the processor.
- Layer a few watercress leaves (stems should be removed) in each sandwich.

ROAST BEEF SANDWICHES
MAKES 48 WHOLE SANDWICHES

4 loaves of bread (white, whole-wheat, rye)
2¼ lb. (1 kg) medium-rare roast beef,
    trimmed and very thinly sliced
1 lb. (500 g) butter
Salt and pepper
3 heads Boston lettuce—leaves washed, dried,
    and separated

- Place a single large outer leaf of lettuce on each sandwich and about two thin slices of roast beef. Reserve the small curled inner lettuce leaves for your own use.

   Note: All gristle and fat should be removed and the meat sliced so thin that it is not at all tough. It is wise to use a boneless rib roast.

CHICKEN SALAD WITH WALNUTS
MAKES 48 WHOLE SANDWICHES

4 loaves of bread (white, whole-wheat, pump-
    ernickel, or pita)
2 3-4 lb. (1.5-2 kg) chickens, cooked and
    deboned
2 bunches scallions or chives, chopped
1 cup (250 ml) mayonnaise (approximately—
    add enough to moisten mixture well)
2 Tbs. (30 ml) Worcestershire sauce
1/2 lb. (250 g) walnut pieces, chopped
2 tsp. (10 ml) paprika
Lemon juice
Salt and pepper
1 lb. (500 g) butter, softened

- Chop the chicken very finely and mix with the rest of the
  ingredients, except for the bread and butter.

CURRIED CHICKEN SALAD
MAKES 48 WHOLE SANDWICHES

As for Chicken Salad with Walnuts but omit the walnuts and
paprika.
Add:

1 cup (250 ml) chopped raisins
1 cup (250 ml) finely chopped celery
1–2 Tbs. (15–30 ml) curry powder
1 Tbs. (15 ml) ground cumin

Note: Layer a few watercress leaves or alfalfa
sprouts on mixture before closing sandwiches.

EGG SALAD SANDWICHES
MAKES 48 WHOLE SANDWICHES

4 loaves of bread (white, whole-wheat, pump-
    ernickel, light and dark rye, pita)
2 dozen large eggs, hard-boiled
¾ cup (200 ml) mayonnaise (approximately—
    add enough to moisten well)
1 bunch chives, chopped
2 Tbs. (30 ml) prepared Dijon mustard
2 Tbs. (30 ml) lemon juice
Salt and pepper
1 lb. (500 g) soft butter
¾ cup (200 ml) finely chopped gherkins or
    finely chopped stuffed green olives
    (optional)

- Put coarsely chopped hard-boiled eggs in processor and pulse until finely chopped.
- Remove from processor and stir in the other ingredients, except for the bread and butter.

CURRIED EGG SALAD

Same ingredients as for Egg Salad except omit mustard and add:

2 Tbs. (30 ml) curry powder
1 Tbs. (15 ml) ground cumin
2 Tbs. (30 ml) Worcestershire sauce

HAM AND SWISS CHEESE
MAKES 48 WHOLE SANDWICHES

4 loaves of bread (whole-wheat, rye, or pump-
    ernickel)
1½ lb. (750 g) thinly sliced, smoked roast ham
1½ lb. (750 g) thinly sliced Swiss cheese
Mustard (optional)
½ cup (125 ml) mayonnaise (optional)
1 lb. (500 g) butter

Notes: You can put a little mustard on one type of bread only so that those who want it know which to choose.

I put a little mayonnaise between the ham and the cheese for moistness.

CREAM CHEESE AND RED-CURRANT JELLY
MAKES 48 WHOLE SANDWICHES

Though hosts usually expect these to be eaten only by the children, I've found this a favorite among adults, too.

>   4 loaves of bread (white and/or whole-wheat)
>   2 lb. (1 kg) softened cream cheese
>   12 oz. (350 g) red-currant jelly
>   1 lb. (500 g) butter

Note: After buttering bread, spread a thin layer of cream cheese on *both* slices so that the jelly doesn't soak through.

OPEN-FACE SANDWICHES

Open-face sandwiches (a Danish specialty) are single slices of bread with a filling or spread on top. You can be very creative with garnishes creating designs with the sliced white of egg, capers, anchovies, sliced olives, pimentos, etc.

For a children's party, you could make a clown's face on a ham spread.

For hors d'oeuvres, cut each slice into small, decorative shapes.

Here are some of the coverings I use:

>   Pâté de Campagne or de Foie (available at delicatessen stores)—garnish with olives and parsley.
>   Tuna Salad Spread—garnish with sieved egg, capers, and olives.
>   Shrimp Salad Spread—garnish with fresh dill and egg.

Devilled Ham Spread (recipe below)—garnish with sliced pickle, gherkin, egg, or cheese.
Egg Salad Spread—garnish with parsley
sprigs, gherkins, or pickles.
Olive and Cheese Spread (recipe below)—
garnish with chopped parsley.

Note: For spreads, make mixtures as for
sandwiches and process a few seconds in the
food processor until the texture is more uniform. (Don't eliminate the texture!)

DEVILLED HAM SPREAD MAKES APPROX. 3
CUPS (750 ml)—150 PARTY SANDWICHES

2 cups (500 ml) cooked ham, cubed
¼ cup (60 ml) sweet-pickle relish
¼ cup (60 ml) softened butter
¼ cup (60 ml) mayonnaise
2 tsp. (10 ml) prepared mustard
1 Tbs. (15 ml) minced onion
2 Tbs. (30 ml) finely chopped celery
Pepper
Dash of Tabasco

• Put all the above ingredients into the processor and pulse
until the mixture has good consistency for spreading but still
has texture.

OLIVE AND CHEESE SPREAD MAKES
APPROX. 2 CUPS (500 ml)—100 PARTY SANDWICHES

1 lb. (500 g) cream cheese
⅔ cup (165 ml) stuffed green olives
½ tsp. (2 ml) garlic powder
1 tsp. (5 ml) minced onion or onion powder
3 Tbs. (45 ml) chopped parsley
Paprika, salt, and pepper to taste

• Put ingredients into processor and pulse until mixed but not
smooth.

ROLLED SANDWICHES

These are decorative and easy. Prepare and apply fillings as for open-face sandwiches (omitting the garnish) and, after crusts are removed, roll the slice up. Another variation is to have the bakery slice the bread lengthwise and put the spread on the full, loaf-length slice (removing the crusts). Roll this up and then slice it in $1/2$-in. slices (1 cm) for a pinwheel effect. Keep the roll refrigerated until just ready to serve, and then slice.

SOME FINAL WORDS ABOUT SANDWICHES

- When making sandwiches, two or three people radically reduce the time needed for preparation. (Besides, making 350 sandwiches alone would reduce the toughest of us to tears.)
- When packing sandwiches, have separate labelled boxes for each variety. Don't layer two hundred egg sandwiches on top of all of the roast beef sandwiches. At one large wedding I was convinced that I'd left a hundred and fifty ham-and-cheese sandwiches at home, only to discover that after two hours of serving sandwiches we finally got down to—ham and cheese, and...ham and cheese. For some unknown reason, we'd layered the bottom of each box with ham and cheese.
- One of the aspects of sandwiches I like least is the waste. A good sandwich has the crust cut off *after* it has been filled. This way the filling goes right to the edge. But this also means that each piece of crust has a little filling left on it—"contaminating" it for other uses such as bread crumbs, stuffings, and bread pudding. I was brought up to believe that wasting food is a sin, so I dutifully saved these crusts at first and used them for my lunches. (I confess, after a day or two, as they got staler, it seemed like less of a sin to throw them out.)

  As I write this, it occurs to me that these could have fed an army of ducks, squirrels, and birds!

  With that digression I've gone far enough. Back to recipes!

SOUPS

A good soup begins with good stock. There is no real substitute. Start getting into the habit of stocking your freezer with rich stock every time you have chicken, ham, lamb, pork, or beef bones to boil down. Many butchers will give you bones (especially if you are a good customer).

Garnishes for soups are part of the fun of eating them. For smaller dinner parties or large buffets, I like to offer a variety of garnishes: croutons; chopped parsley, cucumber, or chives; sour cream; salted whipped cream; and bacon bits. Guests can help themselves. This is a little more informal, so discuss it with your client first.

Unless otherwise noted, the quantities for these soups can be multiplied to feed larger groups. I have given these recipes in relatively small quantities because soup is more often served at smaller gatherings. It is difficult to serve to large groups because people must stand and balance the bowls.

Most of these recipes are familiar favorites; that is what clients seem to choose most often.

I always make extra soup. Soups freeze well and are a healthful, light food we all love.

> *Note:* To save time chopping and slicing
> vegetables for soups, nothing can match the
> food processor. Blenders are better for purée-
> ing soups to a creamy texture.

172

COLD SOUPS

GREEN SUMMER SOUP SERVES 10-12

5 cups (1250 ml) light, unseasoned chicken
   stock
2 cups (500 ml) zucchini, raw and chopped
2 cups (500 ml) romaine lettuce, raw,
   chopped
2 cups (500 ml) green beans, raw, chopped
2 cups (500 ml) raw or frozen peas
1 cup (250 ml) chopped celery
1/2 cup (125 ml) scallions
1/2 cup (125 ml) parsley
Salt and pepper
1 tsp. (5 ml) sugar (optional)
Dash of lemon juice (optional)
1/2 cup (125 ml) light cream

- Combine all the ingredients but the last four in a saucepan.
- Simmer the vegetables until just tender (about 15-20 minutes).
- Put through the blender in small batches until soup is smooth.
- Add the salt and pepper to taste. (Depending on the natural sweetness of the vegetables, you may find you want to add a touch of sugar.)
- Chill.
- Add the cream (adjust seasoning and add a dash of lemon juice if it is at all bland).

   To Serve: Garnish with chopped chives
   and/or sour cream or croutons

GAZPACHO SERVES 12

There seem to be hundreds of versions of this cold Spanish soup (or liquid salad, as it's sometimes called). I like it thick, with plenty of texture, but not a stringy or seedy texture.

> 5 large, ripe, fresh tomatoes, peeled and seeded (or if no ripe tomatoes are available, use canned plum tomatoes and seed them or a mixture of fresh and canned). Chop finely.
>
> 1 large green pepper, seeded and chopped finely.
>
> 1 cup (250 ml) fresh herbs—a mixture of chives, parsley, basil, chervil, and tarragon (the latter two may be dried since fresh are hard to find, but use half the quantity of the fresh). Chop finely. (You may use your processor for the tomatoes and the pepper, but the herbs are better chopped by hand.)
>
> 2 pressed cloves of garlic

Add to the above:

> ¾ cup (200 ml) oil (a mixture of olive oil and corn oil is what I prefer)
>
> 2 Tbs. (30 ml) lime or lemon juice
>
> 3 Tbs. (45 ml) wine vinegar
>
> 1 very large or 2 medium sweet Spanish onions, *thinly* sliced, then chopped
>
> 2 cups (500 ml) cucumber, peeled and seeded, finely chopped
>
> 1 cup (250 ml) chilled light chicken stock
>
> 4 cups (1 liter) tomato juice
>
> Salt and pepper to taste
>
> Dash of cayenne

- Chill.
- Serve ice cold, garnished with croutons and/or chopped chives or parsley.

To Serve: It is impressive to have small, deep earthenware bowls (chilled in freezer before filling) set into a second, white, soup plate filled with crushed ice. Or you can set a large earthenware tureen on crushed ice at a buffet.

VICHYSSOISE SERVES 8-10

A rich potato-and-leek soup that is always surprisingly refreshing when served cold. (It's good hot, too.)

    4 Tbs. (60 ml) butter (unsalted)
    4 leeks (chop the white part finely)
    1 onion, chopped finely
    5 medium potatoes, peeled and thinly sliced
    4 cups (1 liter) chicken stock
    3 cups (750 ml) milk
    2 cups (500 ml) heavy cream
    Salt and white pepper
    Chopped chives
    Watercress leaves

- Brown leeks and onions very slightly in butter.
- Add potatoes, broth, and about 2 tsp. (10 ml) salt.
- Boil until potatoes are very tender.
- Purée in blender.
- Add milk and half the cream. Bring to boil.
- When cool, blend again and chill.
- Add remaining cream and serve *very* cold.
- Garnish with chopped chives and one or two watercress leaves.

SEAFOOD BISQUE SERVES 8-10

This is delicious hot or cold. You may use shrimp, sea scallops, lobster, or crab.

> 3 cups (750 ml) water
> 3 cups (750 ml) milk
> 4 medium potatoes, peeled and coarsely
>   chopped
> 2 medium onions, coarsely chopped
> 1 bay leaf
> 1/2 tsp. (2 ml) powdered thyme
> 1 clove pressed garlic
> Salt and pepper to taste
> 1 1/2 cups (375 ml) raw seafood, chopped
> 3 egg yolks, beaten
> 1/2 cup (125 ml) heavy cream
> Paprika (if hot)
> Chives (if cold)
> Croutons
> 1 1/2 Tbs. (20 ml) sherry (optional)

- Bring the water to a boil and add vegetables and seasonings. Cook until potatoes are tender.
- Add one cup (250 ml) of the seafood and cook for 5 minutes.
- Take out bay leaf and blend till smooth.
- Add milk, bring to boil.
- Remove from heat and beat in egg yolks.
- Add heavy cream, sherry, and rest of seafood.
- Garnish with chives and/or croutons if cold, or paprika and/or croutons if hot.

TO MAKE CROUTONS

I find Italian bread is the best for croutons.

> 1 large Italian loaf, cut up into ½-in. (1.5 cm)
>   cubes
> ¾ lb. (350 g) butter
> 2 tsp. (10 ml) salt
> 2 tsp. (10 ml) pepper
> 1½ tsp. (7 ml) thyme
> 1½ tsp. (7 ml) oregano
> 2 cloves pressed garlic
> 1 tsp. (5 ml) paprika
> ½ tsp. (2 ml) cayenne
> 2 Tbs. (30 ml) chopped parsley

- Preheat oven to 325°F (160°C).
- Melt butter in deep, heavy saucepan.
- Lower heat.
- Add everything but the bread; stir.
- Toss the bread cubes in quickly and stir until well coated with butter mixture.
- Turn bread cubes out onto cookie sheet and bake until dark golden brown and completely crisp.
- Freeze until ready to use. Crisp briefly in 250°F (120°C) oven before serving.

> *Note:* I always make extra croutons because
> they keep well in the freezer. An Italian loaf
> makes about 3 quarts (3 liters) of croutons.

HOT SOUPS

MUSHROOM BISQUE SERVES 8-10

I have often served this delicately flavored soup as a first course for buffets with several main entrée choices. I like it best thick and hot.

> 1-1½ lb. (500-750 g) fresh mushrooms. (The broad, flat-topped mushrooms found in Oriental vegetable stores are especially good in this.)
> 1 qt. (1 liter) rich chicken stock
> 1 medium onion, finely chopped
> 8 Tbs. (120 ml) butter
> 6 Tbs. (90 ml) flour
> 3 cups (750 ml) milk
> 1 cup (250 ml) heavy cream
> 1 tsp. (5 ml) salt (adjust to taste later)
> Pepper
> Dash of Tabasco
> 2 Tbs. (30 ml) sherry

- Wash mushrooms. Cut off dried ends of stems. Reserve 10 caps and slice them for garnish.
- Put the rest of the mushrooms and stems in food processor and chop finely.
- Sauté onions in 2 Tbs. (30 ml) butter.
- Toss the mushrooms into this and stir for a minute.
- Add broth and simmer, covered, for 20 minutes.
- Cook flour in remaining butter.
- Add milk, and stir until thick; remove from heat; add mushrooms and broth.
- Add cream.
- Season to taste.

> To Serve: Sauté the sliced caps in a very hot pan with butter until just brown, not fully cooked. Add sherry to soup just before serving. Garnish with the mushroom slices.

SPINACH SOUP SERVES 10-12

Delicious hot or cold, and so easy to make.

> 4 packages (2 lb., or 1 kg) fresh spinach (well
>   cleaned, large stems discarded)
> 2 Tbs. (30 ml) finely grated lemon peel
> ¾ cup (200 ml) water
> 2 chicken-stock cubes
> 3 cups (750 ml) light cream
> Salt and pepper to taste
> Fresh dill, chopped (for garnish)

- Cook spinach in water and seasoning until just cooked.
- Put in blender and purée.
- Add cream and chill (or heat without boiling if to be served hot).
- Garnish with fresh dill before serving.

FRENCH ONION SOUP SERVES 10-12

> 4 cups (1 liter) thinly sliced onions
> ¾ cup (200 ml) butter
> 3 quarts (3 liters) beef stock. (This must be good stock.)
> Salt and pepper
> 1 loaf French bread
> 1½ cups (375 ml) grated Parmesan cheese
> 3 Tbs. (45 ml) cognac or sherry

- Preheat oven to 400°F (200°C).
- Sauté the onions in butter until slightly browned.
- Add stock and boil for about 10 minutes; then season to taste.
- Slice and toast French bread.
- Divide soup into small bowls or put into large oven-proof tureen.
- Place bread in each bowl and sprinkle on the cheese. Add a dot of butter on top of cheese.
- Bake until brown and bubbling.
- Add cognac or sherry.
- Serve immediately.

> *Note:* Be careful not to over-salt the soup.
> (Remember, the cheese is salty.) Onions have a
> sweetness that shouldn't be hidden with too much salt.

POTAGE CRESSONNIÈRE (CREAM OF WATERCRESS SOUP) SERVES 10-12

½ cup (125 ml) butter
2 cloves garlic, minced
4 cups (1 liter) chopped onions
2 lb. (1 kg) potatoes
Salt and pepper
2 cups (500 ml) light chicken stock
2 bunches watercress
3 cups (750 ml) milk
2 cups (500 ml) water
1 cup (250 ml) light cream
Lemon juice

- Sauté garlic and onions in butter until transparent.
- Add stock, potatoes, and seasonings; simmer about 20-25 minutes.
- Chop watercress finely in processor, reserving a handful of leaves for garnish.
- Add watercress, milk, and water; cook 20 minutes (add more milk if it appears too thick).
- Purée mixture in blender. (Soup may be made the day before and kept ready at this stage.)
- Heat to boiling and stir in cream. Remove from heat before it boils.
- Add lemon juice to taste.
- Garnish with watercress leaves.
- Serve.

MINESTRONE SERVES 10-12

While the other soups described so far are good for accompanying a meal, minestrone can be the center of the meal itself. When served with crusty garlic bread and sliced salamis, it is perfect for a winter supper with an Italian flair.

I like a minestrone that has all the many vegetables cut up into small, delicate pieces. Choose the vegetables according to what is in season; many different combinations are good.

⅓ lb. (150 g) white beans

⅓ lb. (150 g) red kidney beans

4 qt. (4 liters) boiling salted water

5 qt. (5 liters) rich beef stock

1 lb. (500 g) shin beef or other inexpensive cut, chopped into small pieces (or ground beef)

¾ lb. (400 g) bacon or salt pork, diced into small pieces

4 Tbs. (60 ml) oil (mixture of corn oil and olive oil)

3 cloves of garlic, minced

2 large onions, chopped

4 large stalks celery, diced

4 carrots, peeled and chopped

2 cups (500 ml) (or ½ head) of shredded cabbage

4 cups (1 liter) canned tomatoes

2 zucchini or yellow squash, finely chopped

3 Tbs. (45 ml) tomato paste

1½ cups (375 ml) red wine

1 cup (250 ml) spaghetti, broken into small pieces

½ cup (125 ml) chopped fresh parsley and basil

Salt and pepper

2 cups (500 ml) frozen peas

2 cups (500 ml) grated Parmesan cheese

- Either cook the dried beans in pot with bones while making stock or put them in boiling, salted water for 5 minutes and then let stand for an hour before draining.
- Sauté garlic, onion, and meat in oil.
- Stir in other vegetables except peas and cook for 10 minutes.
- Add stock and wine. Cook for 25 minutes or until vegetables are tender.
- Add spaghetti, peas, and salt and pepper to taste.
- Cook briefly until spaghetti is tender.
- Serve hot, and let guests garnish with Parmesan cheese.

SPLIT-PEA SOUP SERVES 20

Also a hearty soup for cold winter evenings, this soup is best when made from the stock in which a ham or a ham bone has been boiled.

If a boiled ham is used to make the stock, taste before adding salt.

4 qt. (16 cups) (4 liters) ham stock
3-4 cups (750-1000 ml) split peas. For very
     thick soup use 4 cups.
3 onions, chopped
3 stalks celery, chopped
3 carrots, diced
2 cloves garlic
2 bay leaves
Dash of cayenne
$\frac{1}{2}$ tsp. (2 ml) thyme
Salt and pepper
2 cups (500 ml) finely diced ham
Croutons for garnish

- Simmer all the ingredients except the finely diced ham for about 3 hours.
- Remove cloves of garlic and bay leaves.
- Stir in diced ham and keep hot until ready to be served.
- Garnish with hot croutons.

ENTRÉES
BEEF

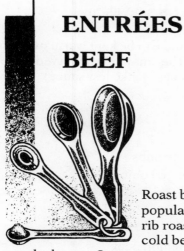

Roast beef, served either hot or cold, is a popular item for large buffets. Boneless rib roasts are what I choose when serving cold beef because it is easier to slice without the bones. One or more meat thermometers are essential, especially if you are cooking more than one roast in the oven at a time. (The number of minutes per pound changes with several roasts in the oven at one time.) For large gatherings, have some of the meat rare and some medium. The meat continues to cook once it is out of the oven, so I remove it just *before* the temperature reads for either rare or medium beef. It should all be *thinly* sliced with a meat slicer if you want to feed the maximum number of people per pound.

- Salt and pepper the roasts.
- Get extra fat from the butcher to cover them.
- Set them on racks in fairly deep pans.
- Preheat oven to 475°F (240°C).
- Cook meat for 15 minutes at that temperature (this seals in the juices).
- Lower temperature to 325°F (160°C) and cook until approximately 140°F (60°C) for rare and 150°F (65°C) for medium.

> To Serve: Cold roast beef is good with Horse-radish-and-Sour-Cream Sauce (made by stirring 2 Tbs. (30 ml) of horseradish into 1½ cups (375 ml) sour cream). Also put out a dish of hot mustard.
>
> Hot beef is good with pan gravy and Yorkshire pudding.

SWEDISH MEATBALLS SERVES 20

These work well for large numbers and can be kept warm over long periods without deteriorating. They may also be served with toothpicks for appetizers (but in that case make less sauce).

2 lb. (1 kg) ground beef
2 lb. (1 kg) ground veal
2 lb. (1 kg) ground pork
3 cups (750 ml) fresh breadcrumbs
1 1/2 cups (375 ml) finely minced onion
3/4 cup (180 ml) chopped parsley
1 1/2 cups (375 ml) milk
4 eggs
2 tsp. (10 ml) finely grated lemon peel
2 Tbs. (30 ml) lemon juice
2 Tbs. (30 ml) Worcestershire sauce
1 tsp. (5 ml) paprika
Salt and pepper
5 Tbs. (75 ml) butter
1/2 cup (125 ml) flour
1 cup (250 ml) beef stock
1 cup (250 ml) cream
3/4 cup (180 ml) sour cream
Sherry
Parsley

- Mix the meat, seasonings, breadcrumbs, milk, and eggs very well and roll into 1 1/4-in. (3.5 cm) balls.
- Brown these in small batches in butter and remove to warm serving dish.
- Add flour to fat and stir until well cooked.
- Add beef stock and cream and bring to a boil.
- Remove from heat, add sour cream and sherry, and adjust seasoning.
- Pour over meatballs. Just before serving, sprinkle on chopped parsley.

BOEUF BOURGUIGNON SERVES 12

A traditional classic, this remains a favorite with several of my clients. I use a fairly good Burgundy wine, as the flavor of the wine predominates.

> 5 lb. (2¼ kg) lean stewing beef (remove all
>   gristle)
> Flour (to dredge meat)
> Salt and pepper
> Butter and oil (to brown meat)
> ¾ lb. (350 g) smoked bacon, diced
> 3-4 cloves garlic, minced
> 3 large carrots, coarsely chopped
> 6 medium onions, coarsely chopped
> 1 cup (250 ml) chopped parsley
> 3 bay leaves
> 2 tsp. (10 ml) thyme
> 1 bottle Burgundy wine
> ¾ cup (195 ml) flour
> ⅓ lb. (200 g) butter
> Lemon juice
> Salt and pepper
> ¼ cup (60 ml) butter
> 1 lb. (500 g) mushrooms—small; cut larger
>   ones in half
> 1 lb. (500 g) baby onions
> Cognac
> Parsley

- Preheat oven to 350°F (180°C).
- Cut the meat into 1½-in. (4 cm) cubes.
- Toss in a flour, salt, and pepper mixture.
- Brown in small batches in half butter, half oil.
- Remove to Dutch oven or deep casserole dish.
- Fry the bacon until crisp and add to beef.
- In bacon fat, brown the garlic, carrots, and onions.
- Add vegetables to beef and cover with wine. (Add water if wine doesn't cover.)
- Bake about an hour.

- Make a *beurre manié* (a paste) with butter and flour and stir this in well. Add a dash of lemon juice.
- Continue to bake until meat is tender (about 2 hours).
- Lightly brown the baby onions in 2 Tbs. (30 ml) butter, add a little water, cover, and simmer them until they are cooked.
- Just before serving, melt 2 Tbs. (30 ml) butter and sauté whole mushrooms briefly over high heat.

> To Serve: Spread about half of onions and mushrooms over top of beef; sprinkle on chopped parsley. Warm cognac and pour it over casserole. Ignite the cognac in front of the guests. Pass separate, warmed bowls of extra mushrooms and onions for the guests to help themselves once the beef has been served.

BEEF STROGANOFF SERVES 8

This is best when the most tender meat is used, cooked quickly, and served immediately. It is better prepared for smaller groups.

> 2 lb. (1 kg) beef fillet or sirloin steak
> Salt and pepper
> 2 large onions, finely minced
> 5 Tbs. (75 ml) butter (approximately)
> 2 Tbs. (30 ml) flour
> 1½ cups (375 ml) beef stock
> 2 tsp. (10 ml) Dijon mustard
> 5 Tbs. (75 ml) sour cream
> 1 lb. (500 g) mushrooms, sliced
> 1 Tbs. (15 ml) sherry
> Parsley

- Slice the beef into strips 2 in. (5 cm) long; salt and pepper them.
- Heat 2 Tbs. (30 ml) butter in skillet. Add onion and beef in batches. Brown quickly.
- Remove to heated platter.
- Melt 2 Tbs. (30 ml) butter in the pan and add flour; stir with whisk until cooked. Add stock and stir until thick and smooth.
- Add mustard and sour cream; heat without boiling.

- Adjust seasoning and pour over meat.
- Sauté mushrooms quickly in 1 Tbs. (15 ml) butter, then add the sherry.
- Stir these into meat and sauce.
- Put in serving dish and sprinkle with parsley.
- Serve with buttered noodles.

WINTER STEW SERVES 12

This is a very easy and delicious stew. It cooks so slowly for so long that the flavors penetrate the meat and vegetables. Leave the pieces of meat and vegetable fairly large. A thick, brown gravy forms magically from the juices.

> 4½ lb. (2 kg) stewing beef, cubed
> 6 cups (1.5 liters) canned tomatoes, undrained
> 8 large carrots, peeled and cut into large chunks
> 4 medium onions, quartered
> 1½ cups (375 ml) chopped celery
> 4 Tbs. (60 ml) Minute Tapioca
> 5 tsp. (25 ml) sugar
> 1 Tbs. (15 ml) salt
> 2 tsp. (10 ml) pepper
> 1 tsp. (5 ml) thyme
> 1 tsp. (5 ml) marjoram
> 1 tsp. (5 ml) rosemary
> 8 oz. (250 ml) red wine
> 2 cups (500 ml) frozen peas
> 1 bunch of parsley, chopped

- Combine all of the ingredients except the peas and the parsley in a casserole.
- Cook for 6 hours in a 225°F (110°C) oven (check occasionally and add water if it appears dry).
- Fifteen minutes before it is finished, add the peas.
- Before serving, stir in some parsley and sprinkle the rest on top.

LAMB

LEG OF LAMB WITH GARLIC AND HERBS CALCULATE ½ lb. (250 g) PER PERSON

1 leg of lamb
3 cloves of garlic, sliced
1½ tsp. (7 ml) ground rosemary
½ tsp. (2 ml) thyme
½ tsp. (2 ml) marjoram
Salt and pepper
1-2 Tbs. (15-30 ml) corn oil

- Preheat oven to 300°F (150°C).
- Wash leg of lamb and pat dry. Trim if there is excess fat.
- With a sharp, pointed knife make slits all over the leg and insert slices of garlic.
- Mix the herbs, salt, and pepper with the oil and coat the leg of lamb.
- Cook until thermometer reads 140°F (60°C) for rare or 150°F (65°C) for medium.
- Serve with fresh mint sauce and pan gravy.

HERBED LAMB CHOPS SERVES 8

½ lb. (250 g) softened butter
2 cloves of crushed garlic
Salt and pepper
½ tsp. (2 ml) ground rosemary
2 tsp. (10 ml) *finely* chopped parsley
½ tsp. (2 ml) tarragon
8 loin lamb chops, 1½ in. (4 cm) thick,
    trimmed

- Make a paste with the butter and herbs.
- Slit open lamb chops horizontally; fill cavity with butter mixture and close with oiled toothpicks. Calculate 1 Tbs. (15 ml) of herbed butter for each lamb chop.
- Place chops on a rack 3 in. (8 cm) from a preheated broiler and broil until brown on both sides, 10-15 minutes.
- Pour any melted butter that dripped into the pan over the chops.
- Remove toothpicks. Garnish with fresh chopped parsley and ground pepper.

SHISH KEBAB SERVES 12

4½ lb. (2 kg) lean lamb, cut into 1½-in. (4 cm)
   cubes
2 Tbs. (30 ml) soy sauce
4 cloves of garlic, coarsely chopped
Tabasco sauce
Salt and pepper
2 cups (500 ml) oil
2 Tbs. (30 ml) lemon juice

- Mix all the ingredients except the lamb, and then marinate the lamb in this mixture several hours or overnight.
- Put meat on skewers and broil over charcoal or in the oven, turning frequently. The lamb is cooked when it feels firm to the touch.
- Serve it with rice and a side dish of grated cucumber mixed with yogurt, crushed garlic, salt, and pepper.

Notes: Vegetables can be alternated with the meat.

Blanch by dipping briefly in hot water: mushrooms, onion quarters, and green pepper squares.

Then dip these and tomato wedges in the marinade oil before skewering with the meat.

LAMB CURRY WITH COCONUT AND GINGER SERVES 12

This is one of the most succulent, elegant, and unusual curries I've ever eaten.

4½ lb. (2 kg) stewing lamb (usually from the
    shoulder)
¼-½ lb. (125-250 g) butter
4 onions, finely chopped
½ cup (125 ml) chopped crystallized ginger
Salt and pepper
3 Tbs. (45 ml) curry paste or 6 Tbs. (90 ml)
    curry powder
1 Tbs. (15 ml) fresh mint, chopped finely, or 1
    tsp. (5 ml) dried
1½ cups (375 ml) dried coconut
4 cups (1 liter) milk
½ cup (125 ml) freshly squeezed lime juice
1 cup (250 ml) heavy cream
Dash of sugar

- Cut the lamb into 1½-in. (4 cm) cubes, removing all excess fat and gristle.
- Melt butter in a large, heavy cast-iron skillet. Add the onions and cook until transparent.
- Remove the onions and brown the meat in batches.
- Return all the meat and onions to the pan along with the ginger, salt and pepper, curry paste, mint, ½ cup (125 ml) of the coconut, and three cups of milk.
- Heat the remaining cup (250 ml) of milk and, just before it boils, add the remaining cup (250 ml) of coconut and remove from the heat. Let it stand for 30 minutes, then strain and discard the coconut. Add the milk to the meat.
- Cover and simmer meat for one hour.
- Stir in the lime juice and then the cream and heat without boiling until ready to be served.
- Adjust to taste, adding more lime juice and/or sugar.
- Serve on hot rice.

MOUSSAKA SERVES 40

This is a very popular and practical meal for large buffets. It actually improves by being prepared ahead of time and reheated. It freezes very well. I usually make it with a mixture of beef and lamb, though it can be made with either one or the other.

12 eggplants, thickly sliced, peel left on
2 cups (500 ml) oil
12 large onions, chopped
4 lb. (1.75 kg) ground beef
4 lb. (1.75 kg) ground lamb
1/2 cup (125 ml) tomato paste
3-4 cups (750 ml-1 liter) red wine
1 1/2 tsp. (7 ml) cinnamon
Salt and pepper
2 28 fl. oz. (796 ml) cans of plum tomatoes, undrained
3 cups (750 ml) chopped parsley
3/4 lb. (375 g) butter
1 1/2 cups (375 ml) flour
4 qt. (4 liters) milk
16 eggs, beaten
8 cups (2 liters) ricotta or cottage cheese
Nutmeg
6 cups (1.5 liters) fresh breadcrumbs
5 cups (1.25 liters) grated Parmesan cheese

- Heat 2 Tbs. (30 ml) of the oil at a time in heavy skillets and brown the eggplant slices quickly.
- Set them on racks so that excess oil drains off.
- Brown the onions, beef, and lamb each in separate batches in more oil.
- Add wine, tomato paste, tomatoes, parsley, cinnamon, salt, and pepper to meat and onions and simmer over low heat until most of the liquid is absorbed. (It shouldn't be dry, however.)
- Melt the butter, add the flour, and stir until cooked.
- Add the milk and stir until thick; remove from heat and add the beaten eggs, ricotta, and nutmeg.
- Grease long, deep baking pans (I use two pans 10 in. by 15 in. by 3 in. or 25 cm by 37.5 cm by 7.5 cm) and sprinkle the bot-

tom with breadcrumbs. Layer meat mixture, eggplant slices, meat, breadcrumbs, Parmesan cheese, eggplant, meat, cheese.

- Pour custard mixture on top and sprinkle with the remaining Parmesan cheese.
- Bake at 350°F. (180°C) until the top has risen and browned (be sure to leave room for the custard to rise). Cool.
- Reheat before serving.

PORK AND HAM

PORK ROLLS WITH APPLE AND PRUNE STUFFING SERVES 12

Though time-consuming to make, this is an unusual and delicious winter meal. I've served it at Christmas Eve parties.

> 4½ lb. (2 kg) boneless pork loin
> 6-8 tart apples, peeled, cored, and chopped
> 1 dozen pitted prunes, softened by cooking in
>   water for 20 minutes
> 1 tsp. (5 ml) ginger
> Grated rind of one orange
> Seasoned flour
> 4 Tbs. (60 ml) butter
> 1 cup (250 ml) apple juice or cider
> 2 cups (500 ml) chicken stock
> Lemon slices and finely chopped parsley for a garnish
> *For Sauce:*
> 1½ cups (375 ml) sugar
> 2 cups (500 ml) red wine
> 3 cups (750 ml) cranberries
> 1-2 Tbs. (15-30 ml) cornstarch

- Slice the pork loin into ¼-in. (1.25 cm) slices and pound these slices until they are ⅛ in. (.65 cm) thick.
- Cook the apples with the prunes until just soft and mash them together. Add the ginger and the orange rind.
- Turn apple-and-prune mixture into a sieve, so that all extra moisture is drained (conserve this for later).

- When the apple-and-prune purée is fairly "dry", spread it on the slices of pork and roll them up. Tie with string and dredge them in flour.
- Melt the butter in a heavy skillet and brown the rolls on all sides.
- Add the chicken stock and cider and simmer pork rolls, covered, about 40 minutes.
- While pork is cooking, heat the sugar and wine in the pan, and when it comes to a boil, add the cranberries.
- Cook these until they pop, and then strain cranberries from the liquid.
- Remove pork rolls from their pan. Cut the strings and set them on a warmed platter.
- Add wine, apple-and-prune liquid, and cranberry liquid to the pan juices.
- Thicken with cornstarch. (Mix cornstarch with a little water before adding it in a thin stream.)
- Pour the thickened fruit sauce over the pork rolls and arrange the hot cranberries around the edge of the platter.
- Sprinkle with parsley and set lemon slices around.

BAKED GLAZED HAM

    1 uncooked ham
    Whole cloves
    1 cup (250 g) brown sugar
    1 Tbs. (15 ml) dry mustard
    Pineapple rings
    ½ cup (125 ml) raisins

- Preheat oven to 325°F (160°C).
- Bake the ham for approximately 20 minutes per pound, or until it registers done on a meat thermometer.
- Cut off the rind and slit the fat diagonally.
- Insert the cloves where the cuts intersect.
- Mix the brown sugar and mustard with a little of the fat from the pan and coat the ham with this.
- Raise oven to 350°F (180°C) and put ham back in.
- When the sugar has formed a glaze, place the pineapple rings with the raisins set in each ring on the ham and baste the fruit with brown-sugar mixture and fat.
- Bake for 15 or 20 minutes more.

SWEET-AND-SOUR PORK CHOPS
SERVES 6

6 trimmed pork chops
1 tsp. (5 ml) powdered ginger
1 tsp. (5 ml) paprika
1 tsp. (5 ml) salt
Pepper
1/4 cup (60 ml) flour
3 Tbs. (45 ml) butter
1 green pepper, diced
1 onion, finely chopped
1 cup (250 ml) pineapple juice
1 Tbs. (15 ml) cider or white vinegar
3 Tbs. (45 ml) brown sugar
2 ripe tomatoes, peeled
Watercress

- Mix the seasonings and the flour and coat the pork chops in this.
- Melt the butter and cook the onion and green pepper until soft. Remove vegetables and brown the chops (add more butter or oil if necessary).
- Add the pineapple juice, vinegar, brown sugar, and vegetables and simmer uncovered over low heat for 35-40 minutes (the sauce will be thick).
- Serve with sliced tomatoes and watercress sprigs on top.

HAM AND LEEK ROLLS IN WINE SAUCE
SERVES 20

4 lb. (1.75 kg) cooked smoked ham
1 doz. medium-size leeks or 24 small ones
2 lb. (1 kg) mozzarella cheese
3 Tbs. (45 ml) butter
3 Tbs. (45 ml) flour

2 cups (500 ml) milk
1 cup (250 ml) slightly sweet white wine
Salt and pepper
Dash of nutmeg
Parsley

- Slice the ham and cut cheese into strips.
- Clean the leeks well, removing the outer leaves and the green tops. Cook until they are soft.
- Cut leeks in half lengthwise and then to the width of the ham slices and set one large half or two small halves and two strips of mozzarella on the ham before rolling it up and securing it with a toothpick.
- Arrange the ham rolls in an attractive casserole.
- Preheat oven to 350°F (180°C).
- Melt butter; stir in flour, and when flour is mealy rather than gooey, it is cooked. Add milk and wine and bring to a boil, stirring constantly as the sauce thickens. Add a little salt and pepper and a dash of nutmeg.
- Pour over the ham rolls and bake for 30-40 minutes.
- Garnish with chopped parsley.

VEAL

VITELLO TONNATO (VEAL IN A TUNA SAUCE) SERVES 20

I've found this is a delicious and different cold-meat entrée at a buffet. The rich sauce (only a part of which is tuna) keeps the meat moist and has interesting flavors. It is ideal for large groups because it can be done ahead and it keeps well. When multiplying this recipe, be careful not to multiply the tuna and anchovies even *nearly* as many times as you multiply the rest of the recipe. If the recipe is tripled, I'd add only one and a half times the tuna and anchovies. Their strong and salty flavors can quickly dominate.

7 lb. (3.25 kg) boneless rolled leg of veal (you
    will probably need more than 1 roast)
4 Tbs. (60 ml) oil

4 chopped onions
6 chopped carrots
5 stalks of celery, chopped
4 large cloves of garlic
1 2-oz. (60 g) can of anchovies
8 oz. (250 g) canned tuna fish
2½ cups (625 ml) of dry white wine
1 bunch parsley
4 bay leaves (whole)
1 tsp. (5 ml) thyme
1½ cups (375 ml) mayonnaise
1 cup (250 ml) sour cream
Pepper
Lemon juice
Dash of sugar
Sliced black olives, chopped parsley, capers,
    and sieved egg for garnishing

- Heat the oil in a large Dutch oven(s) and brown the roasts on all sides.
- Remove the meat and sauté the vegetables and garlic in the oil from the meat.
- Add the bay leaves, thyme, parsley, wine, tuna, and anchovies and return veal to the Dutch oven(s).
- Simmer covered about 2 hours.
- Remove the meat from the pot and chill.
- Reduce the vegetable-fish sauce by ⅓ to ½. Remove the bay leaves and purée the sauce in the food processor. Chill the sauce.
- Add mayonnaise, sour cream, lemon juice, pepper, and sugar to taste.
- Slice the veal very thinly and serve with the sauce and garnishes.

OSSO BUCO (LITERALLY THE "HOLE IN THE BONE") SERVES 10

This hearty Italian meal consists of thick chunks of stewed veal in a tomato sauce with the bone and its succulent marrow left in for flavor.

10 slices of veal shank 1½ in. (4 cm) thick
Flour for dredging
Oil for browning
2 onions, chopped
2 bay leaves
3 carrots, sliced thinly
2 stalks of celery, diced
¾ cup (175 ml) white wine
4 cups (1 liter) canned tomatoes, undrained
2 tsp. (10 ml) tomato paste
¼ cup (60 ml) parsley, chopped
2 cloves of garlic, crushed
1 Tbs. (15 ml) finely grated lemon peel
Salt, pepper, lemon juice, and sugar to taste

- Dredge the shank slices in the flour and slit the outer membrane so the meat doesn't curl while browning in the oil.
- Brown meat over medium-high fire.
- Remove meat to a warm platter and cook the vegetables over medium heat for 10 minutes in more oil.
- Add wine and simmer for about 15 minutes.
- Return the meat to the pan and add the tomatoes and tomato paste.
- Cover and simmer two hours. Add extra liquid if necessary.
- Remove shanks to warm serving platter and either strain or purée the sauce (after removing the bay leaves).
- Return the shanks to the pan with lemon peel, parsley, salt, and pepper; cook 10 minutes.
- Adjust to taste with lemon juice and sugar.
- Sprinkle with fresh parsley and serve with peas and a Rice Pilaf.

BLANQUETTE DE VEAU
(RICH VEAL STEW) SERVES 20

7 lb. (3.25 kg) stewing veal, cut into 1½-in.
   (4 cm) pieces.
Water
40 small white onions, left whole
8 carrots, cut into largish chunks
½ bunch parsley
3 stalks celery
Onion studded with cloves
3 bay leaves
3 cloves garlic
1 tsp. (5 ml) peppercorns
1 tsp. (5 ml) thyme
Salt
½ cup (125 ml) butter
½ cup (125 ml) flour
1½ cups (375 ml) heavy cream
5 egg yolks
80 small white mushrooms

- Clean veal and rinse, then cover in water and parboil for about 5 minutes. Drain, rinsing away the scum.
- Add enough water to cover meat and put in baby onions and carrot pieces. Add some salt.
- Divide the parsley, celery, onion with cloves (cut in three pieces), bay leaves, garlic, thyme, and peppercorns into three piles and tie these up into three cheesecloth bags.
- Put the bags in with the meat and vegetables and simmer, covered, for about 1½ hours. Test to see if veal is tender.
- Remove meat, carrots, and onions and put these into a warm serving dish. Discard cheesecloth bags.
- Reduce the broth to about half its original volume.
- Cream the butter and flour together and stir this into the boiling broth until the broth is thickened.
- Beat together the egg yolks and the cream and add to thickened broth. Do not let this boil.
- Pour this over the meat and vegetables.
- Sauté the mushrooms in butter and use them for garnish along with some chopped parsley.
- Serve with rice.

ESCALOPES DE VEAU
(BREADED VEAL CUTLETS) SERVES 10

Good for luncheons, this is better served to smaller groups because it should be eaten immediately once it is cooked.

> 10 5-6 oz. (175-200 g) veal cutlets
> Flour seasoned with salt and pepper
> 2 eggs
> 2 tsp. (10 ml) water
> 2 cups (500 ml) fine, fresh breadcrumbs
> 1/4 tsp. (1 ml) oregano
> 1/4 tsp. (1 ml) ground rosemary
> 3/4 cup (180 ml) butter
> 2 lemons
> Chopped parsley

- Pound cutlets until they are very thin.
- Dredge them in seasoned flour.
- Mix the eggs and water and dip the cutlets into this egg mixture before patting on the breadcrumbs that have been mixed with the herbs.
- When the cutlets are well coated, set them on racks in the refrigerator and chill for several hours.
- Divide the butter among several heavy skillets.
- When it is hot but not yet brown, add the cutlets and brown on both sides.
- Serve immediately with a lemon wedge and a sprinkling of parsley.

POULTRY

MOIST-COOKED CHICKENS

Many recipes call for pieces of cooked chicken. Here is what I've found to be the best method for getting tender, moist, and very flavorful cooked meat.

- Clean well however many roasting chickens you will need.
- Choose a deep baking pan and place the chickens close together.
- Add enough water to come 1/4 in. (.60 cm) up the side of the pan.

- Set a sheet of aluminum foil over the chickens.
- Do not seal the foil; you want the steam to escape.
- Roast in preheated 350°F (180°C) oven until the juice from a pricked breast is clear, not pink, and the legs move easily when pulled. Give chicken approx. 20 minutes per pound (500 g). When roasting more than 15 lb. (7 kg), reduce to approx. 15 minutes per pound (500 g).
- If cooking only one or two chickens, you may need to add more water.
- Debone chickens as soon as they are cool enough to handle, mix with seasonings, and chill.

PARMESAN CREAM CHICKEN
SERVES 30 [SERVES 100]

One of the most popular dishes I offer, this can be served to almost any size group.

> 5 3-4 lb. (1.5-2 kg) [15] chickens
> ½ lb. (250 g) [2 lb. (1 kg)] smoked ham
> ⅔ lb. (300 g) [1½ lb. (750 g)] butter
> 1⅓ cups (330 ml) [3 cups (750 ml)] flour
> 2 qt. (2 liters) [4 qt. (4 liters)] milk
> 2 cups (.5 liter) [4 cups (1 liter)] dry white wine
> 3 Tbs. (45 ml) [½ cup (125 ml)] lemon juice
> Salt and pepper to taste
> ½ lb. (250 g) [1 lb. (500 g)] medium Cheddar
>   cheese, grated
> ⅔ lb. (300 g) [1½ lb. (750 g)] Parmesan
>   cheese, grated
> 4 cups (1 liter) [10 cups (2.5 liters)] fresh
>   breadcrumbs
> 1 cup (250 ml) [2½ cups (625 ml)] melted butter

- Roast chickens (see Moist-Cooked Chicken recipe).
- When cool enough to handle, remove meat from bones and cut into largish bite-size pieces. (Boil down bones and skin for stock.)
- Melt butter and stir in flour until cooked.
- Add milk and stir until thickened.
- Add wine.

- Add Cheddar and half the Parmesan cheese and stir until melted.
- Season to taste and add lemon juice.
- Chop ham into small bits and mix with chicken pieces. Set the meat in deep baking pans.
- Pour sauce over meat.
- Mix remaining Parmesan cheese and breadcrumbs with melted butter.
- Sprinkle bread-and-cheese mixture over chicken.
- Bake in preheated 350°F (180°C) oven until sauce bubbles at edges.
- Just before serving you may broil the top briefly to brown it.

> *Note:* The breadcrumbs should not be the fine, dry, commercial ones. It's best if you process fresh slices of bread, leaving some coarse chunks.

CHICKEN CURRY WITH GINGER
SERVES 20

3 3-4 lb. (1.5-2 kg) chickens
4 Tbs. (60 ml) butter
5 medium onions, chopped
2 cloves garlic, crushed
4 stalks celery, chopped
2 Tbs. (30 ml) fresh ginger root, peeled and
    finely chopped
5 Tbs. (75 ml) curry powder (curry paste is
    even better)
3 Tbs. (45 ml) ground cumin
1 Tbs. (15 ml) Worcestershire sauce
1 Tbs. (15 ml) honey
1 cup (250 ml) raisins
6 tart apples, peeled, cored, and coarsely
    chopped
4 cups (1 liter) chicken broth
4 Tbs. (60 ml) cornstarch
Lime or lemon juice to taste
Salt and pepper

- Cook chicken as in Moist-Cooked Chicken recipe.
- Debone and cut up in large, bite-size pieces. Set aside.
- Melt butter in large, deep Dutch oven.
- Add onion, garlic, celery, and ginger.
- When onion is transparent, add curry and cumin. Cook for several minutes, stirring.
- Add apples, raisins, honey, and Worcestershire sauce.
- Add broth and chicken and simmer, covered, for 30 minutes.
- Make a mixture of water and cornstarch and add this to the bubbling chicken in a thin stream; stir until thickened.
- Season to taste and add lime juice.
- Remove from heat. This may be served immediately but improves if served the next day.

To Serve: Part of the fun of eating curry is the condiments you can serve with it. Here are some suggestions:

mango or tomato chutney	crisp bacon bits
sliced banana	chopped egg
grated coconut	chopped Spanish onion
chopped nuts	raisins
(peanuts or cashews)	crushed pineapple

CURRIED CHICKEN SALAD SERVES 18-20

3 or 4 3-4 lb. (1.5-2 kg) chickens
8 stalks celery, finely chopped
2 bunches spring onions, finely chopped
4 cups (1 liter) seedless green grapes (approx.
    1¼ lb. (310 g))
1 16 oz. (250 g) can water chestnuts, sliced
2 cups (500 ml) mayonnaise
1½ cups (375 ml) sour cream
5 Tbs. (75 ml) curry powder
3 Tbs. (45 ml) ground cumin
1 Tbs. (15 ml) honey
2 Tbs. (30 ml) lime or lemon juice
2 Tbs. (30 ml) Worcestershire sauce
Chopped parsley—large bunch
1 lb. (500 g) toasted slivered almonds
Lettuce

- Cook chickens as in Moist-Cooked Chicken recipe.
- Debone, cut into largish bite-size pieces, and chill.
- Mix together all the rest of the ingredients except the toasted almonds and the lettuce and parsley.
- Stir this mixture into the chicken and adjust seasoning.
- Just before serving, fold in two-thirds of toasted almonds and arrange chicken on a platter. Sprinkle the remaining toasted almonds and the chopped parsley over the chicken. Arrange lettuce leaves and sprigs of parsley around the edge.

> *Note:* To toast slivered almonds, spread them evenly on a cookie sheet and place them in a preheated 250°F (120°C) oven, checking frequently until they turn a golden brown. I know they are ready when the toasted-almond smell fills the kitchen. It usually takes about 15 minutes.

JAMBALAYA SERVES 16

This is a spicy rice-and-meat dish that is perfect to cook if you are not certain when the guests will eat, as it can be kept warm without deteriorating.

> 8 strips smoked bacon
> 2 cups (500 ml) chopped onion
> 2 cups (500 ml) finely chopped green pepper
> 1 cup (250 ml) chopped celery
> 4 cloves garlic, crushed
> 2 cups (500 ml) sliced mushrooms
> 1 Tbs. (15 ml) thyme
> ½ tsp. (2 ml) chili powder
> Salt and pepper
> 2½ cups (625 ml) raw white rice
> 2 cups (500 ml) cooked chicken pieces
> 1½ cups (375 ml) cooked diced ham
> ½ lb. (250 g) chorizo or Spanish sausage
> 3 cups (750 ml) chicken broth
> 3 cups (750 ml) canned tomatoes, undrained
> Chopped parsley for garnish

In deep skillet or Dutch oven:

- Fry the bacon; remove strips and crumble for garnish.
- In bacon fat, sauté until cooked the onion, green pepper, celery, and garlic.
- Toss in the mushrooms, thyme, chili powder, salt, and pepper.
- Add the rice and stir until it is coated with fat.
- Add meats, broth, and tomatoes.
- Turn the mixture into attractive casserole dish.
- Cover and bake at 350°F (180°C) until rice is tender, about an hour and a quarter.
- Serve, garnished with chopped fresh parsley and crisp bacon bits.

> *Note:* If the Jambalaya will be left to keep warm, turn off oven after an hour and set lid ajar so that some steam will escape and the rice won't become mush.

CANARD À L'ORANGE
(DUCK IN ORANGE SAUCE) SERVES 16

4 roasting ducks
3 Tbs. (45 ml) butter
4 cloves of garlic, crushed
2 onions, chopped
2 carrots, chopped
2 stalks of celery, chopped
2 tsp. (10 ml) thyme
2 bay leaves
2 tsp. (10 ml) rosemary
4 Tbs. (60 ml) orange rind, grated
2 cups (500 ml) chicken or duck stock
4 Tbs. (60 ml) cornstarch
4 Tbs. (60 ml) vinegar
4 Tbs. (60 ml) sugar
1 cup (250 ml) orange juice
1 Tbs. (15 ml) lemon juice
4 Tbs. (60 ml) curaçao

Salt and pepper to taste
2 oranges
1 bunch watercress

- Preheat oven to 400°F (200°C).
- Wash and dry the ducks; prick the skins and sprinkle with salt and pepper.
- Place ducks on their sides on racks and cook 20 minutes. Cook 20 minutes on other side and then, with the ducks breast up, reduce heat to 350°F (180°C) and cook 30 to 40 minutes longer.
- Test for doneness by pricking the thigh. Clear juices should run out.
- Split the ducks in quarters, removing the breastbone and ribs. Set on serving dish in warm oven 100°F (40°C).
- Melt butter and lightly brown garlic, onions, carrots, and celery. Toss in herbs and grated orange rind.
- Heat stock and add to roasting pan and scrape up all of the brown bits.
- Add stock and pan scrapings to vegetables and simmer for 30 minutes.
- Strain out the vegetables and thicken broth with cornstarch.
- In separate pan, cook together the vinegar and the sugar until they are pale brown.
- Add this to thickened broth.
- Add lemon and orange juices and curaçao.
- Adjust seasonings. Thicken with additional cornstarch if necessary.
- Peel oranges and slice into paper-thin slices. Place these on hot duck pieces and pour over some of the sauce.
- Serve the remaining sauce separately.
- Garnish with watercress.

FISH AND SEAFOOD

WINE-BAKED SALMON SERVES 20

This can be eaten either hot with a hollandaise sauce or cold
with a fresh dill mayonnaise and is universally popular. The key
to delicious fish is to not overcook it. To test for doneness, I slip
a fork in along the dorsal fin in toward the backbone (the thick-
est part of the fish). If the flesh lifts up easily and is opaque, the
fish is done.

> 9-11 lb. (4-5 kg) of whole salmon. (Use the
>   larger weight if the fish are small; the waste
>   is greater with several small fish.)
> 1/2 bottle dry white wine
> 1/2 bunch parsley
> Celery leaves
> 2 bay leaves
> 2 lemons, sliced
> 2 small onions, chopped
> 1/2 tsp. (2 ml) *each* dried thyme, rosemary,
>   basil, tarragon
> Dash of black pepper

- Have head and tail removed from salmon.
- Clean very thoroughly, removing all the brown substance (it
  looks almost like blood) along the spine as this has an
  unpleasant, bitter flavor. I run a small, sharp knife along the
  spine to break the membrane that holds this substance.
- Preheat oven to 350°F (180°C).
- Simmer together the rest of the ingredients for about 30
  minutes.
- Place the salmon on extra-wide, heavy-duty foil set in a deep
  baking pan, two or three fish to a pan. Turn up the edges.
- Pour on the wine-and-herb mixture.
- Sprinkle with salt and wrap fish up tightly in the foil.
- Bake in oven. Because the size of the fish determines how
  quickly it is cooked, I check each fish after about 40 minutes.

To skin and fillet the salmon:

- Leave the fish uncovered to cool; this way the skin dries slightly and pulls off in one piece.
- Scrape off the dark flesh. (It comes off easily if you scrape in the direction of the grain of the fish.)
- Slide two long spatulas in at the top of the back along the dorsal fin, being careful not to disconnect the "rib cage" bones from the backbone.
- Gently lift off the fillet and place it on a platter.
- Remove the backbone and all rib bones from the remaining half and flip over this fillet to skin it.

FLOUNDER, SOLE, OR PLAICE WITH CRAB-MEAT STUFFING SERVES 10

¾ cup (190 ml) butter
2 small onions, chopped finely
½ lb. (250 g) mushrooms, sliced
1½ cups (375 ml) fresh breadcrumbs
½ bunch parsley, chopped
Salt and pepper
¾ lb. (350 g) frozen crab meat, thawed and
    squeezed dry
10 fillets of firm, small-grained white fish
Lemon juice

- Melt about half a cup of butter in a skillet and sauté onions until transparent.
- Toss in mushrooms and cook briefly.
- Stir in breadcrumbs, parsley, salt, and pepper.
- Remove from heat and add crab meat.
- Preheat oven to 350°F (180°C).
- Wash and dry fillets. Butter 10 cups of a muffin pan and set a fillet on its edge in each cup to form a cylinder.
- Fill the opening with crab-meat stuffing.
- Melt remaining butter and some lemon juice and brush this over the exposed fish.
- Bake for approximately 30 minutes.
- Serve with white wine sauce on the side.

WHITE WINE SAUCE

4 Tbs. (60 ml) butter
3 Tbs. (45 ml) flour
1 cup (250 ml) each white wine and water (or
    fish stock)
1/2 cup (125 ml) heavy cream
2 egg yolks
Salt and pepper to taste

- Melt the butter and stir in the flour.
- When flour is cooked, add wine and water (or stock) mixture and bring to boil. Remove from heat.
- Add egg yolks beaten into cream and stir until thick.
- Season and serve in a sauce bowl with the fish.

SHRIMP WITH GARLIC AND HERBS
SERVES 6-8

30-36 jumbo shrimp
1 cup (250 ml) lemon juice
1 cup (250 ml) olive oil
6 cloves of pressed garlic
2 tsp. (10 ml) dry mustard
2 tsp. (10 ml) oregano
Salt and pepper
1/4 cup (60 ml) fresh parsley, chopped
1 cup (250 ml) butter

- Shell and devein raw shrimp.
- Combine all the ingredients except the butter and marinate the shrimp for several hours or overnight.
- Melt butter in a deep, heavy skillet and toss in the marinated shrimp, turning and cooking it until pink.
- Serve immediately, spooning the butter over the hot shrimp.

LOBSTER IN A PERNOD
CREAM SAUCE SERVES 10

This is one of the most elegant (and expensive) of entrées. Have the host check that none of the guests are allergic to seafood.

8 or 9 1½-2 lb. (750 g-1 kg) live lobsters
1 Tbs. (15 ml) tarragon
1 Tbs. (15 ml) chervil
2 Tbs. (30 ml) chopped parsley
8 egg yolks
1 cup (250 ml) butter
¾ cup (190 ml) heavy cream
Salt and pepper
2 cups (500 ml) dry white wine
1 cup (250 ml) Pernod
3 cups (750 ml) light cream
Dash of Tabasco
Chopped parsley for garnish

- Drop live lobsters one at a time into boiling salted water. Cook for about 12-15 minutes.
- Cut open when cool enough to handle and remove the green liver, or tomalley; set this aside in a bowl. (Discard if it isn't bright green.)
- Mix 3 livers with 6 Tbs. (90 ml) softened butter, egg yolks, heavy cream, and the herbs. Set aside.
- Remove meat from large claws and tail and cut this up into bite-size pieces. (Reserve small claws for other use.)
- Melt remaining butter in a heavy skillet and stir in lobster pieces.
- Add wine and cook uncovered until wine has mostly evaporated.
- Heat half of the Pernod in a separate pan, pour it over lobster, and ignite it.
- Lift lobster out with a slotted spoon and set into a warmed casserole or Dutch oven.
- Add the light cream and a dash of Tabasco to the lobster broth. Heat until almost boiling.
- Remove from heat and add liver mixture and stir vigorously with a wire whisk until it is thick.
- Season with salt and pepper.
- Add rest of Pernod and pour sauce over the lobster.
- Garnish with chopped parsley.

PAELLA SERVES 12-14

This was originally a peasant dish from Spain, but more elegant versions have been developed that still utilize some of the same flavors. You can use almost any combination of seafood, chicken, ham, and sausage. It is surprisingly easy to expand this recipe to feed larger numbers of people. The choice and quantity of various ingredients can be varied to fit a client's budget. This is fun, outdoor food.

> 1 cooked lobster, shelled and cut up
> 1½ lb. (750 g) raw shrimp, shelled and deveined
> 20 cherrystone clams, well scrubbed
> 1½ qt. (1.5 liters) mussels, well scrubbed
> 1 3-4 lb. (1½-2 kg) roasting chicken, with
>   breasts deboned and cut into quarters, and
>   legs cut up (they don't need to be boned)
> 2 pressed cloves of garlic
> 1 Tbs. (15 ml) oregano
> 2 tsp. (10 ml) wine vinegar
> Salt and pepper
> 1 cup (250 ml) olive oil or corn oil, or a mix-
>   ture of the two
> 3 onions, chopped
> 1 green pepper, seeded and chopped
> 1 tsp. (5 ml) ground coriander
> ¼ lb. (125 g) smoked ham, cut into strips
> ¼-½ lb. (125-200 g) hot Spanish sausage, sliced
> 2½ cups (625 ml) long-grain rice
> ½ cup (125 ml) tomato sauce
> 4 cups (1 liter) light chicken stock
> 1½ tsp. (7.5 ml) saffron
> 2 cups (500 ml) frozen peas, thawed
> 1 small jar of red sweet pimentos cut into strips
> Chopped parsley

- Mix garlic, oregano, vinegar, salt, and pepper with a ¼ cup (60 ml) oil and marinate chicken for several hours.
- Brown chicken quickly in remaining hot oil.
- Add onion, green pepper, coriander, ham, and sausage. Stir until hot.

- Add rice and tomato sauce and stir for about 10 minutes.
- Boil the stock; add saffron and a little salt.
- Pour this onto chicken and ham mixture; add shrimp and cook about 20 minutes until rice is tender.
- Turn this mixture into hot serving dish, stirring in the thawed peas; set the lobster on top. Keep warm, covered, in oven.
- Steam mussels and clams until they open.
- Arrange these with the lobster on rice with strips of pimento.
- Sprinkle lightly with chopped parsley.

SHRIMP AND RICE SALAD WITH FRESH PINEAPPLE SERVES 12

48 fresh medium shrimp, cooked, shelled, and deveined
2 cups (500 ml) Mustard Vinaigrette (see Salad Dressings, Sauces, and Butters)
2 cups (500 ml) long-grain rice
4 cups (1 liter) salted water
1 fresh pineapple, cut up into chunks
1 cup (250 ml) celery, finely diced
1 bunch spring onions, chopped
1 packed cup (250 ml) golden seedless raisins
2 cups (500 ml) frozen peas, briefly steamed
2 Tbs. (30 ml) lemon juice
Salt and pepper
2 cups (500 ml) toasted slivered almonds
Chopped parsley
Parsley sprigs and lemon twists for garnish

- Pour some of the vinaigrette onto the cooked shrimp while they are still hot.
- Cook rice in salted water; while hot, stir in a little of the vinaigrette.
- When shrimp and rice are cool, combine all the ingredients but the nuts and garnish, and chill. Reserve some shrimp for decoration.
- Just before serving, stir in the nuts.
- Decorate with reserved shrimp, parsley sprigs, and lemon twists.

CURRIED FISH SALAD SERVES 40

A good choice for one of the main entrées at a cold summer buffet. As one of three choices at a buffet, I'd calculate 2 to 4 ounces (60-125 g) of fish fillet per person. At a luncheon, where it is the only entrée, I'd calculate just under 1/2 lb. (250 g) per person. Use any firm-textured, fine-grained white fish.

> 8-10 lb. (3.5-4.5 kg) of flounder, plaice, or sole
>   fillets
> 1/2 bottle white wine
> 2 Tbs. (30 ml) oil
> 4 medium onions
> 1 heart of celery, chopped—approximately 4
>   cups (1 liter)
> 1 large bunch of parsley
> 2 cans water chestnuts, drained and sliced
> 3 Tbs. (45 ml) lemon juice
> 1 lb. (500 g) seedless green grapes, halved if
>   large
> 2 cups (500 ml) mayonnaise
> 1 cup (250 ml) sour cream
> 4 Tbs. (60 ml) curry powder
> 2 Tbs. (30 ml) ground cumin
> 2 Tbs. (30 ml) dark honey
> Salt and pepper
> 1 Tbs. (15 ml) Worcestershire sauce
> 1 1/2 lb. (750 g) toasted, slivered almonds

- Preheat oven to 350°F (180°C).
- Set fillets into greased baking pans. Sprinkle on some salt and pour on wine.
- Bake for 15-20 minutes or until fish is barely cooked. Leave to cool in the wine; fish will continue to cook after it is removed from oven.
- Drain the stock and freeze it for future use.
- Chill fish in baking pan, so fillets remain whole.
- Heat oil in skillet and sauté onions until transparent. Cool.
- Mix well: onions, celery, parsley, water chestnuts, lemon juice, grapes, mayonnaise, sour cream, curry, cumin, honey, and salt and pepper.

- In deep glass bowl layer curried mayonnaise mixture, fish, curried mayonnaise, almonds, fish, curried mayonnaise, almonds, fish, etc.
- Garnish the top with toasted almonds and chopped parsley.

SALMON MOUSSE SERVES 12

Using freshly cooked salmon for this improves it vastly, though canned salmon may be substituted. (Use same quantity but add less salt.) Serve it as a starter or a main course.

> 1½ envelopes unflavored gelatin
> ¾ cup (190 ml) cold water
> ½ cup (125 ml) mayonnaise
> ½ cup (125 ml) sour cream
> Pinch of sugar
> ½ tsp. (2 ml) cayenne
> ½ tsp. (2 ml) paprika
> Salt and pepper
> 2 Tbs. (30 ml) lemon juice
> 2 Tbs. (30 ml) grated onion
> Dash of Tabasco
> Dash of Worcestershire sauce
> 3 cups (750 ml) cooked salmon
> 2 Tbs. (30 ml) capers
> 1 cup (250 ml) heavy cream

- Soften the gelatin in cold water in top of double boiler. Dissolve over hot water. Cool.
- Add mayonnaise, sour cream, seasonings, lemon juice, onion, Tabasco, and Worcestershire sauce.
- Chill until just beginnning to thicken.
- Finely chop the salmon and beat this into gelatin mixture with the capers.
- Whip the cream and fold it into the salmon.
- Turn this into an oiled mold.
- Chill for several hours until set.
- Unmold onto serving platter and garnish with watercress, lemon twists, sieved egg, and sliced black olives.
- Serve with Cucumber Sauce (see Salad Dressings, Sauces, and Butters).

RICE, PASTA, AND A SOUFFLÉ

SOME NOTES ABOUT PASTA

I am fortunate to be able to go to a number of stores which make their own fresh pasta. It is much better than the dried boxes of pasta available at the store—though more expensive. (It also cooks in less than half the time.)

Probably the most important points to remember in cooking pasta are:

- Use plenty of boiling, salted water and cook pasta in small batches. (A little oil keeps pasta from sticking.)
- Leave pan uncovered.
- Test frequently, and drain and rinse the moment the pasta is firm but no longer chewy. *Don't overcook!*
- Toss in a little butter with some oil to keep the pasta separate after cooking.

TAGLIATELLI WITH PESTO

PESTO

Ideally pesto is made with fresh basil, but a mixture of fresh parsley and dried basil is a possible substitute. Stirred into fresh pasta, it makes a good starting course or serves as a dish to accompany minestrone. (Leave out the pasta when making minestrone to go with this.)

It's easy to make pesto in the food processor. It may be frozen or stored in the refrigerator, so make extra in the summer while fresh basil is available.

> 1½ cups (375 ml) fresh basil leaves—or parsley and 2 tsp. (10 ml) dried basil
> 2 cloves garlic
> ½ cup (125 ml) pine nuts

¾ cup (180 ml) grated Parmesan cheese
¾ cup (180 ml) olive oil
Salt and pepper

- In food processor purée basil, garlic, and pine nuts, and then add cheese. The mixture will be thick.
- With motor running, pour in olive oil and process until the pesto has the consistency of whipped butter.
- Calculate 2 Tbs. (30 ml) per person.

TAGLIATELLI (EITHER SPINACH OR EGG)

Calculate 2 or 3 nests per person.

- Boil pasta in uncovered pan of rapidly boiling, salted water until *al dente*.
- Drain, and, while still hot, stir in pesto.

LASAGNE SERVES 30

Though somewhat time-consuming to make, lasagne can be made in large quantities. Because it keeps (and freezes) well, it can also be made ahead of time. This recipe is very moist.

MEAT SAUCE

MAKES APPROXIMATELY 6 QUARTS—6 LITERS

This is an excellent spaghetti sauce, too.

¼ cup (60 ml) oil
4 lb. (1.75 kg) ground beef
3 lb. (1.25 kg) onions
3 carrots, finely chopped
4 stalks celery, finely chopped
4 cloves garlic, minced
4 large cans plum tomatoes, undrained
2 cans tomato paste
1 bottle dry red wine
Salt and pepper
1 Tbs. (15 ml) dried basil
2 bay leaves
1 Tbs. (15 ml) oregano
½ cup (125 ml) chopped parsley
(Dash of sugar if sauce is sour)

To make sauce:

- Brown the meat in the oil in small batches and set aside.
- Lightly brown all the fresh vegetables and basil, bay leaves, oregano, and parsley and return meat to pan.
- Add tomatoes, paste, wine, and seasoning and simmer covered for two hours.

LASAGNE NOODLES

2 lb. (1 kg) green lasagne noodles

- Have three or four *large*, deep pots with boiling salted water and in each pot put 2 Tbs. (30 ml) of oil.
- Divide the noodles among the three pots. Add them gradually, keeping the water at full boil.
- Cook uncovered, stirring occasionally so that the pasta doesn't stick to the bottom.
- When pasta is still firm (*al dente*), drain and rinse with cold water.
- Hang each noodle to dry around edge of cooled pans.

CREAM SAUCE:

3/4 lb. (350 g) butter

1 1/2 cups (375 ml) flour

Approximately 6 cups (1.5 liters) milk

1/2 cup (125 ml) white wine

Salt and pepper

Dash of lemon

Dash of nutmeg

- Melt butter; stir in flour.
- When flour is cooked, stir in milk.
- Continue stirring until thick and beginning to bubble.
- Add wine, seasoning, lemon, and nutmeg.

CHEESES:

1 1/2 lb. (750 g) grated Parmesan cheese

3 lb. (1500 g) ricotta cheese

3 lb. (1500 g) mozzarella cheese, grated

TO ASSEMBLE LASAGNE:

- Butter the bottom of four baking pans 10 in. (25 cm) by 15 in. (37.5 cm) by 3 in. (7.5 cm).
- Spread a thin layer of meat sauce on the bottom and arrange a layer of noodles on top.
- Dot some ricotta on the noodles and sprinkle on some Parmesan and mozzarella.
- Continue layering meat sauce, noodles, and cheese, ending with a layer of noodles.
- Pour on cream sauce and sprinkle heavily with grated cheeses (not the ricotta).
- Bake for about 40-45 minutes at 350°F (180°C) until bubbles form around edges. The lasagne may be reheated later.
- Broil the cheese to brown slightly just before serving.

CHEESE SOUFFLÉ SERVES 6

This is one of the lightest and most delicate-tasting of soufflés. It should be eaten the moment it comes out of the oven, and it creates a feeling of excitement as it's set on the table. I like it made with a mixture of Gruyère and Cheddar cheese, but experiment with your own combinations.

> ½ cup (125 ml) butter
> ½ cup (125 ml) flour
> 2 cups (500 ml) milk
> 2 Tbs. (30 ml) white wine
> Salt and pepper
> ½ tsp. (2 ml) paprika
> ½ tsp. (2 ml) dry mustard
> Dash of cayenne
> Dash of Worcestershire sauce
> ¼ lb. (125 g) sharp Cheddar, grated
> ¼ lb. (125 g) Gruyère, grated
> 8 eggs, separated

- Preheat oven to 450°F (230°C).
- Melt butter; stir in flour until cooked.
- Add milk and bring to boil.
- Add wine, seasonings, and cheeses. Stir until cheese melts.
- Remove from heat and add beaten egg yolks.

- Beat egg whites until stiff but not dry; fold into yolk-and-cheese mixture.
- Pour into well-buttered 2½-3 qt. (2.5-3 liter) soufflé dish.
- Bake for ten minutes and then reduce heat to 350°F (180°C).
- Total baking time is usually 30-35 minutes. Top should be brown and well risen. Soufflé should not wobble when moved.

To increase quantity: This recipe may be doubled, but it should be cooked in two 3-qt. (3 liter) soufflé dishes rather than in one large one.

FETTUCCINI PRIMAVERA (EGG NOODLES WITH SPRING VEGETABLES) SERVES 20

This is an unusual accompaniment to meats at a cold buffet. Fettuccini are thin egg noodles; they are best if bought fresh.

> Fresh fettuccini (1-2 oz. per person) (30-60 g
>   per person)
> Oil
> Mustard Vinaigrette—approximately 1½ cups,
>   or 375 ml (see Salad Dressings, Sauces, and
>   Butters)
> 1 doz. fresh asparagus spears, cut into small
>   pieces
> 2 cups (500 ml) peas
> 5 carrots, chopped
> 1 head broccoli, cut into small flowerets
> 1 bunch spring onions, chopped
> ¾ lb. (350 g) mushrooms, sliced
> 1 bunch fresh parsley, chopped
> Salt and pepper

- Cook fettuccini in boiling salted water with oil until *al dente*.
- Drain and rinse under cold water. Drain thoroughly and toss in enough vinaigrette to coat lightly.
- Steam separately: asparagus, peas, carrots, and broccoli. Refresh each under cold water to stop cooking. Vegetables should be slightly crisp.

- Add cooled vegetables to pasta along with raw vegetables and chopped parsley.
- Toss in a little more vinaigrette and adjust seasonings.
- Chill until an hour or two before serving; serve at room temperature.

RICE AND VEGETABLE SALAD SERVES 20

Like Fettuccini Primavera, this is a delicious and practical side dish at a cold buffet. The key to making this well is to pour the vinaigrette over the rice before it has cooled completely. The tangy flavor penetrates the rice this way. A cup (250 ml) of rice will feed approximately 8 to 10 people in this recipe.

> 1 cup (250 ml) white rice
> 1 cup (250 ml) brown rice
> Mustard Vinaigrette—approximately 1 1/2 cups,
>   or 375 ml (see Salad Dressings, Sauces, and
>   Butters)
> 1 head broccoli, cut up into small flowerets
> 1 head cauliflower, cut up into small flowerets
> 5 medium carrots, chopped
> 2 cups (500 ml) peas
> 1/4 lb. (125 g) young green beans
> 1 bunch spring onions
> 1/2 cup (125 ml) finely chopped fresh mint or 2
>   Tbs. (30 ml) dried oregano
> 1/2 bunch fresh parsley, chopped
> 1 red pepper, finely diced
> 1/2 lb. (250 g) mushrooms, sliced
> 6 stalks celery, finely chopped
> Salt and pepper

- Cook white rice in 2 cups (500 ml) and brown rice in 2 1/4 cups (560 ml) salted water. Drain and rinse with cold water.
- Toss in vinaigrette while rice is still warm.
- Steam the broccoli, cauliflower, carrots, peas, and beans, separately, and chill them quickly under cold water.
- Toss the raw and cooked vegetables and the fresh herbs and seasonings with the rice, adding more vinaigrette as necessary.
- Chill.

HERBED WHITE AND WILD RICE
SERVES 10

This is especially good with duck or Cornish game hens. The wild rice gives the mixture a nutty flavor and a firmer texture. Be sure not to overcook the wild rice. Cook the different rices separately.

> ³/₄ cup (190 ml) white rice
> ³/₄ cup (190 ml) wild rice
> *In the water of each type of rice put*:
> ¹/₄ tsp. (1 ml) ground thyme
> 1 chicken bouillon cube
> ¹/₄ tsp. (1 ml) ground rosemary
> Black pepper
> 2 tsp. (10 ml) butter
> *For garnish*:
> 2 Tbs. (30 ml) fresh parsley, finely chopped.

- Add each of the white and wild rice separately to 1²/₃ cups (415 ml) boiling, seasoned water. Reduce heat so that the rice will barely simmer. Stir only once when the water comes back to the boil.
- Check frequently for doneness after 15 minutes; the kernels should not become too soft.
- Toss the two types of rice together with butter and fold in the chopped parsley.
- Leave rice uncovered in oven on warm setting.

RICE PILAF SERVES 20

This is delicious served with broiled or grilled meats, fish, or poultry.

> 4 Tbs. (60 ml) butter
> 2 medium onions
> 3 cups (750 ml) long-grain white rice
> Pinch of saffron
> 1/2 tsp. (2 ml) paprika
> Approximately 1 1/2 tsp. (7 ml) salt
> Pepper
> 5 1/2 cups (1.375 liters) chicken, lamb, or beef
>   stock, boiling
> Chopped parsley for garnish

- Sauté the onions in the butter until transparent.
- Stir in the rice, saffron, paprika, salt, and pepper and cook, stirring, until rice is opaque.
- Pour on the boiling broth and simmer, partially covered, until the rice has absorbed the liquid.

HOT VEGETABLES

Many vegetables I cook in a pressure cooker. It not only saves time but helps vegetables retain their vitamins as well. Modern pressure cookers have features which make them very safe and easy to use.

ZUCCHINI WITH DILL SERVES 12

This is a recipe demonstrated to me years ago by a Danish friend; it's been one of my favorites for zucchini ever since.

> 6-8 young zucchini
> ¼ lb. (125 g) butter
> 1 medium onion
> 1 Tbs. (15 ml) flour
> 1 Tbs. (15 ml) lemon juice
> 1 tsp. (5 ml) sugar
> 2 tsp. (10 ml) chopped fresh or 1 tsp. (5 ml)
>   dried dill
> Salt and pepper

- Make a *beurre manié* (i.e. a flour-and-butter paste) with 2 Tbs. (30 ml) of the butter and the flour.
- Wash and slice the zucchini fairly thinly.

- Melt 2 Tbs. (30 ml) of butter in a heavy skillet and sauté the onion until transparent.
- Add zucchini, stirring constantly until it begins to cook.
- Add lemon juice, sugar, dill, salt, and pepper.
- Stir in the beurre manié and continue stirring until the butter glaze has thickened.
- This is best served immediately. The zucchini should remain slightly crisp.

BRANDIED MUSHROOMS SERVES 10

The key to good mushrooms is to sear them in a very hot pan quickly. It seems to seal in the juices.

> 1 lb. (500 g) mushrooms, thickly sliced or
> halved
> 6 Tbs. (90 ml) butter
> 1 clove garlic, pressed
> 1 medium onion, finely chopped
> 2 tsp. (10 ml) brandy
> Salt and pepper
> Parsley, finely chopped

- Melt 4 Tbs. (60 ml) of butter in a very hot pan.
- Toss in mushrooms, turning over frequently.
- Remove when golden to warm platter.
- Lower heat and melt remaining butter. Sauté onion and garlic. Return mushrooms to the pan.
- Add brandy, salt, pepper, and parsley.
- Serve immediately.

PARSNIP PURÉE

This homely root can be a delight.

- Peel and boil parsnips until a fork enters easily.
- Drain and mash very thoroughly.
- Add a dash of lemon juice, nutmeg, salt, and pepper.
- Either stir in some heavy cream or whip the cream and fold it in for an extra-light consistency. Add cream gradually until the color and consistency is attractive and palatable.

ASPARAGUS

The difficulty with cooking asparagus is getting the stems thoroughly cooked without overcooking the tips. Here is my method.

- Peel the base of the stems.
- Holding one end in each hand, bend the stalk; it will naturally break where the stalk is too tough.
- Gather the asparagus into bunches and tie with a string.
- Set these bunches in boiling salted water in a deep, narrow saucepan, so that the top two inches of the tips are out of the water. Cover. This way the tips steam slowly while the stems boil.
- Serve hot with Hollandaise Sauce or Hot, Herbed Mayonnaise (see Salad Dressings, Sauces, and Butters), or cold with fresh mayonnaise mixed with a little extra lemon juice.

GLAZED BRUSSELS SPROUTS WITH CARAWAY

- Cut the brussels sprouts in half and cook until just tender.
- Melt plenty of butter in a heavy skillet and add a dash of brown sugar, lemon juice, caraway seeds, salt, and pepper.
- Toss the brussels sprouts in this until covered with a shiny glaze.

VIENNESE SPINACH

Spinach reacts to aluminum. Use stainless steel or enamel.

- Cook fresh spinach that has been washed and has had the stems removed. Chop finely and drain well.
- For every two pounds (1 kilo) of spinach, use one Tbs. (15 ml) each of butter and flour. Melt butter; add flour and cook the mixture.
- Add ½ cup (125 ml) sour cream and some minced onion to this quantity of mixture.
- Stir in spinach with a dash of lemon, salt, pepper, nutmeg (and a pinch of sugar if spinach is acid).

SCALLOPED POTATOES SERVES 12

8 cups (2 liters), approximately 3-4 lb. (1.5-
    2 kg), peeled and thinly sliced potatoes
2 medium onions, grated
2 tsp. (10 ml) salt
Pepper
½ lb. (250 g) smoked bacon, fried and broken
    up into bits
½ lb. (250 g) butter
6 Tbs. (90 ml) flour
4 cups (1 liter) hot milk
1 tsp. (5 ml) paprika
1 tsp. (5 ml) dried mustard

- Butter a 14 in. (35 cm) flat baking dish and arrange layers of potatoes, sprinkling each with salt and pepper, grated onion, and most of the bacon. Dot with butter.
- Put flour in a sieve and tap a thin sprinkling of flour on each layer.
- Put mustard and paprika in hot milk and pour over potatoes.
- Bake in a 350°F (180°C) oven for about 1½ hours. Cover for first hour.
- Garnish with bacon bits and paprika.

BAKED STUFFED POTATOES

- Bake large potatoes for one hour in preheated 450°F (230°C) oven. (Calculate approximately one half potato per person if the potatoes are large. You may want to make extra if you expect a hungry crowd.)
- Slice in half lengthwise and scoop out insides.
- Mash potato and mix with milk, butter, and a dash of mustard, cayenne, salt, and pepper.
- Pile mixture back into the skins and garnish with paprika.
- Depending on what the potatoes are to accompany, you may wish to sprinkle them with grated Cheddar and grill them.

CARROTS VICHY

Carrots have a wonderful butter flavor when cooked this way.

- Peel and cut carrots lengthwise into thin, finger-length sticks.
- For every 8 medium carrots, put 2 Tbs. (30 ml) water, 1 Tbs. (15 ml) lemon juice, and a dash of nutmeg, sugar, salt, and pepper into 4 Tbs. (60 ml) of melted butter.
- Add carrots and cook, covered, very gently until they are tender. Check frequently to see that they don't scorch. All the liquid will be absorbed.
- Toss in plenty of chopped parsley before serving.

GRILLED TOMATOES

These often add a tangy flavor and bright color to meals with grilled meats.

- Wash and slice off the top and bottom of large, ripe tomatoes, then slice in half. Calculate half a large tomato per person or a whole small one.
- Sprinkle with salt, pepper, a dash of brown sugar, and a couple of drops of Worcestershire sauce.
- Toss seasoned breadcrumbs and chopped parsley in plenty of melted butter.
- Pile this crumb mixture on top of each tomato.
- Bake at 250°F (120°C) for approximately 20-30 minutes.

PETITS POIS À LA FRANÇAISE SERVES 8

4 Tbs. (60 ml) butter

5 or 6 outside leaves of lettuce

4 strips of uncooked bacon, cut into small
    pieces

5 cups (1.25 liters) fresh or frozen peas

10 tiny, baby onions

Salt and pepper

3 or 4 Tbs. (45 or 60 ml) water

Dash of sugar (optional)

- Melt the butter in a skillet and layer the lettuce leaves in the pan.
- Mix together the rest of the ingredients and put on top; cover very tightly and simmer over a *low* heat.
- Check to make sure that the mixture hasn't gone dry, and add more water if necessary.

SALADS AND COLD VEGETABLES

MANDARIN ORANGE AND AVOCADO SALAD SERVES 6

3 large, ripe avocados, peeled and thinly sliced
1 large can mandarin orange sections, drained
¾ cup (190 ml) Lemon and Honey Vinaigrette
  (see Salad Dressings, Sauces, and Butters)
1 bunch watercress for garnish

- Arrange the crescent-shaped slices of avocado on a plate and set the mandarin orange sections on top.
- Dribble on lemon dressing; decorate each plate with one or two sprigs of watercress.

BROCCOLI VINAIGRETTE, OR WITH CURRIED MAYONNAISE

- Briefly steam broccoli flowerets, chill.
- When cold, pour on Mustard Vinaigrette (see Salad Dressings, Sauces, and Butters) or mayonnaise mixed with curry, cumin, lemon juice, and a dash of sugar, salt, and pepper.

TOMATO, CUCUMBER, AND MINT SALAD
SERVES 10

5 large, ripe tomatoes, peeled
2 large cucumbers (the English variety),
     peeled and thinly sliced
1 bunch fresh mint leaves, washed and
     chopped
Salt and pepper
Wine vinegar
Corn or olive oil

- Slice tomatoes thinly and arrange with slices of cucumber.
- Sprinkle on salt and pepper and chopped mint.
- Just before serving, sprinkle on drops of vinegar and oil.

> *Note:* To peel the tomatoes more easily, first
> dip one at a time in boiling water, then in ice-
> cold water.

GREEK SALAD SERVES 20

Good as accompaniment to grilled meats, or with crusty bread
as a light meal on its own.

4 large, ripe tomatoes, cut into wedges
2 large heads Boston lettuce, cut into small
     wedges
1/2 lb. (250 g) Greek feta cheese
1/2 lb. (250 g) ripe black olives (deli-store vari-
     ety)
2 Tbs. (30 ml) dried oregano
Salt and pepper
Wine vinegar
Olive oil

- Mix together vegetables and cheese and toss in the oregano.
  Season with salt and pepper.
- Sprinkle liberally with vinegar and oil.
- Toss again and serve immediately.

WATERCRESS AND ENDIVE SALAD
SERVES 10

> 3 large bunches watercress, cleaned and
>   dried, with large stems removed
> 2 large or 3 small endives with the bases
>   removed, quartered lengthwise
> ⅓ cup (75 ml) Mustard Vinaigrette (see Salad
>   Dressings, Sauces, and Butters)

- Toss watercress and endives together with dressing just before serving.

GERMAN POTATO SALAD SERVES 20

The key to why this salad is so good lies in pouring the vinaigrette over the potatoes while they are still hot. The tangy flavor
is absorbed this way.

> 4 lb. (2 kg) mature potatoes
> 1 large bunch spring onions, chopped
> 2 Tbs. (30 ml) fresh mint or fresh basil,
>   chopped
> 1 large red pepper, finely diced
> 1 green pepper, finely diced
> 2 stalks celery, finely diced
> 1½ cups (375 ml) Mustard Vinaigrette (see
>   Salad Dressings, Sauces, and Butters)
> 1-1½ cups (250-375 ml) sour cream
> Approximately ½ cup (125 ml) mayonnaise.

- Cut the potatoes in half or in quarters and boil with skins on.
- Drain the potatoes, and as soon as you can handle them, peel them and cut them up into large cubes.
- Pour on vinaigrette; let cool.
- When cold, toss in herbs, vegetables, sour cream, and mayon- naise. Add enough of the sour cream and mayonnaise for the salad to be moist and coated.

CRUNCHY VEGETABLE ASPIC SERVES 10

I like to serve this with a dish of Creamy Blue Cheese Dressing (see Salad Dressings, Sauces, and Butters) set in the center of the ring mold.

2 envelopes unflavored gelatin
1 cup (250 ml) cold water
1 clove garlic, pressed
2 cups (500 ml) vegetable juice
1/4 cup (60 ml) lemon juice
1 Tbs. (15 ml) sugar
1 tsp. (5 ml) salt
1 Tbs. (15 ml) Worcestershire sauce
Pepper
Dash of Tabasco
3 Tbs. (45 ml) fresh dill, finely chopped
1/2 bunch of spring onions, finely chopped
1 stalk celery, finely diced
1/2 cucumber, coarsely shredded
1/2 green pepper, finely diced

- Soak the gelatin in the cold water until softened, and then heat until melted.
- Stir in garlic, the juices, and the seasonings, and chill until just beginning to set.
- Fold in the chopped vegetables and the dill, and chill until firm.
- Unmold onto a bed of lettuce.

SALAD DRESSINGS, SAUCES, AND BUTTERS

SALAD DRESSINGS

MUSTARD VINAIGRETTE
MAKES 2½ CUPS (625 ml)

This is the salad dressing that I use most often. Whether it's for a tossed green salad for two or two hundred, people always say how delicious it is. The Dijon mustard makes it creamy. I like corn oil best for its unobtrusive flavor. Occasionally I mix corn oil and olive oil.

> ½ cup (125 ml) wine vinegar
> 2½ Tbs. (40 ml) sugar or honey
> 1 tsp. (5 ml) salt
> Plenty of ground black pepper
> 2½ Tbs. (40 ml) Dijon mustard
> 1¾ cups (435 ml) corn oil

- Pour the vinegar into a jar with a tight-fitting lid.
- Add sugar, salt, pepper, and mustard and shake well, until sugar is dissolved.
- Add oil; shake well. (Always shake just before serving.)

LEMON AND HONEY VINAIGRETTE

MAKES 2½ CUPS (625 ml)

I use this dressing with spinach, watercress, or avocado salads.

> ¼ cup (60 ml) lemon juice
> ¼ cup (60 ml) white vinegar
> 2 Tbs. (30 ml) honey
> 1 tsp. (5 ml) salt
> Plenty of ground black pepper
> 1¾ cups (435 ml) corn oil

- Combine the honey, lemon juice, and vinegar with the salt and pepper and shake vigorously.
- If dressing is to be used immediately, you may want to set the jar in warm water to help the honey mix more quickly.
- Add oil and shake well.

CREAMY BLUE CHEESE DRESSING

MAKES ABOUT 2 CUPS (500 ml)

I make this in the processor, but I add the crumbled blue cheese last and don't pulse it long enough to eliminate all the small chunks of blue cheese.

> 8 oz. (250 g) cream cheese
> ½ cup (125 ml) mayonnaise
> ¼ tsp. (1 ml) salt
> ½ tsp. (2 ml) pressed garlic.
> 2 tsp. (10 ml) sugar
> ½ cup (125 ml) buttermilk (plain milk may be
>   used)
> 6 oz. (200 g) blue cheese, broken up in 1-in.
>   (2.5 cm) pieces

- Process the first five ingredients until smooth.
- Add the buttermilk through the chute with the processor running.
- Add the blue cheese pieces and process to desired consistency.

PAT'S CREAMY GARLIC DRESSING
MAKES APPROXIMATELY 2 CUPS (500 ml)

This is my mother-in-law Pat Harris's recipe.

> 1 egg, beaten
> 1/2 cup (125 ml) olive oil
> 1 Tbs. (15 ml) grated Parmesan cheese
> 1 Tbs. (15 ml) lemon juice
> 1 tsp. (5 ml) sugar
> 1/2 cup (125 ml) mayonnaise
> 2 or 3 cloves of crushed garlic
> Salt and pepper

- Combine all of the ingredients and shake well. This gets better if left in the refrigerator overnight.

COLD SAUCES

MINT SAUCE MAKES ABOUT 1 1/2 CUPS (375 ml)

When I was growing up, making the mint sauce was a yearly ritual performed by my father, whose taste for mint sauce was developed during a youth spent in England. We'd harvest and clean large bunches of fresh mint he'd planted on our property. (To get the leaves off, hold the top of the stalk and pull down.) The mint was always chopped with the sugar until it was very fine and then mixed with enough vinegar to preserve it in the fridge. Small batches of this mint concentrate were diluted with a little more vinegar and water just before serving, but it was thick, never watery. Our family joke was that we liked a little lamb with our mint sauce.

If you can't grow your own, fine fresh-produce stores sell bunches of mint during the summer.

> 4 bunches of fresh mint, about 3 cups (750 ml)
> 3/4 cup (180 ml) sugar
> 1/2 cup (125 ml) cider vinegar
> 1/4 cup (60 ml) water

- Chop the cleaned and de-stemmed mint leaves on a large board.
- When the pieces are becoming small, dump the sugar on top. The sugar absorbs the mint oil and juices and helps you to chop the leaves *very* finely.
- Put the sugar-and-leaf mixture in a jar and add the vinegar and water.
- Let this stand at least overnight before serving. It will keep almost indefinitely and actually improves with age.

CUCUMBER SAUCE MAKES 2 CUPS (500 ml)

This is ideal for hot or cold fish and seafood. I especially like it with salmon.

> 1 large cucumber, peeled and seeded
> 1½ cups (375 ml) sour cream
> 1 Tbs. (15 ml) fresh chopped dill
> 1 Tbs. (15 ml) grated onion
> Salt and pepper to taste

- Grate the cucumber and drain off excess liquid.
- Mix together all ingredients and chill.

MAYONNAISE MAKES 2½ CUPS (625 ml)

This is the best homemade mayonnaise I've ever tasted—and the quickest and most foolproof. I make it in the processor and use it frequently with entrées.

> 2 eggs
> 1½ tsp. (7 ml) sugar
> 2 Tbs. (30 ml) white vinegar
> 2 Tbs. (30 ml) lemon juice
> 1 tsp. (5 ml) dry mustard
> 1 tsp. (5 ml) salt
> 2 cups (500 ml) corn oil

- Put all the ingredients and ⅔ cup (165 ml) of oil in the completely dry processor bowl.
- Process about 5-10 seconds.

- With processor running, add remaining 1⅓ cups (330 ml) of the oil. Process only until the mixture is thick and smooth (about 10-15 seconds).

VARIATIONS:

DILL MAYONNAISE

This is great on cold salmon.

- Add 4 Tbs. (60 ml) of chopped fresh dill to basic mayonnaise recipe.

HOT, HERBED MAYONNAISE

Good with vegetables, especially artichokes.

- Warm mayonnaise in top of double boiler.
- Stir in *finely* chopped fresh tarragon, and/or chervil, and/or parsley, and/or chives. (Soak dried herbs in a little lemon juice if no fresh are available.)
- Serve from a warmed bowl. (It can also be served cold.)

HOT SAUCES

BÉCHAMEL

See basic béchamel recipe, page 101.

VARIATIONS:

WINE SAUCE

- Substitute wine for part of the milk.

CHEESE SAUCE

- Add grated Cheddar, Parmesan, or Gruyère to bubbling sauce. Remove from heat and stir until cheese is melted. Less salt will be needed.
- A dash of paprika is good in cheese sauces.
- Wine and cheese together in the sauce is also delicious (omit the paprika).

HOLLANDAISE SAUCE MAKES 2 CUPS (500 ml)

For a really good "light" hollandaise, I haven't (yet) found any shortcuts; it must be beaten by hand.

> 1 cup (250 ml) unsalted butter
> 3 Tbs. (45 medl) lemon juice
> 6 egg yolks
> Boiling water
> $\frac{1}{2}$ tsp. (2.5 ml) salt
> Dash of sugar (optional)
> Pinch of cayenne

- Put the butter in a Pyrex measuring cup in a warm oven. (When melted, the milky substance sinks to the bottom and isn't used. There is less chance of curdling this way.)
- Warm the lemon juice, and keep it warm.
- Boil a pan of water and have it ready, at the boil, with a tablespoon to measure out the water a little at a time.
- Put the yolks in the top of a double boiler over hot, but not boiling, water.
- Beat the egg yolks with a whisk until they begin to thicken.
- Add boiling water 1 Tbs. (15 ml) at a time up to 8 Tbs. (120 ml), beating until hollandaise is thick after each addition.
- Gradually beat in warmed lemon juice.
- Remove the sauce from the heat and gradually beat in the melted butter.
- Add salt, sugar, and cayenne and beat until thick.

> *Note:* I have actually added small amounts of boiling water at the very end if I felt the sauce wasn't quite light enough.

HERBED OR SEASONED BUTTERS

Depending on its use, herbed butter can be made with almost any variety of herbs. When using fresh herbs, I chop them by hand and fold them into softened butter. Dried herbs can be mixed with butter in the processor. Some of the uses of herbed butter are:

HOT, HERBED ITALIAN BREAD

- Mix finely chopped fresh dill, parsley, and oregano (use dried if no fresh is available) with softened, salted butter and spread on bread that has been sliced not quite through. Wrap in foil and warm.

HERBED LAMB OR PORK CHOPS

- Mix softened butter with parsley, rosemary, and tarragon (and a little minced garlic).
- Slit open or spread chops with this herbed-butter mixture before grilling or broiling.

STEAKS

- Mix softened butter with salt, pepper, freshly chopped parsley, and a dash of lemon juice, Worcestershire sauce, and Tabasco.
- Spread this on steak after it has been cooked.

BREADS, MUFFINS, AND CRÊPES

HERBED BISCUITS MAKES 2 DOZEN

3 cups (750 ml) flour
2½ Tbs. (40 ml) sugar
4½ tsp. (20 ml) baking powder
¾ tsp. (3 ml) baking soda
¾ tsp. (3 ml) salt
½ cup (125 ml) cold butter, cut up
¼ cup (30 ml) lard or shortening, cut up
¾ cup (180 ml) buttermilk
½ cup (125 ml) finely chopped parsley
3 Tbs. (45 ml) chopped chives
½ tsp. (3 ml) dried oregano
1 egg, beaten
(1 egg yolk for wash)

- Put butter, lard, and flour mixed with baking powder, soda, salt, and sugar in food processor and process until the flour resembles meal. Turn this into a large bowl.
- With a fork, stir in ½ cup (125 ml) buttermilk and the herbs.
- Beat the egg in ¼ cup (62 ml) buttermilk and stir this in to bind dough.
- Knead the dough once or twice in the bowl and then turn out onto a floured surface.

- Press the dough with the heel of your hand until it is ³⁄₄ in. (2 cm) thick. Using a cookie cutter or a glass 2 in. (5 cm) in diameter, cut out circles of dough.
- Brush with egg wash of one yolk and a little water beaten together.
- Set biscuits on a greased cookie sheet and bake at 400°F (200°C) for approximately 15 minutes, until they are lightly browned.

HOT, HERBED ITALIAN BREAD SERVES 30

2 large Italian loaves
¹⁄₂ lb. (250 g) Herbed Butter, softened (for
    mixture of herbs, see Salad Dressings,
    Sauces, and Butters)

- Slice thick slices of the bread, butter them, reassemble them, then slice loaf lengthwise.
- Wrap in foil with opening for steam to escape.
- Heat in 350°F (180°C) oven for about 20 minutes.
- Turn off oven; bread can be held for about half an hour.

SWEET CORN MUFFINS
MAKES APPROXIMATELY 2 DOZEN

1³⁄₄ cups (435 ml) finely ground cornmeal
2¹⁄₄ cups (560 ml) flour
1 cup (250 ml) sugar
8 tsp. (40 ml) baking powder
2 eggs
¹⁄₂ cup (125 ml) oil
2¹⁄₂ cups (625 ml) milk

- Mix dry ingredients well.
- Beat together eggs, oil, and milk and stir this into the flour mixture.
- Stir until just well mixed. Do *not* overbeat, as the muffins become denser if you do.
- Fill greased muffin tins ³⁄₄ full and bake in a 400°-425°F (200°-220°C) oven for about 20 minutes. Muffins are cooked when lightly browned and split open on top.

BRAN, RAISIN, AND WALNUT MUFFINS
MAKES APPROXIMATELY 2 DOZEN

2 cups (500 ml) flour
$^3/_4$ cup (180 ml) packed brown sugar
5 tsp. (25 ml) baking powder
1 tsp. (5 ml) baking soda
$^1/_2$ tsp. (2 ml) salt
$2^1/_2$ cups (625 ml) bran cereal
2 cups (500 ml) milk
2 eggs
$^1/_2$ cup (125 ml) corn oil
2 cups (500 ml) raisins
$1^1/_2$ cups (625 ml) chopped walnut pieces

- Combine flour, sugar, baking soda, baking powder, and salt.
- Put the bran cereal in a bowl, pour the milk over it, and let stand for 5 minutes.
- Beat the egg and oil into the cereal and milk mixture and stir in the flour mixture, nuts, and raisins until *just* combined.
- Fill muffin pans about $^2/_3$ full.
- Bake in 400 F (200°C) oven about 20 minutes or until the centers of the muffins spring back when touched.

BUTTERMILK BUTTERFLY ROLLS
MAKES APPROXIMATELY 2 DOZEN

2 cups (500 ml) buttermilk
1 Tbs. (15 ml) yeast
$^1/_4$ tsp. (1 ml) baking soda
2 tsp. (10 ml) salt
$^1/_4$ cup (60 ml) sugar
4 cups (1 liter) flour
$^1/_2$ cup (125 ml) melted butter

- Warm buttermilk until it is just warmer than body temperature.
- Pour about $^1/_2$ cup (125 ml) of the buttermilk into a warmed cup and dissolve the yeast in this, then add it to the rest of the warm buttermilk.

- Add the sugar, salt, and soda and beat well.
- Add ½ the flour and 2 Tbs. (30 ml) of melted butter and then the rest of the flour.
- Greasing your hands and a warm bowl, turn the batter into the bowl and knead it lightly until it just barely forms a ball.
- Cover the ball with a damp cloth and keep it in a warm place until it has doubled in bulk.
- Knead lightly for one minute, then divide the dough in half. Roll out each half into squares ⅛ in. (.3 cm) thick on a floured board.
- Cover the squares with melted butter and cut them into strips 1½ in. (3.7 cm) wide. Stack these strips in groups of five.
- Cut the stacks of dough at 2½-in. (6.2 cm) intervals by sliding a piece of string underneath it and crossing it over before pulling.

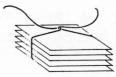

- Set these sliced layers into greased muffin pans so that the layers look like leaves in a book.
- Leave to stand covered in a warm place until the bulk is doubled once again.
- Brush tops with butter and bake in a 400°-425°F (200°-220°C) oven for 15 to 20 minutes.

> *Note:* These freeze well and may be warmed in a paper bag before serving.

CRÊPES MAKES 75 CRÊPES

BASIC RECIPE:

9 eggs
3 cups (750 ml) flour
3¾ cups (925 ml) milk
1 tsp. (5 ml) salt

- Put all of the ingredients in a blender or processor until they are very smooth, then refrigerate the batter for one hour.
- Heat a crêpe pan over medium-high heat, and when drops of water bounce, it's ready.

- Put some butter in the pan and quickly spread it around with a paper towel, wiping away excess butter. (Between making each crêpe, wipe the pan with a butter-soaked towel.)
- Pour in a little batter, swirl it around, and pour off the excess.
- As soon as crêpe is firm, turn it over and cook it briefly on the other side.
- Slide crêpe out onto a plate.
- When cool, put a piece of wax paper between each crêpe and either refrigerate or freeze them until ready for use.

> *Note:* I intentionally made this recipe for a large number of crêpes because they keep so well in the freezer. It makes sense to make extra for future use.

WHAT TO PUT IN CRÊPES:

There are countless varieties of fillings for crêpes. For light, savory meals, mix any of the following with a seasoned cream sauce.

chopped spinach, bacon, and Parmesan cheese and/or ricotta
chicken, onions, and mushrooms
poached salmon or sole pieces
ham, pineapple, and raisins

Dessert crêpes are delicious filled with fresh fruits such as peeled peaches marinated with sugar and kirsch. Sprinkle extra kirsch over the crêpe before putting whipped cream on top. Serve immediately.

DESSERTS

As a rule, if the meal is quite a simple one, I suggest a more lavish and rich dessert. For dinners with rich main courses, a light dessert like Citron Fromage (lemon mousse), Zabaglione, or Drambuie Dream is more appropriate. Most of us really love a wickedly extravagant dessert, so I'm not *too* restrained about them. At buffets, however, I will often have a dessert of fresh fruit such as strawberries and kiwi or sliced oranges in kirsch with candied peel to offer as an alternative to a rich dessert like the Chocolate Silk Pie.

BOMBE SURPRISE SERVES 10-12

This is quick, easy, and very impressive.

> 1 thin layer of sponge cake 12 in. (30 cm) in diameter (you can buy this or make your own; it should have a raised, fluted rim)
> 2 cups (500 ml) strawberries (sliced), blueberries, raspberries, or peaches (peeled and sliced)
> 3 Tbs. (45 ml) kirsch (optional)
> 1 qt. (1 liter) good-quality vanilla ice cream
> 6 egg whites

$^1/_2$ cup (125 ml) of sugar

2 tsp. (10 ml) vanilla extract

- Preheat oven to 475°F (250°C).
- Put cake on a wooden board covered with aluminum foil.
- Just before serving, spread the berries to cover the cake and dribble on the kirsch.
- Cover the berries with a layer of *firm* ice cream.
- Beat the egg whites in two batches; when they are beginning to stiffen, fold in sugar and vanilla; then beat until they are really stiff.
- Pile the meringue on top of the ice cream.
- Place in oven until meringue is just a light brown. (Stand by to watch; it happens quickly!)
- Serve immediately.

> *Notes:* It is important to use a wooden board which will not conduct the heat. I use an old cutting board and cover it with foil so that flavors from the board don't seep up through to the cake.
>
> Be sure to leave the fluted edge of cake uncovered; it is delightful if this is crisp. But the meringue should completely cover the ice cream, as it acts as insulation and keeps the ice cream from melting.

FROZEN DRAMBUIE DREAM SERVES 12-14

The Drambuie makes this expensive, but it has been one of the most universally popular of all my desserts.

2 cups (500 ml) milk

4 egg yolks

$^1/_2$ cup (125 ml) sugar

3 Tbs. (45 ml) clear, dark honey

$^3/_4$ cup (200 ml) Drambuie

2 Tbs. (30 ml) orange juice

3 cups (750 ml) whipping cream

Toasted almonds

- While heating the milk until it is hot but not boiling, beat together sugar and egg yolks until light lemon-colored.

- Pour on the hot milk and return mixture to saucepan.
- Heat until just thickening. Add honey and remove from heat.
- Add the Drambuie and the orange juice and stir to let the steam escape (this prevents the custard from curdling).
- Chill.
- Whip the cream until it forms soft peaks.
- Fold it into cooled mixture.
- Pour into 1½-quart mold and freeze until firm.

An hour before serving:
- Dip the mold briefly in hot water and turn it onto a cold plate.
- Garnish with whole toasted almonds or almond slivers and any of a variety of candied or brandy-soaked fruits cut into attractive shapes.
- Return to freezer until ready to be served.
- Slice if you wish.

I serve this with wafers, and I dribble on more Drambuie and sprinkle toasted almonds on top of each serving as I am dishing it up.

> *Notes:* If multiplying this by 2, add only 1½ times the sugar and honey.
>
> This dessert should have the consistency of not-too-hard ice cream. If frozen custard has been in the deep-freeze, put it into the refrigerator freezer the day before it will be served. If your freezer is very cold, you may want to leave it in the refrigerator an hour before serving it.

PROFITEROLES WITH CHOCOLATE SAUCE (CHOCOLATE-COVERED CREAM PUFFS)

MAKES ABOUT 75 CREAM PUFFS,

ENOUGH FOR 15-20 PEOPLE

These are time-consuming, but always popular.

> Choux pastry as for Seafood-Stuffed Éclairs in Appetizers section. Pipe dough into balls 1¼ in. (3 cm) in diameter before baking.

For Whipping Cream:
2 cups (500 ml) whipping cream
½ cup (125 ml) sugar
2 tsp. (10 ml) vanilla

- When cream puffs are cooled, pierce a hole in the bottom. (I find the tip of a corkscrew is good for this.)
- Fill a pastry piping bag (equipped with the small, round tip) with whipped cream, and insert the tip into the hole in the cream puffs.
- Fill all the puffs with whipped cream and refrigerate.
- Just before serving, stack the filled puffs and dribble on the chocolate sauce.

CHOCOLATE SAUCE

16 oz. (500 g) semi-sweet chocolate
½ cup (250 ml) sugar
Approximately 1 cup (250 ml) heavy cream
2 tsp. (10 ml) vanilla extract
2 Tbs. (30 ml) cognac (optional)

- Melt the chocolate in a double-boiler.
- Add the sugar.
- When mixture has cooled slightly, stir in half the cream.
- When completely cool, add the vanilla, cognac, and enough cream for a good, smooth consistency.

Note: Serve the extra sauce that hasn't been dribbled over the profiteroles in a small cream pitcher.

CITRON FROMAGE
(LEMON MOUSSE) SERVES 20 [SERVES 125]

This is a light, Danish recipe, excellent as an accompaniment to wedding (fruit) cakes or fresh seasonal fruits such as raspberries, strawberries, or blueberries. Though this dessert works well for over a hundred people, the ingredient quantity ratios do change radically when it is multiplied.

> 9 eggs [45 eggs] separated
> 1½ cups (375 ml) [5 cups (1250 ml)] sugar
> 2 [8] envelopes of unflavored gelatin
> ¾ cup (180 ml) [3 cups (750 ml)] cold water
> Juice of 6 lemons [30 lemons—approximately
>   4 cups lemon juice]
> Rind of 3 lemons, finely grated [15 lemon rinds]
> 6 cups (1.5 liters) [2 qt. (2 liters)] whipping
>   cream
> Sprigs of mint and paper-thin lemon slices for
>   garnish

- Beat egg yolks and sugar until pale yellow and fluffy.
- Soak gelatin in cold water, then melt over hot water.
- Beat together well the gelatin, egg-yolk mixture, lemon juice, and rind.
- Refrigerate until *just* beginning to set.
- Fold in whipped cream and beaten egg whites.
- Put in deep glass bowls and chill until set.

> To Serve: Decorate with sliced lemons and sprigs of mint. Chopped crystallized fruit adds color if no fresh mint is available.

> *Notes:* The only tricky part of this recipe is the gelatin. After it is completely dissolved, don't let it become entirely cool before adding it to egg-yolk mixture because it may start to set.
>   If you stir the refrigerated gelatin, lemon, egg, and sugar mixture occasionally, it keeps a more uniform coolness and won't become too set at the outer edges while still liquid at the center. These problems only exist when it is made in large quantities.

SHERRY TRIFLE SERVES 10-12

When made with plenty of fresh berries, this classic is both refreshing and luxuriously rich.

> 1 sponge cake
> Raspberry or strawberry jam or jelly
> 1 qt. (1 liter) fresh raspberries or strawberries, halved
> Approximately ½ cup (125 ml) sherry (a cream sherry is good)
> Custard (recipe below)
> Whipped cream, toasted almonds, candied or crystallized bits of fruit, or fresh berries for decoration.
>
> *For custard*:
> ½ cup (125 ml) sugar
> 2 Tbs. (30 ml) cornstarch
> 2 cups (500 ml) milk and cream combined
> 5 egg yolks
> 2 Tbs. (30 ml) butter
> 2 tsp. (10 ml) vanilla
> 2 cups (500 ml) whipping cream

- Mix sugar and cornstarch with milk and cream in top of double-boiler. Stir until thickened.
- Add egg yolks and butter. Cook for three minutes.
- Cool, stirring to let steam escape.
- Add vanilla.
- When chilled, fold in whipped cream, reserving ⅓ for decoration.

To assemble trifle:

- Cut cake into fingers or wedges and put a single layer of these in a pattern on the bottom of a crystal bowl.
- Spread half the cake with a little jam and sprinkle on as much sherry as you desire—without completely soaking the cake.
- Layer in half the berries.
- Pour on half the custard.
- Repeat layer of cake, jam, sherry, berries, and custard.
- Pipe on whipped cream.

- Sprinkle with toasted almonds or crystallized fruit, or arrange fresh berries on top.

  To Serve: There is no neat way to present single portions of trifle unless you layer individual portions in glass goblets.

  Note: Trifle is a feasible choice for feeding large numbers, but make sure you add enough cornstarch to the custard for it to be fairly firm when chilled.

PUMPKIN SOUFFLÉ PIE
MAKES 3 PIES. SERVES 24 TO 30

This is the lightest and most delicious pumpkin pie. It can be served either hot or cold, but I love serving it just out of the oven before it has fallen. It freezes very well, so I usually make four at a time, but here's the recipe for three pies.

Basic short pastry crust. Make and cook pastry as for spinach pie (see Appetizers section) and line three 9-in. (23 cm) pie plates. Flute edges and moisten pie-plate rims so that the crust doesn't pull away during pre-baking.

> 3 cups (750 ml) canned, *unsweetened* pumpkin
> 8 eggs, separated
> 3 cups (750 ml) heavy cream or evaporated milk
> ¾ cup (180 ml) brown sugar
> ¼ cup (60 ml) white sugar
> ½ tsp. (2 ml) salt
> 2 tsp. (10 ml) cinnamon
> 1 tsp. (5 ml) ground ginger
> ¼ tsp. (1 ml) cloves
> 2 tsp. (10 ml) vanilla
> 4 Tbs. (60 ml) rum
> Toasted walnuts and/or raisins plumped in brandy (optional)
> Whipped cream for garnish

- Preheat oven to 375°F (190°C).
- Heat the pumpkin, all the spices, and the sugar with the beaten egg yolks.
- When this has thickened, remove from heat.
- Add vanilla and rum. Stir to let steam escape.
- Beat egg whites until stiff but not dry.
- When pumpkin mixture has cooled slightly, fold in beaten egg whites and pour into pie shell.
- Bake until set (about 30 minutes).

> To Serve: Chopped, toasted walnuts and/or raisins plumped in brandy can be sprinkled over the top.
>
> Slightly sweetened whipped cream should be passed around for people to help themselves.

ZABAGLIONE SERVES 4-6

This is an unusual and light dessert which may be used as a sauce over fruit or eaten in goblets plain. It only works well if you serve it to small groups of people.

> 8 egg yolks
> 6 oz. or ¾ cup (165 ml) cream sherry or Marsala wine
> 6 Tbs. (90 ml) powdered sugar

- In top of double-boiler, beat egg yolks and gradually add wine and sugar.
- Put pan over boiling water and whisk (preferably by hand) until thick and foamy.
- Serve immediately from glass goblets either plain or poured over berries.

> To Serve: I like to arrange a few assorted wafers on the plate under each goblet, or pass a plate of these around.

> *Note:* It is important to use a good-quality wine, as the flavor is almost entirely that of the wine.

UPSIDE-DOWN APPLE
AND DATE CAKE SERVES 12-14

Apple and Date mixture:
3 Tbs. (45 ml) butter
½ cup (125 ml) dark brown sugar
6 oz. (200 g) pitted dates, chopped coarsely
12 medium apples, peeled, cored, and thinly
  sliced
Dash of cinnamon
1 tsp. (5 ml) lemon juice

- Melt butter in a 9 in.-by-13 in. (23 cm-by-31 cm) baking pan.
- Sprinkle on the brown sugar.
- Scatter on the chopped dates.
- Toss the sliced apples in the cinnamon and lemon juice and spread these on top of the dates and brown sugar.

Cake:
½ lb. (250 g) butter
1 cup (250 ml) sugar
4 eggs
2 tsp. (10 ml) vanilla
1½ cups (375 ml) flour
1½ tsp. (7 ml) baking powder

- Preheat oven to 350°F (180°C).
- Cream the butter and the sugar.
- Add eggs one at a time; then add vanilla.
- Combine flour and baking powder.
- Fold in flour mixture.
- Spread cake batter over the apples and bake for 30-45 minutes until cake springs back when touched at center.

To Serve: This upside-down cake is delicious when served hot with whipped cream. You may make it the day before and reheat it, or serve it at room temperature.
   Turn it out onto an oval or a rectangular plate with a decorative edge for buffets.

APPLE NUT CRUNCH SERVES 8-10

This is a country dessert, good for cold weather and informal suppers.

 1 1/2 cups (375 ml) flour
 1/2 cup (125 ml) sugar
 2 oz. (60 g) butter, chilled
 1/2 cup (125 ml) finely chopped toasted wal-
    nuts or almonds
 12 medium tart apples, peeled, cored, and
    sliced
 1/2 tsp. (2 ml) cinnamon
 1/4 tsp. (1 ml) ground cloves
 1/4 tsp. (1 ml) nutmeg
 1 Tbs. (15 ml) lemon juice
 6 oz. (200 g) seedless raisins
 Sugar (depending on tartness of apples)
 1/2 cup (125 ml) water

- Combine the flour and the sugar.
- Cut the chilled butter into the flour and then rub with your fingertips until it has the texture of fine breadcrumbs.
- Stir in the nuts.
- Set aside.
- Preheat oven to 350°F (180°C).
- Toss together the apples, spices, lemon juice, sugar (if desired), and raisins.
- Put into an attractive, deep casserole.
- Add water.
- Sprinkle the flour-and-nut mixture on top of the fruit. *Do not press down*.
- Bake until topping is a light brown—about an hour.
- Serve hot with ice cream or whipped cream.

    Note: Oven should not be too hot; this causes
    the juice to bubble up and spoil the topping.

CHOCOLATE SILK PIE SERVES 10

This is a rich dessert for chocolate lovers. A little goes a long way.

Crust:
1½ cups (375 ml) graham cracker crumbs
2 Tbs. (30 ml) sugar
1 cup (250 ml) chopped, toasted almonds or
    walnuts
3 Tbs. (45 ml) butter, melted

- Combine ingredients and *press* into 9-in. pie plate.
- Bake in a 350°F (180°C) preheated oven until it is beginning to brown—about 10 minutes.
- Cool.

Chocolate filling:
¾ lb. (350 g) butter
1 cup (250 ml) confectioner's (icing) sugar
5 egg yolks
3 squares unsweetened chocolate, melted and
    cooled
1 Tbs. (15 ml) vanilla
5 egg whites, stiffly beaten
2 cups (500 ml) whipping cream
Toasted nuts and/or chocolate curls

- Cream the butter and sugar.
- Beat in egg yolks, one at a time.
- Stir in chocolate and vanilla.
- Fold in egg whites.
- Fill cooled pie crust and chill several hours.
- Beat whipped cream and pile on top. Sprinkle with toasted nuts and/or chocolate curls.

Note: This may also be made with a short crust instead of the crumb-and-nut crust.

PINEAPPLE RUM SORBET
SERVES 10

This is amazingly light and refreshing and can be served either alone or to accompany other desserts or fruits.

> 2 whole fresh pineapples, peeled, cored, and
>   chopped coarsely
> $\frac{1}{2}$ cup (125 ml) lemon juice
> $\frac{1}{4}$ cup (60 ml) orange juice
> $\frac{3}{4}$ cup (200 ml) sugar
> $\frac{1}{2}$ cup (125 ml) rum

- Purée the pineapple in a blender.
- Put through a sieve to remove fiber.
- Stir in fruit juices, sugar, and rum.
- Freeze.
- When crystallized, but not solid, blend again. (This gives an almost creamy consistency to the sorbet.)
- Refreeze.

To Serve: It is very attractive to serve the sorbet from the pineapple shell. You can cut the pineapple in half lengthwise and scoop out the insides to form a boat. Put these halves in the deep-freeze so that they are frozen solid. Fill them with the sorbet just before serving. If they are to be served at a buffet, set the pineapple boats one at a time in crushed ice in a large silver or glass bowl. Otherwise, the sorbet will melt too quickly.

This is excellent with Rich Chocolate Brownies (recipe below) or chocolate-coated wafers.

Note: The amount of sugar will depend on the sweetness of the pineapple. Taste before adding full amount. Remember: freezing makes food taste *less* sweet.

RICH CHOCOLATE BROWNIES
MAKES BETWEEN 50 AND 60 BROWNIES

½ lb. (250 g) butter
8 oz. (250 g) semi-sweet chocolate
8 eggs
Dash of salt
3 cups (750 ml) sugar
2 tsp. (10 ml) vanilla (or 2 Tbs. (30 ml) brandy)
1¾ cups (430 ml) flour
2 cups (500 ml) pecans or toasted walnuts,
    chopped (optional)

- Preheat oven to 350°F (180°C).
- Melt the butter and chocolate together and let cool completely.
- Beat eggs and salt until light and add sugar gradually until creamy.
- Combine the chocolate-and-egg mixture.
- Fold in vanilla or brandy.
- Fold in flour by hand until just mixed. *Do not beat*.
- Fold in nuts (if desired).
- Bake in two 9 in.-by-13 in. (23 cm-by-31 cm) greased and floured pans.

> To Serve: Arrange brownies on a plate. If they will be eaten immediately, scoop a dollop of whipped cream on each and sprinkle on chocolate shavings.

BERRY CREAM CRUNCH SERVES 12

1 10 oz. (325 g) package shortbread cookies
¾ cup (180 ml) butter
1 cup (250 ml) confectioner's (icing) sugar
2 eggs
½ cup (125 ml) chopped nuts (either almonds,
    pecans, or walnuts), toasted
1 qt. (1 liter) fresh strawberries, raspberries,
    or blueberries
1½ cups (375 ml) whipping cream

- Put cookies into processor to crush to about the size of dried peas.

- Cover the bottom of a deep 9-in. square pan with a little more than half the crumbs.
- Beat butter and sugar together and add eggs one at a time, beating until each is incorporated.
- Spread butter mixture on the crumbs, sprinkle the nuts over it and then a layer of berries (reserve a few whole berries).
- Spread the whipped cream over the berries.
- Sprinkle the remaining crumbs on the top, and before serving decorate with reserved berries.
- Chill several hours until firm.

APRICOT CREAM SERVES 8

10 oz. (325 g) dried apricots
1 1/2 cups (375 ml) water
1/2 cup (125 ml) sugar
3 Tbs. (45 ml) lemon juice
1/4 cup (60 ml) Grand Marnier
16 lady fingers, or sponge cake sliced into
　　3 in.-by-1 in. (7.5 cm-by-2.5 cm) strips
1 cup (250 ml) whipping cream
2 oz. (60 g) toasted slivered almonds

- Cook apricots in the water. When plump, strain, reserving the liquid. Add enough water to make 1/2 cup (125 ml).
- Add sugar and 2 Tbs. (30 ml) lemon juice and beat until sugar dissolves. Cool, and add 2 Tbs. (30 ml) Grand Marnier.
- Layer the cake in a crystal bowl or in individual glass goblets. Drizzle on the liquid.
- Reserve 8 apricots for decoration and pulp the remaining ones in processor, adding 1 Tbs. (15 ml) lemon juice and 2 Tbs. (30 ml) Grand Marnier.
- Fold pulp into unsweetened whipped cream.
- Pour over cake and chill.
- Decorate with reserved apricots and toasted slivered almonds just before serving.

> *Note:* To toast slivered almonds, put a thin
> layer of blanched slivers onto a cookie sheet
> lined with aluminum foil. Bake in a slow 250°F
> (120°C) oven until they are a pale tan color.
> Check after ten minutes. I always toast extra
> and freeze them. In fact, I keep spare toasted
> nuts of all sorts in the freezer.

BRANDIED CHOCOLATE TORTE SERVES 10

A very rich, different chocolate dessert.

> 7 oz. (225 g) semi-sweet chocolate
> 1/4 lb. (125 g) butter
> 1/2 cup (125 ml) sugar
> 7 eggs, separated
> 1/4 cup (60 ml) brandy
> 2 cups (500 ml) whipping cream
> 1 cup (250 ml) toasted walnuts

- Preheat oven to 325°F (160°C).
- Melt butter and chocolate together.
- Beating chocolate and butter at high speed in saucepan over heat, add sugar and egg yolks.
- When thick, remove from heat and fold in the brandy and then the beaten egg whites.
- Pour 2/3 of batter into a greased pie plate or springform pan.
- Bake for 30 minutes.
- Let torte cool (it will fall) and remove carefully from springform pan or leave in pie plate.
- Pour remaining chocolate cream on top and chill.
- Before serving, whip unsweetened cream until stiff and pile on top of chocolate. Decorate with toasted nuts.

COOKIES

One of the biggest problems in making cookies is burning the bottoms, because the oven must be quite hot. When you introduce the cold cookie tray into a preheated oven, the temperature drops and requires the heating element to come on to maintain the required heat. By preheating the oven to 400°F (200°C) (hotter than is needed) and then lowering it, as I put in the cookies, to 350°F (180°C) (lower than the 375°F (190°C) normally used) I've found that the right temperature is maintained and the element doesn't need to come on.

For quick cleaning and convenience, I cover the cookie trays with foil (shiny side down) and grease the foil. When I remove cookies from the oven, I lift up the edges of the foil and slide out the trays, which allows the cookies to cool quickly so they can be lifted off and set on racks. I reuse the greased foil until all the batches are made, then discard it and put the clean cookie trays back in the cupboard.

RICH CHOCOLATE CHIP COOKIES MAKES APPROXIMATELY 3 DOZEN COOKIES

½ lb. (250 g) butter
¾ cup (180 ml) dark brown sugar
¼ cup (60 ml) white sugar
2 eggs
2 tsp. (10 ml) vanilla essence
1 cup (250 ml) flour
½ tsp. (2 ml) baking soda
½ tsp. (2 ml) salt
1 cup (250 ml) chocolate chips
1 cup (250 ml) chopped nuts (optional)

- Preheat oven to 400°F (200°C).
- Cream together softened butter and sugars until light and fluffy.
- Add eggs, one at a time, and vanilla.
- Combine flour, baking soda, and salt.
- Add to butter-and-egg mixture, folding in until just mixed.
- Fold in chips and nuts.
- Grease cookie sheet and drop on spoonfuls of batter.
- Reduce heat to 350°F (180°C) and bake cookies until they begin to brown around the edges (12-15 minutes).
- Cool on racks.

HEARTY OATMEAL AND RAISIN
COOKIES MAKES APPROXIMATELY 3 DOZEN
COOKIES

½ lb. (250 g) soft butter
¾ cup (180 ml) dark brown sugar
2 eggs
2 tsp. (10 ml) vanilla
1 cup (250 ml) whole-wheat flour
2 cups (500 ml) quick-cooking oats
½ tsp. (2 ml) baking soda
½ tsp. (2 ml) baking powder
½ tsp. (2 ml) salt
1½ cups (375 ml) raisins

- Preheat oven to 400°F (200°C).
- Cream the butter and sugar until light and fluffy.
- Add eggs, one at a time, and vanilla.
- Combine flour, oats, baking soda, baking powder, and salt and fold this mixture into batter.
- Fold in raisins.
- Drop by spoonfuls onto greased cookie sheet.
- Reduce oven to 350°F (180°C).
- Bake until they begin to brown at edges.
- Cool on racks.

DESSERT SALADS

I prefer fruit salads that are a combination of only two or three colors and flavors rather than half a dozen. Make up your own combinations, depending on what is in season. Here are some of my favorites:

> Honeydew Melon and Strawberries with Fresh
>   Mint
> Peaches and Blueberries
> Strawberries and Kiwi Fruit
> Sliced Oranges with Kirsch and Candied
>   Orange Peel

Notes for Preparation:

- Fresh ripe fruit deteriorates quickly. Don't prepare it too far in advance.
- Peaches are better peeled.
- Lemon juice keeps fruits in better condition and adds a tangy taste.
- While I often sprinkle a little sugar on fruit salads, I'm careful not to drown the delicate flavors in too much sugar. The same thing when using liqueurs: a little may add an interesting flavor, but too much drowns the flavor of the fruit. (Kirsch and Cointreau are my favorites with fruit.)
- Keep fruit salads well chilled; they keep better that way and are more refreshing.
- It's attractive to have fresh fruit served from crystal or silver set in crushed ice.
- Cut up the fruit into several different shapes (i.e., crescents, balls, wedges). Larger pieces survive better than small ones, which quickly become mush.
- I drain the juice from a fruit salad and serve it from a chilled silver pitcher at the side. It is more appetizing this way.

INDEX

plums, 71
potatoes, 97
pots and pans, 29, 32-3
poultry, 96
poultry dealers, 67
presentation. *See* decoration and presentation
pressure, 9-10
price bids, 51
pricing: sample menus, 41; calculations involved, 48-54; first conversation, 56-7
professional image, 56
profits, 50-1, 52-3
publicity, 23

rabbit, 42
rates of pay: help for food preparation, 77; serving help, 81-2
recipe trials, 20
records: deductible expenses, 20; as reference, 20; shopping receipts, 50
refrigerators, 19, 27, 37-8
rental companies, 30, 104-6, 107
retail business, 122-3
rice, 97-103

salads, 97
salmon, 42
salt, 99
sandwiches, 46
sauces, 96
seafood. *See* fish and seafood
serving, 78-88

serving dishes, 30, 93-4
shopping, 62-74
shrimp, 42
size of group, 43, 52-3
smoked salmon, 42
soft drinks, 107-8
soufflés, 46
soups, 91
specialty shops, 22, 23, 65
spices. *See* herbs and spices
stove and sink area, 32
stoves, 27
string beans, 38, 69
sugar, 99-100
supermarkets, 63-4

table decorations, 92-3
time: of day, 44; of year, 44-5, 92-3
tomatoes, 70, 73
transportation fee, 53

uniforms, 81, 84
utensils, 28-9, 32

vegetables, 97

waiters, 53, 81-3
washing up, 37
wedding receptions, 44, 57, 84-6
weight watchers, 45-6
whipping cream, 101
wholesale buying, 12, 65-7
wine, 70-1, 107

zoning, 18-19

RECIPE INDEX

HARCFYK99